THE POTSDAM
FÜHRER

THE POTSDAM FÜHRER

Frederick William I, Father of
Prussian Militarism

By ROBERT ERGANG

OCTAGON BOOKS

A DIVISION OF FARRAR, STRAUS AND GIROUX

New York 1972

Copyright 1941 by Columbia University Press

Reprinted 1972

by special arrangement with Columbia University Press

OCTAGON BOOKS

A DIVISION OF FARRAR, STRAUS & GIROUX, INC.

19 Union Square West

New York, N.Y. 10003

Library of Congress Cataloging in Publication Data

Ergang, Robert Reinhold, 1898-
   The Potsdam führer. ~~New York. Octagon Books, 1972.~~
   ~~Bibliography:~~ p. 290
   1. Friedrich Wilhelm I, King of Prussia, 1688-1740.
   2. Militarism—Prussia. I. Title.

DD
399
E7
1972

DD399.E7 1972   943'.052'0924 [B]   72-8922
ISBN 0-374-92623-9

Printed in U.S.A. by
NOBLE OFFSET PRINTERS, INC.
New York, N.Y. 10003

To CARLTON J. H. HAYES

in token of my gratitude
and esteem

Acknowledgments

THIS BOOK owes much to the generous help of others. To Professor Charles Woolsey Cole, of Columbia University, and Professor Walter L. Dorn, of Ohio State University, each of whom read several chapters of the typescript, I extend my sincere thanks for suggestions and emendations. Professor Ernest J. Knapton, of Wheaton College (Norton, Mass.), generously interrupted his own work to read the entire typescript and to give me the benefit of his wide knowledge. I am also under a host of obligations to the librarians of Columbia University Library, Harvard University Library, New York University Library, and the New York Public Library for courtesies shown and assistance rendered. Above all, I am indebted to my wife, Mildred Overbeck Ergang, for her unfailing devotion and her untiring assistance. Finally, the ethics of the profession demand that I state the self-evident, namely, that I alone am accountable for all errors of fact or interpretation.

ROBERT ERGANG

Washington Square College
New York University
July 1, 1941

Contents

Contents

THE POTSDAM
FÜHRER

CHAPTER ONE

Introduction

THE HISTORY of Prussia presents the novelty of a
group of unpromising little provinces speedily growing up in the eighteenth century to a great kingdom which in
the nineteenth united Germany under its rule. The major
factor in this rise was the strength and the efficiency of its
military forces. So large a part did successful war play in the
rise of Prussia that Mirabeau was moved to declare: "War is
the national industry of Prussia." [1] Emperor William II himself proclaimed the Prusso-German army "the rock on which
rests the might and greatness of Germany." [2] It was by
means of his army that Frederick the Great made Prussia
not only the rival of Austria for leadership in Germany but
also a first-rate power in the councils of Europe. In the
nineteenth century Prussia was able to accomplish the work
of German unification by virtue of its efficient army, aided
by the cunning of Bismarckian statecraft. A national assembly, sitting at Frankfort in 1848–1849, had endeavored
to unify Germany by peaceful methods, but the attempt
failed. Gustav Freytag, the Prussian historian and play-
wright, who seemed to feel as early as 1848 that the question

[1] Cited in Lavisse, *Etudes sur l'histoire de Prusse*, p. 72.
[2] *Die Reden Kaiser Wilhelms II*, edited by J. Penzler, II, 185.

of German unity could not be solved by peaceful methods, wrote in *Die Grenzboten:*

If it should be necessary for Prussia to solve this problem herself and to march against Germans and their foreign allies; then we shall carry out our will against all conspiracies, nay against all Europe. We are accustomed to battling with the whole world and to risking everything in order to achieve everything. And perhaps that is what distinguishes us Prussians from other Germans; we are ready to shed the last drop of blood to have our way. . . . We do not fear, for we are a nation of warriors.[3]

Bismarck himself saw no other road to German unity than the defeat of German particularism and foreign opposition by force of arms. "The great questions of the day," he said to the Prussian diet in 1862, "cannot be settled by speeches— that was the great mistake of 1848 and 1849—but by blood and iron." [4] In 1891 Emperor William II said in retrospect: "The soldier and the army, not parliamentary majorities or parliamentary resolutions, have welded together the German Empire. My trust is in the army." [5]

During the years immediately following 1871 the Prussian spirit was infused into German life as a whole. Prussian discipline became the keynote of the new state. The German army was, in fact, Prussianized so completely that Von Treitschke could say: "What is our German imperial army? It is undoubtedly the Prussian army." [6] In addressing a battalion of the German army William II proudly stated: "The spirit of this battalion is the good old Prussian one. It is my wish and hope that it will remain so." [7] Gradually the spirit of the German people was also militarized, until

---

[3] Freytag, *Politische Aufsätze*, I, 86.
[4] Bismarck, *Die gesammelten Werke*, X, 140.
[5] *Die Reden Kaiser Wilhelms II*, I, 175.
[6] *Die Politik*, II, 345.
[7] *Die Reden Kaiser Wilhelms II*, I, 199.

that Prussian discipline which Prince von Bülow styled "one of the greatest of German virtues," [8] became an all-pervading attitude. "It was one of the outstanding characteristics of German thoroughness," Werner Bruck writes, "that this idea of a military machine permeated the whole social life, public and private, and even to a certain degree, influenced German culture. This militarism has rightly been called the cement that bound the whole structure of society into an entity." [9] In short, the new German Empire became the prolongation of the shadow of Prussia.

The task of converting the German people as a whole to the Prussian military point of view was not undertaken solely by professional militarists. Many philosophers, teachers, historians, and writers contributed much of their energy to this cause. These men did not tire of proclaiming the righteousness and the necessity of war and of expounding the "logic" and the "virtue" of the *Machtpolitik* (policy of power) which Bismarck had expressed in the words: "Might makes right; war is a law of nature." [10] The most fanatical and at the same time the most popular exponent of the philosophy of militarism was Heinrich von Treitschke. "War," he stated, "is political science par excellence. Over and over again it will be demonstrated that it is only in war a people becomes in very deed a people." [11] Armed conflict between nations was to him a permanent feature of civilized life. "In this eternal conflict of separate states," he wrote, "lies the beauty of history. The wish to do away with this rivalry is simply unintelligent." [12] Upon the ideas expressed by Von Treitschke, Friedrich von Bernhardi avowedly based his

[8] *Imperial Germany*, p. 188.
[9] *Social and Economic History of Germany*, p. 39.
[10] *Deutsche Worte*, p. 38. Von Moltke's version of the same idea was: "War is sacred; it is ordained of God."
[11] *Die Politik*, I, 90. [12] *Ibid.*, p. 30.

book *Germany and the Next War*, the purpose of which
was to intoxicate the German people with the love of war.

War [he asserted] is a biological necessity of the first importance, a regulative element in the life of mankind which cannot
be dispensed with. . . . Our people must learn to see that the
maintenance of peace never can or may be the goal of a policy.
. . . The inevitableness, the idealism, and the blessings of war,
as an indispensable and stimulating law of development, must
be repeatedly emphasized. The apostles of the peace idea must
be confronted with Goethe's manly words:

> Dreams of a peaceful day?
> Let him dream who may!
> "War" is our rallying cry,
> "Onward to victory!" [13]

Such statements were repeated over and over again until
they were deeply impressed on the German mind. When the
debacle came in 1918, many thoughtful Germans concluded
that the ideals they had been taught were false. The men who
drew up the Weimar constitution went so far as to include
the following article: "In every school the educational aims
must be moral training, public spirit, personal and vocational
fitness, and, above all, the cultivation of German national
character and of the spirit of international reconciliation."
From the outside the Allied Powers sought to curb the
military spirit of Germany by limiting the total strength of
the German army to one hundred thousand men (Article
160 of the Treaty of Versailles). As Stresemann put it: "In
place of the military service that has entered into our very
flesh and blood we are to form a paid professional army." [14]
To prevent the training of fresh men each year as a means
of building up a large trained reserve, it was stipulated in
the Treaty of Versailles that each man in the German army

[13] *Germany and the Next War*, pp. 10–11.
[14] *Gustav Stresemann: His Diaries, Letters, and Papers*, II, 307.

must serve for a period of twelve years. But the spirit of
Prussian militarism with which the German people had been
so deeply imbued by tradition and practice could not suddenly be extinguished. It was kept alive not only in the
German army, small as it was, but also in many semimilitary
organizations, including the Nazi Brownshirts, the Steel
Helmets, the Volunteer Labor Corps, the Hosts of the Cross,
the Vikings, and the Tannenberg League. These and other
organizations gave at least partial military training to hundreds of thousands of young men. Nor did the war prophets
become extinct. For example, in 1920 Oswald Spengler
wrote: "War is the eternal form of higher human existence;
states exist for the purpose of waging war." [15]

With the accession to power in 1933 of the National Socialist Party the worship of the old Prussian idols was resumed in full. The government began feverishly to build
huge armaments and to revive the spirit of militarism. An
army in itself, Herr Hitler told the German people, was not
enough; they must also have the proper military spirit. "The
question of how we can regain German power," he wrote in
Mein Kampf, "is not: how can we manufacture arms? It is:
how can we create the spirit which renders a people capable
of bearing arms? Once this spirit dominates a people it will
find a thousand paths each of which leads to the necessary
armament." [16] The traditions to which he would return are
those of Prussia. "Was not Germany [he asked] a marvellous
example of an empire built entirely upon a policy of power?
Prussia, the germ cell of the Reich, was created by a brilliant
heroism, not by financial or commercial affairs, and the
Reich itself was again but the most magnificent achievement
of a policy of power and of military valor." [17] He demanded

[15] *Preussentum und Sozialismus*, p. 53.
[16] 1933 edition, pp. 365–366.   [17] *Ibid.*, p. 169.

the reëstablishment of the old Prussian principle of authority from above and obedience from below. "This principle," he stated, "which in its time made the Prussian army the most wonderful instrument of the German people, must in the future become the principle of the structure of our whole conception of the State." [18] He further prescribed that a glorification of the triumphs of war be inculcated in the young. "We want to train them," the *Führer* said, "to veneration for our old army, which they shall think about and reverence again and in which they must see the personification of the greatest performance our German people have achieved." [19] These precepts have been carried out, and Prussian militarism has been revived in all its phases.

The history of militarism in modern Prussia begins with the accession of Frederick William the Great Elector to the rule of Brandenburg-Prussia in 1640. He it was who first organized a small standing army which served as an instrument of aggrandizement as well as of protection. But the real father of the army of modern Prussia is King Frederick William I (1713–1740), who by dint of persistent effort managed to organize a military force that was the fourth largest of Europe in size and the first in efficiency. This army he made the conscious instrument of power politics. He believed, as Napoleon later put it, that God is on the side of the big battalions; that the larger a State's army, the larger the role that State can play in international politics and the more it can exploit other States. As crown prince he had already stated his unqualified belief in force and ridiculed the efforts of his father's ministers to gain territory by diplomacy. "They say," he wrote, "that they will obtain

[18] *Ibid.*, p. 501.
[19] Cited in Ogilvie, "Education under Hitler," in *"Friends of Europe" Publications*, No. 17 (1934), 8.

land and people for the king with the pen; but I say it can be done only with the sword." [20]

More than this, Frederick William I is the founder of Prussian militarism, that militarism which involves the subordination of all interests of the State to military ends. In other words, he organized the Prussian State strictly for purposes of military power. Theretofore nations had merely subscribed to the maintenance of armies, but Frederick William converted all Prussia into a vast military organization and applied the whole intelligence of the nation either directly or indirectly to military affairs. More Prussian soldiers! Better Prussian soldiers! This was the goal of most of his policies. To this end he geared industry, commerce, taxation, and agriculture—in fact, almost every phase of national life. So completely did he center the interests of the Prussian State in the army that contemporaries were wont to say: "Prussia is not a State which possesses an army, but an army which possesses a State."

Nor did he stop at drilling his army. He also imposed upon his officials a discipline no less severe than that of the army, and through them he subjected his people as a whole to a hard, nay hardening, discipline. Under his rule Prussia, as the liberals later expressed it, became "the land of the corporal's stick." The State he bequeathed to his son, Frederick the Great, was the product of drill and discipline not only in military matters but in every other phase of life. No modern nation had previously been drilled so thoroughly in the habits of duty, obedience, and sacrifice. In brief, he cast the whole Prussian nation into a military mold, fixing on his subjects military habits which have continued to characterize Prusso-Germans to this day.

[20] *Briefe an Leopold zu Anhalt-Dessau*, p. 55.

Besides organizing a powerful army and militarizing his subjects, Frederick William also consolidated the Hohenzollern rule. He finished the task, started by the Great Elector, of depriving the nobles of the power they had exercised in the government, establishing an absolutism such as even Louis XIV did not enjoy. As the means of carrying out his autocratic will he created the Prussian bureaucracy and impressed upon it, as already stated, those habits of unquestioning obedience, conscientious performance of duty, and strict attention to detail which made the Prussian official unique. This body of officials gave to the widely scattered Hohenzollern territories an efficient administration as well as an inner unity.

Furthermore, it was Frederick William who in Prussia put the State on the highest pedestal by making it the source of all power. For the individual this meant complete subordination to the State in all matters. The State did not exist for the individual, but the individual for the State. Frederick William even regarded himself as "only the first servant of the State." A subject had no rights and must not presume to form opinions of his own; he had only duties, and the supreme duty was unquestioning corpse-like obedience (*Kadaver-Gehorsam*). As Frederick William curtly put it: "No reasoning, obey orders!" In other words, the State was everything; the individual merely the clay of which the State was formed. Stresemann said of the Germany of 1914: "It was still the Germany of Frederick William I with all its feudal characteristics. But this feudalism was inspired by an iron sense of loyalty to the State and nation. The outward aspect of officialdom was a harsh one, and it was decried throughout the world as a bureaucracy; but it was dominated by one sole idea of honour: subordination to the

State." [21] Spengler, one of the spiritual godfathers of National Socialism, wrote: "The Prussian way requires that the individual merge his will in that of the whole. The individual as such is of no importance; he must sacrifice himself for the whole." [22] To the collectivist idea which Frederick William established in Prussia he gives a socialist interpretation. "In its most profound meaning the idea of socialism," he wrote, "stands for the will to power and the struggle for the welfare of the group, not of the individual. Frederick William I, not Marx, was in this sense the first conscious socialist. From him as the great exemplar the whole world movement emanates." [23] More recently a National-Socialist writer has styled Frederick William "the socialist on the royal throne," stating that "today Frederick William I speaks through Adolf Hitler." [24] "We feel distinctly," the same author writes in the *Nationalsozialistische Monatshefte*, "that Frederick William I is no less than his son the conscience of our National-Socialist organization." [25]

Other Prusso-German writers and historians have also hailed the achievements of the "Royal Drill Sergeant." Frederick the Great, who had every reason to hate his father, paid him the following tribute: "If it is true to say that we owe the shade of the oak that covers us to the virility of the acorn from which it has sprung, then the world must agree that the germs of the prosperity which the royal house enjoyed after his death are to be found in the industrious life and wise measures of this prince." [26] A number of German historians have stated that the entire conception and organi-

[21] *Gustav Stresemann: His Diaries, Letters, and Papers*, III, 494.
[22] *Preussentum und Sozialismus*, p. 31.   [23] *Ibid.*, p. 42.
[24] Weber-Krohse, "Nationalwirtschaft Friedrich Wilhelms I, der Sozialist auf dem Königsthron," *Odal*, III (1935), 506–522.
[25] V (1934), 646.   [26] *Œuvres de Frédéric le Grand*, I, 201–202.

zation of the Prussian State goes back to him, but his work
has been especially lauded by more recent writers. "We
are thankful," one biographer states, "that the military spirit
he infused into the Prussian State has not died out." [27] Another German writer declares:

Not only did he create institutions which still exist and lay the
foundations for the entrance of Prussia into the circle of Great
Powers in Europe; he is also the creator of everything which,
either in a laudatory or denunciatory sense, is commonly called
"Prussian." By means of an unspeakably severe training he
created in the army and the bureaucracy and among the people
generally that specifically Prussian bearing which slowly became typical of the nation as a whole. That Germany was able
to do and to bear during the period of the World War what no
nation had previously done or borne may be ascribed to the
Prussian substance, to the Prussian frame of steel, the foundations of which were laid by Frederick William I.[28]

Finally, a recent writer goes so far as to say: "Posterity
knows that in a wider sense he is what he desired to be: the
father of the Fatherland." [29]

This Frederick William, an historical figure of the first
importance, has received but scant attention from non-
German historians. He has, in fact, been neglected to the
extent that there is no biography of him in the English
language. Even if he had not built the pillars upon which the
Prussian State and the German Empire were reared, this
uncouth and choleric, but well-meaning despot would in
himself be a subject of extraordinary interest.

[27] Oppeln-Bronikowski, *Der Baumeister des preussischen Staates,
Friedrich Wilhelm I*, p. 29.
[28] Hinrichs, "Friedrich Wilhelm I, König von Preussen," in *Die
Welt als Geschichte*, IV (1938), 1 *et sqq.*
[29] Collenberg, "Friedrich Wilhelm I zum 250 Geburtstage," *Militärwissenschaftliche Rundschau*, III (1938), 584.

CHAPTER TWO

The Prussian Court at the Opening of the Eighteenth Century

FREDERICK WILLIAM I, born August 14, 1688, was the only son of Elector Frederick III of Brandenburg [1] and Electress Sophie Charlotte. As heir of the Hohenzollern family Frederick III ruled over an aggregation of provinces which, besides Brandenburg, included such widely-scattered territories as East Prussia, Eastern Pomerania, Cleves, Mark, Ravensburg, Halberstadt, Camin, Minden, and Magdeburg. The cradle of Hohenzollern power was Brandenburg, a district of sandy flats and dreary marshes in the north-eastern part of Germany, with Berlin near its center. It had come under Hohenzollern rule in 1417 when Emperor Sigismund had officially conferred the sovereignty over it upon Frederick of Hohenzollern who had previously been burgrave of Nuremberg. The successors of this first Hohenzollern ruler of Brandenburg were an able rather than a remarkable race. By dogged endurance and subtle intrigue they had managed to hold what they had and to add to it bit by bit

[1] The title derives from the fact that he was one of the electors in whom was vested the hereditary right of electing the Holy Roman Emperor.

until they accumulated the provinces listed. This hodge-
podge of territories, lacking common traditions, common
institutions, and common rights, had until the reign of the
Great Elector (1640–1688) given little promise of ever
growing into a powerful State. However, the Great Elector
had by a vigorous policy greatly increased the military
power, the territory, and the wealth of Brandenburg-Prussia
and had also begun the work of establishing some degree of
uniformity in the administration of the scattered provinces.
By the time of his death in 1688 Brandenburg-Prussia had
become, next to Austria, the strongest power in Germany.

Frederick III, son and successor of the Great Elector, was
a man of a different mold. He was, in sharp contrast to his
sturdy father, deformed, frail, and sickly. Nor was his education of the best. He desired, no less than his predecessor,
to promote the rise and the aggrandizement of his House,
but he lacked the necessary vigor of body and mind greatly
to advance the policies the Great Elector had launched. The
world of action was not his world. In lieu of great achievements he sought to give himself dignity and importance by
surrounding himself with magnificence and ceremony. It
is for this reason that German historians often refer to him
as "Frederick the Ostentatious." Only when he was surrounded by that pomp and grandeur which he regarded as
the highest expression of earthly majesty did he seem happy.
Every event of importance was celebrated with magnificent
splendor, and every function in which he participated was
carried out with elaborate ceremonial—even the most tri-
fling affairs of his court being regulated with the minutest
exactness. Often he would spend hours debating the minutiae
of court etiquette. This meticulous attention to detail later
moved Frederick the Great to remark that his grandfather

had been "great in little things and little in great things." [2]
Too busy with court etiquette to learn the needs of his
territories, Frederick III gradually relinquished the actual
management of state affairs to his ministers, who were not
always above reproach. Hence his reign shows a retrogres-
sion in certain respects.

Frederick's great exemplar was Louis XIV of France.
"Smitten with the desire to attract to himself the praises that
were being lavished on Louis XIV," Frederick the Great
wrote, "he imagined that by choosing this monarch for his
model he could not fail to be praised in like manner." [3]
Imitating Louis XIV was not peculiar to Frederick. In Germany the lesser as well as the greater courts sedulously
mimicked the "Grand Monarque." It was the height of
ambition of almost every German princeling to copy the
buildings, the gardens, and the parks of Versailles and to
mirror its festivities. As Frederick the Great later put it in his
Antimachiavell: "There is not a younger scion of a minor
branch who does not imagine himself to be something like
Louis XIV. He builds his Versailles, has his mistresses, and
maintains his army." [4] But no one was more zealous in imitating the French king than Frederick III. He aimed at nothing short of being the "Grand Monarque" of Germany. Like
Louis XIV he surrounded himself with numerous courtiers,
chamberlains, grooms of the chamber, gentlemen-in-waiting,
pages, footmen, blackamoors, court musicians, artists, and
poets. At Lützenburg, later named Charlottenburg in honor
of Sophie Charlotte, he built a palace which was the last
word in both art and luxury. The gardens were laid out on
the model of those at Versailles, and the rooms were fur-

2 *Œuvres de Frédéric le Grand*, I, 144.
3 *Ibid.*, XXI, 86.   4 *Ibid.*, VIII, 234.

nished with magnificent paintings, beautiful carpets, and rare furnitures of inlaid ebony, ivory, and porcelain. So that he would not be outdone by the French monarch Frederick even felt it necessary to have a mistress *en titre*, although his relations with her were restricted to a dignified promenade before the assembled court each evening.

Sophie Charlotte did not share her husband's passion for pomp and etiquette. Having been carefully educated by her mother, that Sophia of Hanover through whom the Hanoverian dynasty came to occupy the English throne, she was a woman of intellectual attainments that were truly extraordinary for a princess of her time. Not only did she have a speaking knowledge of French, English, and Italian, as well as of German, but she had also read widely in the literatures of the first three languages. She was further an accomplished musician and a patron of the arts. But above everything else she delighted in theological and philosophical discussions, for which purpose she invited men of the most varied schools of thought to her salons. Her favorite among them all was Leibnitz, who became closely connected with the Berlin court. One can therefore understand why Sophie Charlotte, though she was careful to discharge the duties of her position, found the minutiae of court etiquette very wearisome. "Leibnitz lectured me today about the infinitely little," she wrote in a letter to her confidante, Mlle von Pöllnitz, "but who would know more about these things than I?" [5] Both Thiebault and Frederick the Great report that when Sophie Charlotte was on her deathbed one of the ladies-in-waiting remarked that Frederick III would be inconsolable if she should die. "Oh, I feel quite at ease about him," she replied; "he will be diverted by the magnificent funeral which he will provide for me. If nothing goes amiss in the ceremony it

[5] *Mémoires pour servir à l'histoire de Sophie Charlotte*, p. 198.

will console him for everything." [6] The sequel was to prove that the statement was not entirely groundless.

Frederick's desire to emulate Louis XIV in every particular caused him also to foster the development of the arts and the sciences. Like the French monarch he maintained a theater in which troupes of French and Italian actors presented operas and ballets. He employed some of the most famous architects of the time to prepare the plans for the palaces he erected; also painters and sculptors, some of them artists of no mean talent, to adorn his palaces and gardens with paintings and statues. In 1696 he founded the Royal Academy of Arts to encourage the development of native talent, the demand for paintings and art having previously been supplied by Dutch and French artists. [7] Four years later he founded the Berlin Academy of Sciences, a learned institute such as Louis XIV had established in 1666. The idea of founding this academy appears to have originated with Leibnitz, who first won the support of his patroness Sophie Charlotte for it. The latter, in turn, found it easy to convince her husband that such an academy would augment his prestige. No less a person than Leibnitz himself was made its first president. Frederick also transformed the Academy for Young Noblemen at Halle into the University of Halle, an institution which was to play an important role in the intellectual life of Prussia.

Though there was little of greatness in Frederick, he did preserve much of the Great Elector's work. He gave con-

---

[6] Thiebault, *Souvenirs de vingt ans de séjours à Berlin*, I, 160: *Œuvres de Frédéric le Grand*, I, 130.

[7] The quarters Frederick assigned to the members of his academy were located in the upper story of the royal stables. This, the Englishman John Toland, who was in Berlin in 1702, observes, gave occasion to the Berlin wits to remark that Frederick "did very well to lodge his horses and his asses together."—*An Account of the Courts of Prussia and Hanover*, p. 20.

siderable care to the army, and during the two wars in which Prussia participated (War of the League of Augsburg and War of the Spanish Succession) increased its numbers substantially with the help of foreign subsidies. Frederick also consistently upheld the principles of toleration his father had established. He continued to offer hospitality to Protestants who were persecuted in or expelled from other lands, with the result that a fresh influx of French Protestants helped to expand the industries of Brandenburg-Prussia. John Toland, upon entering Brandenburg, was greatly impressed with the marks of good administration he saw.

I may truly say [he wrote] that, without asking questions of anybody, a traveller may distinguish this country by the most sensible effects as soon as he enters it. The highways are kept in better order than elsewhere, the posts are more regular, public carriages are more expeditious; and wherever the ways divide themselves there are strong pillars erected, with as many pointing arms as there are roads, bearing, in letters cut or painted, the names of the next stage, and telling the number of miles to that place, as well as from the last out of which you set forth. . . . I presently took notice, that all the churches as well of the country as of the towns were kept in so good a repair as I never saw the like, being most of them newly plastered, whitened or adorned in some other manner. . . . I could not remark one church that was defective in anything.[8]

He found the villages fairly clean and the people diligently at work. "I perceived," he states, "all men employed about some business or other; everything being at once in perpetual motion, and yet the whole enjoying a most profound repose." [9]

Frederick's great contribution to the rise of the house of Hohenzollern was the acquisition of the royal crown. His father had already established virtual equality with kings as

[8] *Ibid.*, pp. 6–7.   [9] *Ibid.*, p. 9.

regards military affairs, and the splendor and dignity of Frederick's court were already royal in everything except name; but the title "king" was still lacking. To obtain it became the primary object of his endeavors. With his own hand he wrote: "Since I have everything appertaining to the royal dignity, and even more than some kings, why should I not strive to obtain also the name 'king'?" [10] Frederick was not alone in his desire to obtain the royal dignity; in fact, in his day the desire was epidemic among the more important princes of the empire. No less than two in addition to Frederick were successful in gratifying their ambition. In 1696, after the death of John Sobieski, the Elector Frederick Augustus of Saxony was elected king by the Poles and took the title Augustus II. Again, when Queen Anne of England died, in 1714, Elector George Lewis of Hanover ascended the English throne as King George I.

Since Frederick was a vassal of the Holy Roman Empire, he could not assume the royal title without the emperor's consent. Negotiations for the purpose of gaining this consent were started in 1693, but the early efforts were wholly unsuccessful. The emperor, already fearing the growth of Prussia, had no desire to strengthen the position of the Hohenzollern rulers. But Frederick, undaunted by the repeated rebuffs, continued to importune the emperor, until the circumstances finally favored his efforts. In 1700, with the War of the Spanish Succession impending, Austria found itself in need of the military assistance of Brandenburg-Prussia. Frederick, who realized this, made the most of the opportunity. When his aid was solicited, he demanded the royal title in return. As Emperor Leopold could obtain

[10] Berner, "Die auswärtige Politik des Kurfürsten Friedrich III von Brandenburg, König Friedrich I von Preussen," *Hohenzollern-Jahrbuch*, IV (1900), 105.

Brandenburg-Prussia's help on no other terms, he was finally forced to accede. The treaty as concluded (Nov. 16, 1700) specified that Frederick was to furnish eight thousand troops in the event of war, while Leopold, for his part, granted the royal title to Frederick. This title was not, however, to apply to the territories which lay within the boundaries of the empire, but only to the province of East Prussia. So far as the affairs of the empire were concerned, Frederick was still to be regarded merely as the Elector of Brandenburg.

Instead of assuming the title by proclamation or announcement Frederick decided to signalize the event with elaborate and solemn ceremonies. He was so impatient for the title, also fearful lest something might at the last minute interfere with his assumption of it, that he resolved to proceed with the coronation at once, despite the fact that it was the depth of winter and the roads between Berlin and Königsberg, where the coronation was to take place, were well-nigh impassable. As soon as the preparations were completed Frederick, together with his court, set out for Königsberg. Before leaving Berlin he had personally drawn up a detailed program prescribing what festivities were to take place en route and how the coronation ceremony was to be conducted at Königsberg. Nothing which could possibly contribute to the magnificence of the occasion was omitted. For the journey the future king, accompanied by a suite of two hundred persons in gala dress, was attired in a garment of crimson velvet embroidered with gold and adorned with ermine, large diamonds serving as buttons. The triumphal procession was of such length that thirty thousand post horses were required to convey it. Along the road of travel citizens decorated their houses, and in Königsberg triumphal arches were erected and the streets were hung with tapestry. There on January 18, 1701, before an assembly of the highest officials of his court and his states, Frederick placed the crown on his own head, indicating thereby that he was assuming it by his own right, not by the grace of a foreign power. He was now Frederick I, king in Prussia.[11] Thereafter anyone who referred to the king as "His Electoral Highness" instead of "His Majesty" was liable to a fine of a ducat.

As Ranke observes,[12] the coronation of Frederick I marked the first time in the history of the Christian West that a royal crown had not been bestowed by ecclesiastical hands. But the new king did not dispense with the blessings of the Church. After the coronation the royal pair, each under a resplendent canopy of silver brocade embroidered with gold and borne by nobility of the first quality, proceeded to the principal church of Königsberg, where they were received by two bishops created for the occasion. These bishops, assisted by six other clergymen—three Calvinists and three Lutherans—escorted the king and the queen to the altar and there in a prolonged ceremony blessed them and anointed them with sacred oil. All details were carried out so scrupulously that the new king had good reason to be pleased. Only one blot marred the perfect execution of the ceremony. The queen, bored with the gaudy pageantry and the long-winded ceremony, could not resist taking a pinch of snuff at a moment when she thought the king's eyes were turned from her. The king, however, saw the maneuver, much to his consternation, and immediately ordered one of his gentlemen-in-waiting to reprimand the queen in his name.

[11] In order to avoid complications with the king of Poland who still ruled West Prussia, Emperor Leopold permitted Frederick to style himself only "King in Prussia"; however, after the acquisition of West Prussia by Frederick the Great the title was changed to "King of Prussia."

[12] *Sämmtliche Werke*, XXV, 429 *et sqq.*

Although the kingship was to Frederick but another pretext for indulging his penchant for magnificence, its acquisition was a distinct step forward in the growth of the Hohenzollern dynasty.[13] It gave luster to the State and precedence to its ruler in an age when precedence and ceremony were matters of the first importance. The new title, it is true, applied only to the duchy of East Prussia, but since East Prussia was free from any authority except that of the Hohenzollern, this fact gave the new monarchy an independence it would not have enjoyed if the title had rested on the Hohenzollern dominions which were part of the empire. The use of the name Brandenburg soon waned, and the scattered dominions of the Hohenzollern became known collectively as Prussia. Thus Frederick brought with the royal crown the common designation "Prussians" to the peoples he ruled. Frederick the Great, in commenting on the importance of the crown for the house of Hohenzollern, wrote:

What originally was rooted in vanity turned out to be a masterpiece of statesmanship. The royal crown rescued the house of Brandenburg from that yoke of servitude under which the house of Austria then held the princes of Germany. It was a bait that Frederick flung before all his posterity and by which he seemed to say to them: "I have procured you a title, therefore show yourself worthy of it; I have laid the foundation of greatness, it is up to you to complete the work." [14]

The acquisition of the royal crown accelerated the rise of the Hohenzollern so that they soon became the rivals of the Habsburgs for the leadership in Germany. Little wonder, then, that Prince Eugene of Savoy, the great Austrian

[13] Most of the states of Europe were not long in recognizing the new kingdom. Only the king of Poland and the Pope withheld recognition, the former until 1764, the latter until 1787.

[14] Œuvres, I, 119; see also II, 59.

general, exclaimed upon hearing of the agreement that gave Frederick the crown: "The emperor ought to hang the ministers who gave him such perfidious counsel." [15]

The immediate effect of the acquisition of the crown upon Frederick was that it whetted his desire for ostentation and pageantry until it became an overmastering passion for the gratification of which he spent money with reckless prodigality. He would show the world that he was capable of conducting himself as a king. It was said of him that he rose very early in order to have more time to enjoy the pleasure of being king. As Frederick's extravagance steadily increased from year to year, his ministers were often hard put to it to raise the necessary funds. Besides collecting the existing taxes to the last pfennig they had to devise new sources of income. No important source of revenue was overlooked. Thus the "head tax," a kind of income tax which the Great Elector had levied but twice (1677 and 1679), was collected no less than eight times during Frederick's reign. Another important source of income was the tax imposed on luxuries. Those who wished to drink tea, coffee, or chocolate, for example, had to pay an annual tax of two taler, while those wearing clothing embroidered with gold or silver were taxed an equal sum. The tax on a coach was eight taler a year, and there was also an annual tax of two taler on wigs. The latter tax was farmed to a Frenchman, whose inspectors caused much annoyance by stopping citizens on the street to make sure that the wigs they wore had a tax stamp affixed. As the need for money increased, many articles of ordinary consumption, including shoes, stockings, boots, and hats, were taxed. Shoemakers, for instance, were obliged to attach a stamp costing one groschen to each pair of shoes. Finally the king even decreed that all

[15] *Ibid.,* I, 124.

hog bristles must be carefully collected and sent to a designated place. This decree provoked so many witticisms that Frederick issued a supplementary order which threatened dire punishment to all who dared to ridicule the collector of hog bristles. When Frederick died, in 1713, not only was the treasury empty but a considerable debt had also accumulated.[16]

[16] See *Acta Borussica: Behördenorganization*, III, 466. This reference will henceforth be abbreviated as *AB, Beh.*

CHAPTER THREE

Frederick William the Man

FREDERICK WILLIAM I, who succeeded his father to the throne in 1713, was a man of robust frame, a thoroughly healthy constitution, and a prodigious amount of physical energy. There was throughout his life much of the primitive and something of the obsessed in him. Already as a young child he manifested many of the qualities that were to characterize the man. He was aggressive, self-willed, and violent of temper. So headstrong and unruly was he as a young lad that his governess, Madame de Montbeil, was able to do little with him. At the age of four, for example, while she was dressing him, he persisted in putting the silver buckle of one of his shoes into his mouth. When the governess endeavored to take it from him, the young prince swallowed it. Great anxiety reigned at the court for several days, but the buckle finally passed off without any apparent harm. On another occasion, when he was to be deprived of his breakfast as punishment for a misdemeanor he climbed onto a window ledge three stories above the ground and threatened to jump if his breakfast were not given him immediately. The terror-stricken governess gave in and thenceforth abandoned all efforts to break the fury of his temper.[1]

[1] Fassmann, *Leben und Thaten Friedrich Wilhelms* I, pp. 12 *et sqq.*

His parents and tutors were no more successful in their efforts to tame the primitive spirit of the stormy and impetuous boy. The queen, though she grieved to see her son so willful and refractory, failed to adopt proper measures of correction. Instead of prescribing condign punishment when he was guilty of gross misconduct she would dismiss him with only a slight reprimand. Frederick William himself related that on one occasion, when he severely beat the young prince of Kurland, his mother merely said to him: "My dear son, what are you doing?" [2] Again, when he pushed Von Brand, a court official, down a flight of stone steps so violently that the latter sprained his neck, his mother merely told him before the assembled court that he should not have done so. On a number of occasions in later life he accused his mother of having been too indulgent. "My mother was certainly a good woman," he said, "but she was a bad Christian." [3]

When the young prince reached the age of six his education was entrusted to Count Alexander Dohna and a staff of tutors in the hope that they might break the fury of his temper. By this time, however, he had become so overbearing that he feared only God and his own father. But, while the question as to whether he was pleasing God caused young Frederick William considerable worry, it wrought little change in his conduct toward men. Even the fear of his father could be put to little use, for Frederick I had written in the instructions for his son's education: "If the prince is disobedient, he is not to be threatened with his father, but only with his mother." [4] So self-willed and refractory was the young prince that if his tutors requested

[2] Morgenstern, *Ueber Friedrich Wilhelm I*, pp. 5 *et sqq.*
[3] *Ibid.*, p. 4.
[4] Instructions in Cramer, *Zur Geschichte Friedrich Wilhelms I und Friedrichs II*, pp. 11 *et sqq.*

him to do something for which he had no inclination he
would fly into a rage and release a shower of denunciations
and curses or he would threaten to poison or strangle himself in such a way that the tutors would be blamed for his
death. One of his favorite threats was: "May the devil take
me if I don't have all of you hanged or your heads cut off
when I grow up." [5] At times the robust lad would become
violent and kick his tutors, tear off their wigs, butt them
with his head, strike them with his fists, beat them with any
appropriate object that was at hand, or try to strangle them.
His temper was so furious that on occasion he would even
ram his head against the wall. Often the only way the tutors
could achieve their ends with the contrary-minded boy was
to order him to do the opposite of what they desired.

Accustomed to having his own way, Frederick William
gained little practice in self-control. As he grew older, all
his desires became passions; he could do nothing moderately.
Thus the report of one foreign ambassador had it: "Quid-
quid vult, vehementer vult (Whatever he desires, he desires
vehemently)." As king he expected blind and unconditional obedience from everyone. The slightest opposition
would throw him into fits of frenzy, in which he would
commit acts of violence which set Europe aghast. During
these outbursts he became a terror to his subjects. With the
stout cane he always carried he would rain blows upon
those who had committed blunders or incurred his displeasure. In this regard he was no respecter of persons, caning young and old, high and low, indiscriminately. It is
therefore not strange to read, as in the report of the Austrian envoy, that "at times the king cannot be in his right
mind." [6] At no time in his life was he able to curb his im-

---

[5] Borkowski, "Erzieher und Erziehung König Friedrich Wilhelms I," in *Hohenzollern-Jahrbuch*, VIII (1904), 115.

[6] *AB, Beh.*, I, 445.

pulsive anger; on the contrary, its fury increased as his physical ills multiplied with advancing age. Frederick William himself realized how ungovernable and furious his temper was, but ascribed it to the innate sinfulness of man. When his confessor chided him because of his perpetual irritability, he replied: "You are right, but that is my nature." [7]

Although he was quick to anger, he was equally quick to forgive, being too naïve to be guileful. No sooner did the paroxysms of anger leave him than he often endeavored to make amends for the injuries he had inflicted. A favorite story of contemporaries was that regarding Joost, the royal coachman, who after having been caned by the king for being late, cursed the clergy that day. In some surprise Frederick William asked the coachman his reason for doing so. "I am cursing them," said Joost, "because they perpetually request God to strengthen the arm of the king. Methinks the royal arm is strong enough. If it grows any stronger only the devil will be able to withstand the blows." The king, it is reported, laughed heartily and gave his coachman a coin of large denomination to soothe his pains. [8] The one hatred of Frederick William's life was his cousin and brother-in-law, George of Hanover, who later became George II of England. The antipathy, which lasted throughout his life, developed while both were boys and playmates at the court of their grandmother, Sophia of Hanover. Frederick William, only five at the time, refused to be bullied by his cousin, who was five years his senior, and the two so frequently engaged in fisticuffs that they had to be separated. Later Frederick William's dislike for his cousin deepened, when

[7] Weber, *Aus vier Jahrhunderten*, N.F., I, 157.
[8] Beneckendorf, *Karakterzüge aus dem Leben König Friedrich Wilhelms I*, VIII, 34–35.

George married Caroline of Anspach, the former's first love. Throughout his life the Prussian king usually referred to George II as "My brother, the dancing-master" or "My brother, the comedian," and the English ruler styled him "My brother, the drill-sergeant." [9] The court preacher, Roloff, reports that when he exhorted the Prussian king, who was dying, to forgive all his enemies, Frederick William retorted that he had no enemy whom he would not gladly forgive except his brother-in-law, George II of England. Since the confessor insisted that he include also his brother-in-law in the forgiveness, the king finally consented, but bade the queen wait until the fact of his own death had been established beyond doubt before writing to her brother that "Frederick William forgives you with all his heart." [10]

Not only was Frederick William lacking in the gentler virtues, he also had little appreciation of the finer things of life. Though nature had endowed him with a vigorous mind, he was so contrary that his tutors were able to teach him but little. Also his mother failed to instill in his mind a love of learning and refinement. His animal spirits were such that he had little inclination to sit still and read. Likewise, he refused to learn music, the practice of which was intolerable to him. His father, who might have induced him to apply himself to his studies, was too busy with pomp and ceremony to give much attention to his education. Consequently Frederick William's intellectual achievements were so meager that he remained a Philistine through and through. This was particularly evident in his pleasures, which went little beyond beer, tobacco, and vulgar guardroom humor. Imagination he had none. Whatever ideas he possessed were

[9] *Œuvres de Frédéric le Grand*, I, 180.
[10] Weber, *Aus vier Jahrhunderten*, I, 156; Förster, *Friedrich Wilhelm I*, II, 154.

strictly bounded by the utilitarian. Having little knowledge and less understanding of all forms of higher learning, he viewed them with contempt. One of his favorite expressions was: "All learned men are fools." Whereas he regarded science as leading to irreligion, he summarily disposed of philosophy as so much "hot air" (*Windmacherei*). In consequence, the pursuit of learning became a devious undertaking. How abject was its state is seen in the fact that Count Seckendorf, the king's bosom friend, had to smuggle books into the royal castle at Wusterhausen and carefully hide them lest their discovery deprive him of the king's confidence and favor.

This, of course, had the effect of discouraging any interest in higher learning in Prussia generally as well as in the circle of the king's immediate friends. Frederick the Great, while he was still crown prince, lamented in a letter to Voltaire:

The arts at present daily wither, and with tears in my eyes I behold knowledge flowing from us, while arrogant ignorance and barbarous manners usurp their place.
> The drooping laurel in our barren fields,
> Now withers in neglect; say why, ye gods,
> Must this my native land remain deprived
> Of science, arts, and heaven-descended fame? [11]

Later in life he said, as recorded by his reader Henri de Catt:

It is a great pity that my father showed so decided a contempt for everything that was related to philosophy and literature; they were really his antipathies. . . . I have never been able to conceive why my father, with so much good sense and intelligence, could not perceive that it was important for a prince to have subjects enlightened by letters and good philosophy, and that the greatest misfortune which could happen to a king

[11] *Œuvres*, XXI, 87.

would be to reign over subjects who are ignorant and for that reason generally superstitious.[12]

A memorable instance of Frederick William's attitude toward learning was his expulsion of the philosopher Christian Wolff, a disciple of Leibnitz, who was teaching his master's theory of preëstablished harmony at Halle. Wolff's enemies, envious of his success and reputation, represented to the king that the theory taught by Wolff might influence the Prussian soldiers to desert, since they could argue that in the existing order of things they were destined to desert and therefore had no choice in the matter. The king, who was naturally suspicious of philosophers because he could not understand their teachings, was readily persuaded and straightway wrote to the rector of the University of Halle: "You are to notify Wolff that within forty-eight hours after the receipt of this order he must quit Halle and all other Prussian territory under penalty of hanging." [13] Moreover, the reading of Wolff's works was for a time made punishable with penal servitude for life. Later Frederick William saw his error, and it is to his credit that he endeavored to make amends by apologizing to Wolff and begging him to return. But the philosopher, unmoved by the entreaties of the Prussian king, postponed his return to Prussia until the accession of Frederick the Great.

Frederick William's distaste for higher learning is also seen in his attitude toward the Berlin Academy of Science which his father had founded. When Leibnitz, the president of the academy, died in 1716, the Prussian autocrat for a time contemplated its dissolution, because he regarded it as an

---

[12] *Unterhaltungen mit Friedrich dem Grossen,* pp. 75–76.

[13] Cited in Winterfeld, "Christian Wolff in seinem Verhältnis zu Friedrich Wilhelm I und Friedrich dem Grossen," *Nord und Süd,* LXIV (1893), 225. See also Beneckendorf, *Karakterzüge aus dem Leben König Friedrich Wilhelms I,* II, 21–26.

unnecessary expense. Only after the chief surgeon of the Prussian army convinced him that it would be useful for the training of army surgeons did he continue to support it. He did, however, show his animus by ridiculing the academy at every opportunity and by entering the salary of its members in the royal accounts under the heading, "Expenses for the various royal buffoons." As Leibnitz's successor he chose Jakob Paul Gundling, a somewhat dull-witted polygraphist, whose admirable qualities as court buffoon recommended him to the king. Thus Gundling served both as president of the academy and as the butt of the coarse practical jokes perpetrated by Frederick William and his cronies. Within the circle of the king's intimate friends Gundling was indiscriminately showered with honors and indignities. One day he would be made a baron or similarly singled out and the next compelled to permit an ape dressed like himself to be seated by his side at the table. On at least one occasion the king and his friends had the door to Gundling's room removed in his absence and the opening filled with masonry; then they plied Herr Gundling with wine until he was inebriated and shook with laughter while he stumbled about seeking the entrance to his room. Another time they chained bear cubs, whose forepaws had been so mutilated that they were not able to lacerate him, to his bed in such a manner that he was forced to share it with them.

When Gundling died in 1731 even his funeral was made an occasion of amusement and hilarity. The king ordered the corpse attired in the former "court jester's" best gala dress of bright red satin with blue trimmings on which were embroidered the letters W U R M (worm), red silk stockings, and a prodigious wig of goats' hair and had it placed in a sitting position in a coffin shaped like a wine cask, reminiscent of Gundling's fondness for wine. The cask, painted black, was decorated with a large white cross and on its sides the following lines were inscribed:

In his own skin here lies
Half swine, half man, a wonder-thing
Wise in youth, foolish in old age
Mornings full of wit, at night full of wine and rage.
"Hark," Bacchus loudly cries;
"This precious child is Gundeling."

Surrounded by twelve burning tapers, the cask was exhibited publicly for twenty-four hours and then interred in the church at Börnstadt, near Potsdam.[14]

In fairness to Frederick William it must be stated, however, that he was not wholly insensitive to the attractions of music and art. At Potsdam he maintained a hautbois band, and whenever he was there this band gave concerts for his special enjoyment. Generally he was the sole auditor. His prime favorites were the operas of Handel. Two of them, *Alessandro* and *Siroe*, had been played for him so often that he knew the choruses and airs from memory. As these concerts were held in the evening, the king would occasionally fall asleep after a heavy meal. When the musicians noticed that he had his eyes closed for some length of time, they often skipped over parts of the music to hasten the end of the concert. The king was not to be trusted, however; frequently he was only feigning sleep and would suddenly shout: "You have omitted something," and order them to start over again. But even in his appreciation of music he showed a trace of buffoonery. Gottfried Pepusch, the conductor of the hautbois band, one day conceived the idea of using an incident which had taken place at a gathering of the king's cronies as the theme for a composition and ac-

[14] See Förster, *Friedrich Wilhelm I*, I, 259 *et sqq.*, 276 *et sqq.*

cordingly composed a piece for six oboes which were super-scribed: *"Porco primo," "Porco secundo,"* etc. ("First pig," "Second pig," and so forth). Delighted not a little with the squeals produced by this pig sextet, Frederick William had it repeated many times, and each time was obliged to hold his sides for laughter. While his interest in music was re-stricted to the role of auditor, he actually tried his hand at painting. The affairs of state permitting, he would fre-quently devote part of an afternoon to this hobby. Later in life, when attacks of the gout confined him to his rooms, he often painted for hours at a time. Since he was at such times racked by severe pains, some of his paintings bore the subscription, "In tormentis pinxit, F.W." His ability as a painter was rather limited, but he did succeed in giving to some of his animals a considerable degree of verisimilitude.

If Frederick William's tutors failed to excite in their pupil any wider intellectual interests, they were able to carry out at least one of the instructions Frederick I had drawn up for the education of his son. It was that which stated: "The electoral prince is to be instructed so thoroughly in the idea of the majesty and omnipotence of God that he will feel at all times a holy fear and veneration of God and his com-mandments." [15] So successfully did they inculcate the fear of God in his mind that throughout life he was never free from it. The arbiter of human destinies was to him the God of the Old Testament, the avenging Jehovah who "visits the sins of the fathers on the children to the third degree." The conviction that he would one day have to give account of his stewardship was, paradoxical as it may seem, the great motivating power of Frederick William's life. His stern Calvinistic training manifested itself in the fact that he re-

[15] Cramer, *Zur Geschichte Friedrich Wilhelms I und Fried-richs II.*

garded most of the ordinary forms of amusement as snares of the devil. Theaters he styled "temples of Satan." Believing them to be detrimental to the morals of his subjects, he ordered them closed when he acceded to the throne in 1713, permitting only marionette shows. "If I were to see a comedy in Bristol or some other place where I do not give orders," he said, "I would make nothing of it; but where the responsibility is mine, I cannot permit it, for I would be guilty of all the evil which would result therefrom." [16] Later he became so liberal as to allow the presentation of comedies in Berlin under strict censorship. Toward the provincial towns and cities he was less indulgent, occasionally permitting the presentation of plays, but most often refusing permission. Balls and masquerades he tolerated at the beginning of his reign, but later he was induced by the clergy to forbid them. In the instructions for his successor he wrote several times, "My dear successor must not permit comedies, operas, ballets, or masquerades in his territories, and must abhor them, for they are godless and satanical, the means wherewith Satan enlarges his dominion." [17]

The one dogma of Calvinism which he did not accept unquestioningly was predestination. In an effort to curb his unruliness, his tutors, it appears, had used this doctrine as a pedagogical weapon. They told him that his vehement temper and his refusal to learn might be indications that he was not predestined. The fear that this was so cast a shadow over his early years, causing him much anxiety and at times making him melancholy. Not until he was twenty did Frederick William conquer this fear, and then only because he came under the influence of Pietism, which taught that salvation

[16] Cited in Hinrichs, "Friedrich Wilhelm I," in *Die Welt als Geschichte*, IV (1938), 22.
[17] *AB, Beh.*, III, 442.

is not the privilege of the few, but is universal. The remembrance of the anxiety he had suffered because of this dogma and his belief that the idea of predestination tended to relieve his subjects of personal responsibility later moved him to forbid the teaching of it to his children. In 1719 he even issued a decree which forbade all Calvinist ministers under the threat of severe punishment to discuss the dogma in their pulpits. As army chaplains he chose only Lutherans, because he feared that the Reformed clergymen might teach the doctrine of predestination to his soldiers, who would then desert, believing they had been predestined to do so.[18]

Sincere as he was, Frederick William often found it difficult to carry out the precepts of his religion in his personal life. His irritability, his passion for the hunt, and particularly his love of food and drink caused him many pangs of conscience. To the younger Francke, for example, he confessed that he felt a great desire to drink to excess and restrained himself only "because God's Word proclaimed that it was sin." [19] Frequent lapses from this chosen path of righteousness are recorded. Count Seckendorf, for instance, reported to Prince Eugene: "Yesterday His Royal Majesty dined with me and made merry until after midnight, becoming somewhat excessively drunk." [20] Such excesses were invariably followed by the deepest contrition. Upon at least one occasion Frederick William's remorse was so great that he resolved to abdicate the throne and retire to a life of prayer and husbandry. Only the remonstrances of his advisers restrained him from actually carrying out the resolve.

[18] See *AB, Beh.*, VI (Part 1), 53; Fassmann, *Leben und Thaten Friedrich Wilhelms*, p. 907; *Briefe Friedrich Wilhelms I an H. R. Pauli*, edited by Frensdorff, pp. 45, 55; Förster, *Friedrich Wilhelm I*, II, 339.

[19] Kramer, *Neue Beiträge zur Geschichte August Herrmann Franckes*, p. 172.

[20] Förster, *Urkundenbuch*, III, 378.

Throughout his life he constantly admonished those about him to be more conscientious in their religious duties. Thus, for example, he urged Leopold of Dessau in 1711 to be more diligent in attending church services. "I am no Pietist," he wrote to Leopold, "but God before everything in the world." [21]

In one respect there was almost complete harmony between creed and conduct in Frederick William's life. In the age of Augustus the Strong and Louis XV, an age in which the private lives of few monarchs would bear investigation, he observed a standard of purity that was extraordinary. Chastity, in fact, was an obsession with the Prussian monarch. The Pietist Francke reports that as a young man of twenty Frederick William flatly contradicted his statement that the sin against the Holy Ghost is the one unforgivable sin with the assertion, "Harlotry, that is the most terrible sin." [22] In his instructions for his successor he stated several times: "My dear successor may be assured that God will shower him with worldly and spiritual blessings if he keeps God ever before him, has no mistresses, better known as whores, and leads a Godfearing life." [23] In 1729, while he was on a visit to Saxony, Augustus the Strong put every temptation in his way, but the Prussian monarch refused to succumb. From Saxony he wrote to his friend Seckendorf: "The life here is anything but Christian. But God is my witness that I have found no pleasure in it and am still as clean as when I left home and with the help of God will persevere until the end." [24] Thiebault relates in his *Memoirs*

[21] *Briefe Friedrich Wilhelms an Leopold zu Anhalt-Dessau*, p. 48.
[22] Cited in Krauske, "Friedrich Wilhelm und Leopold von Anhalt," *Historische Zeitschrift*, LXXV (1895), 32.
[23] *AB, Beh.*, III, 442.
[24] Krauske, "Vom Hofe Friedrich Wilhelms I," in *Hohenzollern-Jahrbuch*, V (1901), 180.

that when the court preacher discussed with the dying
Frederick William the question of forgiveness, the latter
replied: "I was never guilty of the smallest infidelity toward
my wife; and I trust that because of my continence God
will forgive my other sins." [25] That he was not guilty of
infidelity was not due entirely to his self-restraint. There
is at least one recorded instance when he did make advances
to a woman. But his manner was so gruff and his procedure
so blunt that the object of his desires repulsed him.

In his relations with women in general Frederick William
betrayed more of the boor than of the king. He was never
at ease in the presence of members of the other sex. When
a woman addressed him, he would blush deeply and often
become greatly embarrassed. In his embarrassment the naturally blunt and coarse-grained Prussian would become
irresistibly rude. This incivility to women began at an early
age. How deeply it grieved his mother when she heard of it
can be seen from a letter to Mlle von Pöllnitz.

I sent for my son [she wrote] and lectured him well, and as this
does not happen often, I used the opportunity to recall and
dwell upon his many evil doings. I must also add that repeated
complaints have come to me from my ladies that he has often
spoken improperly. This thought angered me to the point of
fury. "Is that the way of refined persons?" I asked. "Is there
any greatness in offending people? What baseness of mind, to
speak improperly to a sex which should be the recipient of
chivalry from men!" [26]

His behavior toward women seems to have become even
more rude after Caroline of Anspach, his first love, who was
five years his senior and who afterward became the wife
of George II of England, refused to take seriously his at-
tentions to her.

[25] French edition, I, 178.
[26] *Mémoires pour servir à l'histoire de Sophie Charlotte*, p. 184.

In 1706, at the age of eighteen, he married Princess Sophie Dorothea, daughter of the elector of Hanover, who soon became George I of England. But the marriage wrought little change in his attitude toward women. During the rest of his life he avoided their company whenever he could. If he attended a wedding, he was wont to permit only the bride and the bride's mother to be present. At the state balls which he attended he would dance only with the queen; on other occasions when there were no women present he would dance with his generals or his giant grenadiers. Baron Bielfeld, who was present on such an occasion, has left a somewhat highly-colored account of it.

After dinner [he wrote] they sent for the hautbois of the regiment and began to dance. I looked this way and that, expecting to see some ladies enter; and I was stupified when one of these descendants of Anak, a giant of ruby and weather-beaten countenance, proferred me his hand to open the ball. I could not but be greatly embarrassed when the proposition was made to me to dance with a man. But they gave me little time for reflection, for dance I must. The commanders of the regiment danced, all the officers danced; and toward the end this masculine ball became very animated, thanks to the repeated bumpers of champagne which they made us drink by way of refreshment. After eight in the evening most of the terrible warriors declined the combat, their huge limbs no longer able to encounter Bacchus and Terpsichore, and they went staggering off.[27]

A good quality in Frederick William was his love of cleanliness. Upon arising in the morning he would wash his body as well as his hands and face, a practice that was truly exceptional in an age in which most people bathed only when they were ill. During the day he would wash and groom himself many times. The number of his ablutions, it

[27] *Letters of Baron Bielfeld*, III, 71.

was said, was in excess of those required of faithful Moslems. "He not only washed himself five times daily," Morgenstern wrote, "but as often as he touched anything that was sticky or whenever his hands perspired." [28] Frederick William also changed his linens daily, and his outer clothing was always scrupulously clean. To protect his uniform from ink spots he wore a large green apron at his writing table, while linen oversleeves kept his sleeves from being soiled. All this was in direct contrast to the habits of his more illustrious son, whose uniform during his later years was usually covered with dirt, gravy spots, and snuff. The use of snuff, which was widespread in his time, Frederick William denounced as an unclean habit. "People who are perpetually choking and polluting their nostrils with tobacco," he said, "are no better than pigs to my mind." [29] In the royal household Dutch cleanliness was the rule. The walls of the king's rooms were painted white, and all the chairs and benches were made entirely of wood. Draperies, upholstered chairs, and even carpets were banished to prevent any accumulation of dust. The linens on the royal table had to be nothing short of immaculate. When in his travels through his territories he stopped to eat in the house of one of his subjects, he would eat whatever food was placed before him, but if the linens were not spotless he would soundly berate the housewife. One of his favorite remarks was: "Dutch cleanliness is needed in this State."

One of Frederick William's characteristics which was to have far-reaching results for the future of Prussia was his frugality. From the age of eight the future Prussian ruler kept an exact account, in a book entitled "Account of My Ducats," of the manner in which he spent his allowance, duly entering every expenditure, however small. In an age

[28] Page 60.   [29] Eulenberg, *Die Hohenzollern*, p. 182.

of princely munificence such thrift was regarded as akin to avarice, and avarice was held to be the most unpardonable of sins. When Sophie Charlotte saw this "ugly tendency" in her son, she unburdened herself to her friend Mlle von Pöllnitz in no measured terms.

I am greatly chagrined, my dear Pöllnitz, [she wrote] and must unburden my heart to you, for besides the worries you know of I have another which your devotion to me foretold long ago. My son, who I thought was only quick and impulsive, has also given proof of a grasping hardness which can only originate in a wicked heart. "Oh no," says la Bülow, "it is only avarice." Ye gods, so much the worse. Avaricious at his tender age! One can correct other faults, but avarice grows with the years and what evil effects it will have later! How can kindness or pity find room in a heart which is dominated by self-interest. Dohna is an honorable man, a man of integrity and noble sentiments, but his failing is also penuriousness, and he cannot well correct a failing which he approves in his heart.[30]

But Sophie Charlotte was wrong in at least one respect. Her son's frugality was not rooted in avarice; it was, at least in large measure, the result of the instruction of Count Dohna, who was doing everything he could to cultivate the habit of frugality in the young prince. Especially did he instill in the mind of his ward an aversion for the excessive pomp and magnificence which, he believed, was ruining Prussia. Soon after Frederick William ascended the throne it became apparent that his frugality was for the best interests of the State as he saw them.

Another respect in which Frederick William differed from his parents was his attitude toward things French. Long before he became king he had evinced a strong repugnance for everything French, probably aroused in the serious-minded lad by the French pomp and frivolity of his father's

[30] *Mémoires pour servir à l'histoire de Sophie Charlotte*, p. 183.

court. Throughout his life he prided himself on being German, and he repeatedly said: "I am a true German." Count Seckendorf reports him as saying: "He is a dastardly scoundrel, even though he be a crowned head, who says I am French." [31] During a visit to Augustus the Strong of Saxony in 1731 he proposed the toast: "*Vivat Germania*. A dastardly scoundrel is he who does not sincerely mean it." [32] Frederick William had for the first six years of his life been in the care of a French governess who, knowing no German, had spoken only French to him. As his mother also conversed with him in this language, French was, so to speak, his mother tongue. But after he had grown to manhood he refused to converse in French, except with strangers. Nor would he employ any language but German in his correspondence, except in extraordinary cases. "I am a German," he said to his secretary on one occasion; "hence I will write in my native language." [33] What he regarded as German, however, was a crude jargon compounded of colloquial barbarisms, High German, French, English, and Latin. He who affected to despise the French language could not express his ideas without borrowing liberally from it, as is evidenced by the following sentence: "Wenn ein junger Mensch *Sottisen* thut im *Courtisiren*, u.s.w., solches kann man ihm als Jugendfehler *pardonniren;* aber mit Vorsatz *Lacheteten* und dergleichen garstige *Action* zu tun, ist *impardonnable*." [34] Again, he who vowed to live and die as a German could not spell the word "Deutschland" (Germany); he invariably wrote it "Deusland."

Frederick William's most outstanding characteristic was his love of soldiers and things military. Aggressive and mili-

[31] Förster, *Friedrich Wilhelm I*, II, 145.
[32] *Ibid.*, p. 12.
[33] *AB, Beh.*, II, 336.
[34] Cited in Preuss, *Friedrichs des Grossen Jugend*, p. 133.

tant by nature, the future Prussian ruler, like most other boys of the time, early took great delight in military games. Count Dohna, a dyed-in-the-wool militarist, fostered this interest at every opportunity, with the result that the games of childhood became the serious policy of his pupil's mature years. As a young lad Frederick William had already assembled at Wusterhausen, the royal hunting lodge, a company of cadets, for the up-keep of which, as the account book shows, he spent much of his allowance. When he was twelve his interest in military things was greatly intensified by a journey to Holland, where he met William III of Orange, and was privileged to review the Dutch troops. At a later time he is reported to have said: "If I had remained with King William he would certainly have made a great man of me." When one of those present remarked: "But you are a great king," he replied: "He would have taught me the art of commanding the armies of all Europe. Do you know anything greater?" [35] At the age of sixteen he was made colonel of a regiment of infantry by his father and thenceforth spent much of his time drilling it. This and the discussion of military affairs soon became his greatest pleasure. At foreign courts it was said of him that he "has little knowledge of anything but the barracks, and knows no other forms of social intercourse but giving orders and obeying orders." [36]

Already during these years he set the goal of his life's endeavors. Whereas his father had tried to give prestige to his new crown by surrounding himself with pomp and by promoting the development of the arts and sciences, he would gain prestige, nay, territory, by means of a large army, one that would be second to none in Europe as regards

[35] Morgenstern, *Ueber Friedrich Wilhelm I*, p. 202.
[36] Cited in Droysen, *Geschichte der preussischen Politik*, IV (Part 2), 7.

efficiency. This plan to create a large, well-drilled, and well-equipped army was motivated not merely by Frederick William's love of soldiers and things military, although he did say: "I find pleasure in nothing in this world except in a strong army"; [37] it was a conscious political policy based on his experiences. The years of his youth were marked by wars—War of the League of Augsburg and War of the Spanish Succession—which involved most of Europe and even extended to remoter parts of the globe. During the latter war he himself participated in the campaign in the Netherlands and was present at the battle of Malplaquet (1709). From his experiences he appears to have concluded that the power and prestige of a prince are exactly equal to the number of troops he is able to maintain. As early as 1711 he ridiculed his father's ministers for thinking they could gain prestige and territory for Prussia by diplomacy. "I can but laugh at the scoundrels," he wrote to his friend Leopold of Dessau; "they say they will obtain land and people for the king with the pen; but I say it can be done only with the sword, otherwise he will get nothing." [38] Later he wrote to the same friend: "If one wishes to decide anything in this world, it cannot be done with the pen if it is not supported by the power of the sword." [39]

Frederick I, it is true, had strengthened the Prussian army which his predecessor had created so that it numbered more than 38,000 at the time of his death. But since he was able to support this army only with the help of foreign subsidies, he had to subordinate his own aims and interests to the aims and interests of the nations that were paying the subsidies. During the War of the Spanish Succession, for example, the Prussian soldiers were sacrificed largely for the ambitions of

[37] *AB, Beh.*, I, 441.
[38] *Briefe Friedrich Wilhelms an Leopold zu Anhalt-Dessau*, p. 55.
[39] *Ibid.*, p. 523.

other nations. The Prussian army demonstrated its fighting prowess in Flanders, in Italy, on the Rhine, and on the Danube, but beyond the royal crown it gained little for Prussia. This led Frederick William to resolve that he would provide for the subsistence of his army without foreign subsidies. In other words, Prussia's army would be supported entirely with Prussian funds and would fight only for Prussian ends. More than this, he would accumulate a reserve fund to support the army in case of war. The French ambassador at Berlin reported Frederick William as saying: "One will always be obliged to court the favor of a prince who has a standing army of one hundred thousand men, and twenty-five million crowns to support it in action." [40] This same idea he stated again and again in the instructions for his successor. "A formidable army and a fund large enough to make this army mobile in times of need," he wrote, "can create great respect for you in the world, so that you can speak a word like the other powers." [41] Once he became king, Frederick William worked persistently and determinedly to achieve these aims. They are the key to his life. Almost everything he thought, said, or did was more-or-less intimately related to them.

[40] Cited in Lavisse, *La Jeunesse du Grand Frédéric,* p. 98.
[41] *AB, Beh.,* III, 456.

CHAPTER FOUR

Frederick William Becomes King

FREDERICK WILLIAM was in his twenty-fifth year when he succeeded his father to the throne. He had an oval and ruddy face, with blue eyes, a high forehead, and a somewhat severe expression. Though his height was only five feet, five inches, he had about him the air of a sovereign. His conception of the kingship was a curious mixture of kind paternalism and unrelenting despotism. With a certain naïveté he declared himself "a true republican" or "only the first servant of the State"; [1] but in practice he adopted the principle of stern autocracy, setting himself above State and law and arbitrarily disposing of honor, life, liberty, and property. On a number of occasions he stated the idea of his absolute supremacy in terms which leave no room for doubt. His version of *L'état c'est moi* was: "We are king and master and can do what we like" or "I need render account to no one as to the manner in which I conduct my affairs." [2] Dire threats were hurled at the Prussian nobles because they were not always as submissive as Frederick William desired. "The authority of the Junkers," he stated determinedly, "shall be destroyed; I will establish the sovereignty like a rock of

[1] Morgenstern, *Ueber Friedrich Wilhelm I*, p. 29.
[2] *AB, Beh.*, III, 295, 573; IV (Part 2), 393.

bronze." [3] The duty of his subjects toward him, as he saw it, was an unquestioning obedience on the part of all, whether of low or of high social standing. This, he believed, they owed him, not because of himself, but because he was God's representative, or *Stadthalter*, as he put it. This idea he not only stated in the phrase "We, Frederick William, by the grace of God King in Prussia," but also in less perfunctory ways. For example, the decree for the reform of the administration of justice which he issued soon after he became king (June 23, 1713), contains the statement: "As the only just Judge will on that great day punish wrong with an inescapable eternal punishment, we shall not be remiss in punishing it with condign severity so long as we are His representative in this temporal existence." [4]

Frederick William's claim to absolute sovereignty was no empty one, for all power in the State actually centered in him. He was at once the supreme lawgiver, the supreme judge, and the supreme administrator. In his case it was quite literally true that "the desire of the prince hath the force of law." Decrees officially issued by him automatically became law. Any objections he summarily overruled with such curt commands as: "I command it," "It is my will," or "I desire it thus." [5] Every show of insubordination he crushed with a remorseless hand. "I am no cipher," he declared; "when I give an order it must be carried out." [6] As supreme judge, Frederick William had the right to change or to nullify the verdict of any court in the land, a prerogative he frequently used. As supreme administrator he personally supervised the administration of all his provinces. All orders,

[3] *Ibid.*, II, 352.
[4] *Corpus constitutionum marchicarum*, II (Part 1), 517.
[5] *AB, Beh.*, II, 470, 476, 535; III, 17, 204; IV (Part 1), 152.
[6] *Ibid.*, IV (Part 1), 156.

even those issued by his ministers and by minor officials, were issued in the king's name.

The artisan to whom the royal guild statute was a solemn guarantee of his economic security; the peasant who received a marriage license; the merchant entrepreneur who was exempted from the payment of duty on importing a specified article, all of them received their privileges from the king. When on Sunday the village pastor read a patent or an ordinance from the pulpit, it was the king who addressed the assembled congregation, even when the document in question had been issued only by a subaltern authority.[7]

The publication of a document in the king's name, however, was not necessarily a fiction; it might well bear the personal signature of the king. The conviction that he was God's stadtholder made Frederick William acutely conscious of his obligation to the Almighty. Next to being a good Christian in his private life he desired nothing more than to be a good ruler, to give his provinces a good administration. But he believed that the administration could be good only if he did most of the administrative work himself. "If one does not stick one's nose into every dirty mess," he wrote to Leopold of Dessau, "things do not go as they should."[8] Hence he decided to do as much of the work as possible himself. In the instructions for his successor he said: "You must work as I have always done; a ruler who wishes to rule honorably must attend to all his affairs himself, for rulers are ordained for work, not for idle effeminate lives such as, alas, are led by a great many people."[9] This left no room for a prime minister or viceroy. At the beginning of the reign Leopold of Dessau had high hopes of tak-

[7] Dorn, "The Prussian Bureaucracy in the Eighteenth Century," *Political Science Quarterly*, XLVI (1931), 408.
[8] *Briefe an Leopold zu Anhalt-Dessau*, p. 338.
[9] *AB, Beh.*, III, 445.

ing complete charge of military affairs. But Frederick William, much as he admired the military ability and rich experience of Old Dessauer, was not the man to abdicate any of his authority even to his best friend. With naïve directness he wrote to General von Grumbkow: "Tell the Prince of Anhalt that I will be his friend so long as he carries out my orders. I am the finance minister and field marshal of the king of Prussia; this will be sufficient to uphold the king of Prussia." [10] He might as well have added that he would also be his own minister of war, diplomacy, education, commerce, industry, agriculture, and home affairs in general.

Frederick William wished to supervise everything—to decide everything. Nothing was too unimportant to pass his attention. "Salvation," he wrote, "is of God; everything else is my affair." [11] No minister or secretary applied himself to petty details more patiently and conscientiously. "He had," Frederick the Great said, "an industrious spirit in a robust body, and perhaps more capacity for entering into the most minute details than any man that ever lived." [12] He would minutely examine an estimate for a new chimney to see if the cost could not be cut down, and he would wrangle with the cook over the price of meat served on the royal table. It is little short of a miracle that he was not overwhelmed by the flood of minutiae. "He who has not witnessed it can hardly believe," Count Seckendorf wrote to Prince Eugene, "that one living person, of whatever intelligence he may be, can dispatch so many different things in one day and can do it himself, as the king does daily." [13] Frederick William's ministers were, of course, mere amanu-

[10] Kessel, "Friedrich Wilhelm I," in *Schöpfer und Gestalter der Wehrkraft*, p. 44.
[11] *AB, Beh.*, II, 128–129.
[12] Catt, *Unterhaltungen mit Friedrich dem Grossen*, p. 34.
[13] Förster, *Urkundenbuch*, II, 42.

enses. The scope of their action was extremely limited; none was permitted any initiative. They decided only those matters which the king deigned to pass down to them; even then the decisions were almost invariably made on the basis of royal decisions of an earlier date. All important matters and untold numbers of unimportant ones were decided by Frederick William himself.

The manner in which Frederick William conducted his administration was that of "cabinet" government. This did not mean, however, as it did in England, that the government was exercised by an inner group of ministers called "the cabinet." In Prussia the expression "cabinet government" was used in an opposite sense. It meant the personal rule of the monarch from his cabinet or private room, not through his cabinet or group of ministers. Both the Great Elector and Frederick I had made their decisions in the council chamber in the presence of their ministers, who as a group were called the Privy Council; but Frederick William I made his in the privacy of his apartment, attended only by his private secretaries, whose principal duty it was to draw up the royal decisions in official form. He saw his ministers infrequently for the purpose of discussing state affairs. Once each year he met with them to discuss or, better, review the affairs of their respective departments. Otherwise the ministers conferred with the king only at his command or by special appointment. Much of the time he was either at Potsdam or Wusterhausen, while his ministers remained at their headquarters in Berlin. The ordinary means of communication between the king and his ministers was the pen, even when he was in Berlin. Not only the voluminous reports of the ministers but also their memorials and petitions were written. These the king answered with his own hand or, more frequently, by orders dictated to his secretaries, called cabinet orders (*Kabinets-Ordres*). Thus the king's apartment was the central bureau or "cabinet" of the Prussian bureaucracy.

The exhaustive reports of his ministers were not, however, the only source of Frederick William's knowledge of his administration and provinces. He had to see with his own eyes what was taking place. Undeterred by the worst kind of roads and by inclement weather, he made frequent journeys to all his provinces. On these journeys he reviewed his regiments, held meetings with his various local officials, examined the accounts of his estates, inspected the military stores and magazines, and in general learned as much as he could about local conditions. "I must know," he stated, "what is going on in my territories." [14] Thus it was not without reason that George II called him "the king of the highroads."

The days Frederick William spent in Berlin or Potsdam were regulated almost with the precision of a time-table. He arose very early, and his secretaries arrived to begin work at five, six, or seven in the morning, according to the season of the year. Sealed letters could be opened only in his presence. After all the correspondence had been opened the secretaries would read the reports and petitions to him, and in most cases he would make an immediate decision. Everything was dispatched with the most punctilious regularity. Frederick William was so methodical in his work that a minister who sent him a petition knew exactly when to expect an answer. If the decision was a long one, he would dictate it; if brief, he would often write it in the margin of the petition with his own hand.[15] Having carefully studied the reports and petitions, a task which usually required from

[14] *AB, Beh.,* V (Part 1), 565.
[15] These marginal notes, of which thousands have survived, afford an excellent insight into the government of Frederick William.

two or three hours, the king would give audience to envoys, ministers, or other important personages. At ten he usually went to the parade ground for purposes of inspection or drill. Those of his subjects who had written petitions to present or oral requests to make could approach the king while he was en route. Often he would make decisions on the spot, particularly if the petitioner was a soldier. Upon the stroke of twelve he would sit down to dinner, at which there were always numerous guests—frequently as many as forty, including generals, ministers, foreign envoys, and others. The discussions at table were usually lively and often lasted an hour and a half to two hours. After dinner, if the weather was good, the king would walk or ride about Berlin or Potsdam accompanied by a general or only by his pages. On these *tours de baton* (as some contemporary wit styled the king's walks, because he applied his cane so often to the backs of his subjects) he would stop to talk with many whom he met, using the opportunities to gain first-hand knowledge of his subjects and of conditions in general. Later in the afternoon he would either return to the parade grounds or again take up matters of state.[16]

The king usually spent his evenings in the so-called *Tabaks-Kollegium* (Tobacco Parliament) which met nightly —in the winter at five and in the summer at seven—at Berlin, Potsdam, or Wusterhausen, in whichever place he happened to be. The Tobacco Parliament was usually composed of from six to twelve people, mostly the king's intimate advisers and high officers of his retinue. Occasionally foreign envoys or distinguished visitors who happened to be in Berlin were also invited. When the weather was mild the group

---

[16] Morgenstern, *Ueber Friedrich Wilhelm I*, p. 162 *et sqq.*; Fassmann, *Leben und Thaten Friedrich Wilhelms I*, p. 876 *et sqq.*; Förster, *Friedrich Wilhelm I*, I, 238 *et sqq.*; Beneckendorf, *Karakterzüge aus dem Leben König Friedrich Wilhelms I*, I, 118 *et sqq.*

met in the open; otherwise around a large wooden table in a large unadorned room. It was the custom to set before each guest a pitcher of beer and a clay pipe. Baskets of coarse tobacco, from which the guests filled their pipes, were placed on the table. All were expected to smoke or at least to go through the motions of doing so. Men like Leopold of Dessau and Count Seckendorf, who had never acquired the habit, were obliged to pretend to smoke with an empty pipe. Frederick William, who was an inveterate smoker, often smoked as many as thirty pipefuls of tobacco during one of these sessions. In these gatherings every kind of ceremony and all restraint were put aside, the king desiring to appear only as a private individual. The time was spent reading German or foreign newspapers, discussing the topics of the day, or reminiscing. Military life and the hunt were the favorite subjects of reminiscence. Frequently prolonged far into the night, the conversation was spiced with guard-room humor or the occasion was enlivened by coarse practical jokes. These gatherings gave so much pleasure to the king that even when he was physically indisposed he had himself carried to the place of meeting, or if too ill for this the company was summoned to his sickroom.[17]

For relaxation Frederick William also turned to hunting. This was his one real luxury, since it called for the maintenance of large game parks, a host of huntsmen attired in livery, and a well-chosen pack of hunting dogs. When he was only a boy of ten the gloomy hunting lodge at Wusterhausen, about fourteen English miles from Berlin, was his favorite abode, and he took great delight in hunting small game. After he became king Frederick usually spent two months of each year there. Frequently he would organize

[17] Fassmann, *Leben und Thaten Friedrich Wilhelms I*, pp. 879 et sqq.; Förster, *Friedrich Wilhelm I*, I, 240 et sqq.

meets in other provinces to hunt deer, wild hogs, bears, wild oxen, herons, quail, hares, pheasants, and other game. It was not unusual for him to rise very early in the bitter cold of winter and to ride two or three leagues in an open carriage in order to begin the hunt at daybreak. Many of these hunting parties turned out to be slaughters, the king often doing all the shooting himself. From an account that was kept it appears that at Wusterhausen alone Frederick William with his own hand killed 25,066 partridges, 1,455 pheasants, and 1,145 hares during the years from 1717 to 1738.[18] Francke made the following entry in his diary for October 4, 1727: "At six the king, highly satisfied with his success, returned with 151 partridges, eighteen rabbits, and two pheasants, all of which he had shot himself." [19] In the year 1729 the king and his party slaughtered no less than 3,602 wild hogs, the hunt for which was often fraught with great danger. Despite the warnings of his close friends, Frederick William continued his hunts with unabated enthusiasm. He took such delight in killing wild hogs that when the dogs cornered one the attendants would hold it by the ears until the king rode up and dispatched it.

It is his custom [Fassmann wrote] to send the boars that have been killed to certain persons, with a note stating how much they are to pay for them. This he does especially in Berlin. First the king takes what is wanted for the use of his own domestic establishment, where a great quantity of smoked hams and wild boars' heads are consumed. Then his majesty makes presents of many to his cousins and other relatives; also to his generals, high officials, and others. The rest are sent to His Majesty's privy councillors, secretaries, or to citizens who pay from three to six taler for each one, according to the size.

---

[18] Förster, *Friedrich Wilhelm I*, I, 351.
[19] Kramer, *Neue Beiträge zur Geschichte August Herrmann Franckes*, p. 165.

It was a favorite prank of the king to compel wealthy Jewish citizens of Berlin to buy a certain number of these hogs. "They pay immediately without making any objections," Fassmann stated, "and send them to the workhouses and hospitals." [20]

One of the first things that Frederick William did after taking up the reins of government was to put an end to the luxury and costly show with which his father had surrounded himself. Thenceforth simplicity and strict economy became the order of the day. This the new king regarded as necessary if Prussia was to defray the expenses of a large army without foreign subsidies. At the funeral of Frederick I the court appeared for the last time in its old magnificence. No expense was spared by the son to give his father a funeral of such splendor as would have met with the approval of the dead monarch. But no sooner was that duty fulfilled than Frederick William proceeded to give the court a new appearance. The twenty-six trumpeters and kettle-drummers who had announced the movements of the king were assigned to various regiments, and the Swiss guards who had so proudly paraded about in uniforms of silk and satin brocaded with gold were simply dismissed. Their place as guards of the palace was taken by regular Prussian soldiers. Even the dress of the courtiers was gradually changed, the gold-brocaded silk and satin garments giving way to the tight-fitting Prussian uniforms as the official state dress. After 1719 the king himself seldom wore anything else. How highly he regarded his uniform is indicated by an incident related by Count von Wartensleben. He reports that when the chaplain sang the hymn, "Naked shall I, too, appear before Thy stern countenance" at the king's bedside during

[20] *Leben und Thaten Friedrich Wilhelms I*, p. 902.

Frederick William's last illness, the latter shouted: "That is not so; I shall be buried in my uniform." [21]

In changing the outward appearance of the court Frederick William also changed its spirit. In fact, the court, if regarded in the usual sense of the word, ceased to exist. The court of Frederick I became, so to speak, the military headquarters of Frederick William I. Not only did army officers replace the courtiers but even the royal parks of Berlin and Potsdam, where the court dames and cavaliers had strolled in the previous reign, were changed into drill grounds which resounded with the clank of arms. Wilhelmina, the king's eldest daughter, states in her *Memoirs:* "The face of everything was changed. Those who wished to insure the favor of the new king assumed the helmet and cuirass; everything became military, not a vestige remained of the old court." [22] Count von Loen wrote during a visit to Berlin in 1717: "I see here a court that has nothing brilliant and nothing magnificent except its soldiers . . . When one speaks of the Berlin court one understands the term to mean little more than the military set, for they alone really compose the royal court. The privy councillors, chamberlains, and similar functionaries are not held in much respect unless they also hold military office." [23]

Here was the beginning of that preponderance of military over civil affairs which became characteristic of Prusso-German history. As indicated, many posts in the civil administration were given to army officers. Von Grumbkow, for example, was Frederick William's minister of finance besides being an active general in the army. Officers sat on many boards and had a voice in most civil matters. If a board was composed of both army officers and civil officials, the

[21] Koser, "Aus den letzten Tagen König Friedrich Wilhelms I," in *Hohenzollern-Jahrbuch*, VIII (1904), 25.

[22] *Memoirs of Frederica Sophia Wilhelmina*, I, 8.

[23] Isaacsohn, *Geschichte des preussischen Beamtenthums*, II, 8.

chair was always occupied by an army officer.[24] The preference was so patent that complaints about it reached the king.
In a letter to Leopold of Dessau, Frederick William wrote:
"Lehmann and Bube (two civil officials) told me to my face
that they are hostile to me. The reason is that I give the best
offices to soldiers and do not esteem men of learning." [25]
Such complaints appear to have effected no change in the
king.

He preferred those [Beneckendorf wrote] who carried a sword,
believing that they were qualified and able to conduct all the
affairs of the state, even the most important. . . . Since he
thought a soldier capable of everything, any development of
the mind was regarded as superfluous. A general was not regarded as uneducated even though he could barely write his
name. Whoever could do more was styled a pedant, inksplasher,
and scribbler. Consequently a stiff and coarse demeanor gradually became widespread, nay, characteristic.[26]

This military demeanor spread from the court to the people,
giving to Prussian life in general a military hue.

But Frederick William did not stop at the changes already
listed; there were others for the benefit of the royal treasury.
The number of court officials and attendants who had
thronged the palaces of his father was drastically reduced.
No official who in the opinion of the new king was not abso-
lutely necessary was retained, no matter how long he had
held his office, while those who were retained had their
salaries greatly reduced. The salary of Von Printzen, the
governor of the palace, for example, was reduced from 1,700
to 400 taler.[27] Other officials had to accept similar reductions. All protests were curtly swept aside with the remark:

[24] See *AB, Beh.,* V (Part 2), 5 *et sqq.*
[25] *Briefe an Leopold zu Anhalt-Dessau,* p. 154.
[26] *Karakterzüge aus dem Leben König Friedrich Wilhelms I,*
VIII, 14.
[27] *AB, Beh.,* I, 320.

"We poor beggars must cut our coat according to our cloth."
Frederick the Great later wrote: "Many who had kept
coaches now walked on foot, which made the people say
that the king had restored to the lame the use of their limbs.
Under Frederick I Berlin was the Athens of the north; under
Frederick William it became the Sparta." [28] How drastic the
curtailment was is shown by the fact that the salaries of the
higher court officials, which during the previous reign had
annually amounted to 276,000 taler, were reduced to 55,000.

Nor did the policy of retrenchment stop here. Whereas
the father had spent five million taler on his coronation, the
son managed to limit the expenses for his own to 2,547 taler
and nine pfennige. Frederick William also decreed that foreign diplomats and even foreign rulers were no longer to be
accorded expensive receptions. In this regard he did not
make an exception even for his friend Peter the Great of
Russia. Thus, when Peter visited him in 1717 the Prussian
monarch informed his director of finances that the state expense for the tsar's trip from Wesel to Memel must not exceed 6,000 taler; then he added the remark: "But before the
world you are to say that it cost me between 30,000 and
40,000 reichstaler." [29] Furthermore, instead of completing
the royal palace at Berlin according to the plan of Frederick
I with its various additions and beautifications, Frederick
William carried out only the essentials of the plan. The
numerous other royal palaces, with the exception of those
at Potsdam, Charlottenburg, and Wusterhausen, were either
rented out, converted into hospitals, or transformed into
living quarters for state officials. The bulk of the jewelry,
silver plate, and valuable furniture which Frederick I had
accumulated was sold; also many of the statues that had been
placed in the parks and the various royal buildings. Three

[28] *Œuvres*, I, 266.   [29] Förster, *Friedrich Wilhelm I*, I, 213.

hundred medals of the large collection his predecessor had made were sent to the mint, together with the silver decorations from the doors of the royal carriages.

In the same manner Frederick William also limited his personal expenses to what was indispensable. Of the many pages who had waited upon the former king he retained only two or three who were required to serve him at table and also to accompany him on his travels and tours of inspection; the rest were put into the army. The same besom of reform also swept into the army the numerous cooks, stewards, and musicians employed by Frederick I. Regarding the menagerie his father had collected as a luxury, the new king sold some animals and gave away the rest. Whereas the father, according to the fodder lists, had kept nearly a thousand horses in the royal stables, the son retained only twelve pairs of carriage horses and thirty saddle horses. Much as he loved hunting, he nevertheless sold most of the four hundred hunting dogs in the kennels of his father.

This scaling down can be observed also in other matters. The daily expenses of the royal kitchen, for example, were limited to 33⅓ taler. If more than the allotted amount was spent during any week for the entertainment of foreign guests, the extra expense was deducted from the allowance for the following weeks. The king himself carefully examined the menu for each week and would strike from it anything that seemed too expensive. He did not even hesitate to haggle with the cook over the price of food. Once when the king was ill, his cook, thinking he would therewith please the king, roasted a woodcock for him. The king enjoyed the treat very much, but later, when he saw the price of the woodcock in the accounts, berated the cook and compelled him to pay for it, declaring that he had not ordered such a delicacy. Whenever rare foods appeared on the royal table they were served so sparingly that not everyone present could partake of them. Usually the king ate the lion's share. Wine was also served sparingly, each guest receiving a small bottle of rhinewine. Only on special occasions did he permit the serving of tokay, which he regarded as a special delicacy. "Would to God," he is reported to have said, "that I could afford a small bottle of this every day." [30]

Some historians have gone so far as to state, on the basis of the *Memoirs* of Wilhelmina, that the thrifty Prussian king did not give the members of his family enough food to satisfy their hunger. Such statements are not founded on fact. True, only seasonable foods were served, and then the simplest and plainest, but the food was wholesome and the quantity sufficient. One glance at the girth of the queen would have dispelled all ideas of undernourishment. Frederick William was himself too much addicted to the pleasures of the table to permit his family to go hungry. A good dinner was one of the great pleasures of his life, that is, if it was served at another's expense. Whenever he wanted a good meal he would have himself invited to the house of his minister Von Grumbkow, whose cook was famous for his tasty dishes. The king had a special fondness for oysters, which nothing but repletion could satisfy. On occasion, contemporaries aver, he gulped down as many as a hundred at one sitting. What caused him to serve homely fare on the royal table was his desire for money to increase the army. To avoid unnecessary expense he even went so far as to forbid special celebrations on the birthdays of the members of his family. He thought of himself, not as the owner, but only as the steward of the royal revenues.

This regime of pitiless economy was also established in

[30] Krauske "Vom Hofe Friedrich Wilhelms I," in *Hohenzollern-Jahrbuch*, V (1901), 176; Beneckendorf, *Karakterzüge aus dem Leben König Friedrich Wilhelms I*, I, 84–105.

every department of the administration. The Prussian diplomatic service was, for example, greatly restricted. From many of the less important courts the Prussian representatives were withdrawn on the principle that "fifty thousand soldiers can accomplish more than a hundred thousand ministers." [31] Even in Vienna the ambassador was replaced by a poorly paid representative. In the internal administration the retrenchment was no less drastic. A Berlin handwritten newspaper of April 22, 1713, states that "the local court of appeal has been reduced by one-half. The members of the government board in Cleves and the members of the board of justice who formerly received 650 taler will in the future receive 500 and 400 taler, respectively." [32] A number of privy councillors had their salaries reduced from 480 to 300 taler, and others had to accept proportionate reductions. Even the salaries of the army officers were reduced. General von Holstein, for example, had his salary reduced from 8,400 to 3,600 taler.[33] No official, not even the higher ones, could spend money without the permission of the king. Time and again he answered the petitions of subsidiary boards by scrawling on them: "I have no money," "Non habeo Pekunia [sic!]," "Where there is no money there is none," or "I shall regard as a dirty dog anyone who asks for more money." [34] On a number of occasions Frederick William

---

[31] See Krauske, "Der Regierungsantritt Friedrich Wilhelms I," in *Hohenzollern-Jahrbuch*, I (1897), 78.

[32] Friedländer, *Berliner geschriebene Zeitungen*, p. 2.

[33] See Schmoller, "Der preussische Beamtenstand unter Friedrich Wilhelm I," *Preussische Jahrbücher*, XXVI (1870), 549.

[34] Förster, *Urkundenbuch*, I, 36; *Acta Borussica, Behördenorganisation*, Vols. I–V, *passim*. On occasion he would state his refusal in verse form with a characteristic coarseness:

> "Eure Bitte kann ich nicht gewähren,
> Ich habe hunderttausend Mann zu ernähren.
> Gold kann ich nicht scheissen,
> Friedrich Wilhelm, König in Preussen."

threatened an entire board with imprisonment because it asked for appropriations he did not regard as necessary.[35] Whenever he did grant appropriations, he usually pared them to a minimum. All complaints regarding the insufficiency of the funds allotted were sharply silenced with, "You must make them do."

Besides reducing the costs of the administration Frederick William applied himself zealously to the management of all possible sources of royal revenue. One of the most important of these were the royal domains. Frederick I and his ministers had as a quick means of raising funds let out a large part of these domains, particularly the great manor farms, on heritable leases. This system of giving the lands on perpetual leases was bound to result in losses for the state if ever the price of the land should increase materially. The new king, who realized this, took measures as early as August, 1713, to regain possession of the lands from such holders. Upon returning the sums they had paid, he ordered them to quit the lands. Thereafter he let out the royal domains only on short-term leases, so that he could demand higher rentals whenever the value of the land increased. The change resulted in an immediate increase of the royal revenue. So spirited was the bidding for the new leases that the revenues were immediately augmented by one-third. As the conditions improved the king raised the rents. Yet the rents he demanded were not excessive. He ordered the royal officials to inform themselves of local conditions and prices so thoroughly that they could set a rent which was neither too high nor too low, but always fair.

In short, by his homely frugality, by curtailing the expenses of the royal court generally, and by extending these rigid economies to all departments of state, Frederick Wil-

[35] See *AB, Beh.,* V (Part 2), 477.

liam greatly reduced the demand on the royal treasury. On the salaries of the higher court officials alone he saved no less than 221,000 taler annually. But the Prussian autocrat did not stop at cutting down expenses. By judicious management he also increased the royal income considerably. Under his careful supervision, for example, the post office alone yielded an annual surplus of 137,000 taler. Furthermore, the income from the royal domains which in 1713 amounted to 1,890,613 taler gradually increased to 3,300,940 before the end of the reign.[36] According to Droysen the total income of the crown rose from 3,655,000 taler in 1714 to 5,483,000 in 1730, and finally to almost 7,000,000 in 1740.[37] This policy of economy and careful management enabled Frederick William not only to provide for the subsistence without foreign subsidies of the army his predecessor had left him but also permitted him to increase the size of this army.

[36] Riedel, *Der brandenburgisch-preussische Staatshaushalt*, p. 61 *et sqq.*
[37] *Geschichte der preussischen Politik*, IV (Part 3), 415.

The Building of the Army

A S FAST AS he was able to gather the necessary funds Frederick William augmented his standing army, composed of professional soldiers who owed allegiance only to him. All other forms of military service were abolished. On March 7, 1713, only twelve days after he became king, Frederick William dissolved the militia which Frederick I had organized. One reason for dissolving it was that many young men joined the militia, which was formed solely for defensive purposes, in order to escape service in the standing army.[1] How much he detested the idea of a militia is shown by the fact that in 1718 he forbade the chancellories, under threat of a fine of one hundred ducats, to use the word *Militz* (militia) as a synonym for *Heer* (army). Early in his reign he also took steps toward commuting into a fixed money payment the old feudal duty of his landholders to do service in wartime. According to an old law each tenant-in-chief of the king was required to furnish one mounted soldier in time of war for each knight's fee he held. This service had been demanded in 1669, 1678, and in 1701, with but little success. As it had ceased to be useful to the state, Frederick I

---

[1] See Courbière, *Geschichte der brandenburgisch-preussischen Heeresverfassung*, p. 80.

had already conceived the idea of transforming the duty of military service into a money tax, but it remained for Frederick William to carry through the idea. In 1717 he offered to renounce his right of escheat as well as his right to the military service in return for an annual contribution to the royal treasury. The amount finally decided upon was forty taler annually for each mounted soldier a tenant-in-chief had been required to furnish.[2] Thus Frederick William abolished at a price the last relics of the feudal ties which still existed between the king and his tenants-in-chief. He himself was proud of his achievement. "I give away nothing but air," he wrote, "and receive forty taler in return. The bargain is a good one. I wish I could conclude a similar one each day." [3]

Meanwhile he was steadily increasing the size of his standing army. In August, 1713, it had numbered 38,459, but by 1715 had grown to 46,000, by 1720 to 56,575, by 1729 to 66,861, by 1738 to 75,124 and finally to 83,446 at the time of Frederick William's death.[4] This gave Prussia, which in the extent of its territory was tenth and in population twelfth of all the countries of Europe, the fourth rank according to the size of its army, only France, Russia, and Austria having larger armies. France had a force of about 160,000, the Russian Empire 130,000, while Austria boasted between 80,000 and 100,000. The steady growth of the Prussian army became a much discussed topic among the foreign representatives in Berlin and at the various European courts. The

---

[2] *Corpus constitutionum marchicarum*, edited by Mylius, II (Part 5), 83 *et sqq.* Will henceforth be abbreviated as *Corp. const.*

[3] Cited in Holtze, *Geschichte der Mark Brandenburg*, p. 96.

[4] Lehmann, "Beitrag zur Geschichte des preussischen Heeres während der Regierung Friedrich Wilhelms I," in *Jahrbücher für die deutsche Armee und Marine*, CXV (1900), 46–59; Osten-Sacken, *Preussens Heer von seinen Anfängen bis zur Gegenwart*, I, 128 *et sqq.*

Dutch representative in Berlin, for example, wrote: "The king is entirely in the hands of a group of impetuous people who advise him to keep as many troops as possible. The worst is to be feared of this monarch, who has expressly stated that his entire affection belongs to the soldiers." [5]

Size, however, was not the only boast of the Prussian army. By dint of persistent effort Frederick William developed an army which for effectiveness and rigorous discipline was soon to be considered the best in Europe. To assist him in the task of improving the army he had the services of Leopold, prince of Anhalt-Dessau, familiarly known as Old Dessauer. Having served under Prince Eugene at Blenheim and Malplaquet and assisted in the training of Marlborough's infantry, Old Dessauer was eminently fitted for the post. He had, in fact, done much to improve the efficiency of the Prussian army before Frederick William became king. At his suggestion the old wooden ramrods had been replaced in some of the regiments by iron ones which permitted faster loading, the bayonet had been improved so that it remained attached to the gun in actual firing, and the practice of marching in step had been introduced. Besides being a person of military experience, he was a man after the king's heart. Like Frederick William, Old Dessauer almost invariably turned his rough side out. He was quick to anger and not infrequently expressed his feelings in sharp invectives and oaths. He was also frugal, interested only in the practical side of life and intensely hostile to all forms of higher learning. Above all, he never tired of discussing military matters. The king and his military adviser would sit for hours on end day after day discussing military affairs and recounting their military experiences. The one thing that Fred-

[5] Cited in Droysen, *Geschichte der preussischen Politik*, IV (Part 2), 13.

erick William seems to have disliked about his friend was Leopold's laxness with regard to praying and attending church services. As the king insisted that his general pray aloud before leading his regiments into battle, Old Dessauer would literally growl a brief rugged prayer. On one occasion, it is reported, the prayer ran: "Dear God, give me, I pray, your gracious support, but if you do not care to help me this time, please do not assist the enemy; just stand by and see what happens. Amen!" [6]

One of the first reforms the two men worked out was the establishment of uniformity in the Prussian army. Under the Great Elector the army had still been loosely organized. It had consisted of a number of regiments which were united only by the oath of loyalty to the ruler. In return for a certain stipend the commander of a regiment was obliged to furnish a specified number of soldiers and to provide for their up-keep. The choice of weapons, of uniforms, and of drill regulations was left to the commanders of the individual regiments. Toward the end of his reign the Great Elector had instructed his regimental commanders to establish a certain uniformity with regard to drill regulations, but the order seems to have achieved little. The first written infantry regulations for the entire Prussian army were not issued until December 18, 1702, and regulated only the manual exercises with the gun. The infantry regulations issued in 1709 still stated: "Such matters as the evolutions and how a battalion is to fire are left to the experience and care of each commander, who is to see that his corps is well-drilled and adept at firing." [7]

Soon after his accession Frederick William, with the as-

[6] Cited in Moeller van den Bruck, *Der preussische Stil*, p. 91.
[7] Linnebach, *König Friedrich Wilhelm I und Fürst Leopold zu Anhalt-Dessau*, p. 98.

sistance of Old Dessauer, put an end to the diversity of weapons, uniforms, and regulations. The regimental commanders could no longer decide which weapons their troops were to use or what kind of uniforms they were to wear. The minuteness of the king's regulations is illustrated by the fact that he did not stop at prescribing the material and color of the uniforms to be worn by all infantrymen and artillerymen; he also regulated their cut down to a fraction of an inch and the exact number of buttons. In 1714 Frederick William drew up with his own hand comprehensive infantry regulations, which included field service and garrison life as well as the manual exercises and evolutions. They were, in fact, so all-embracing that the king himself declared he hoped nothing would turn up that was not covered by them. If one recalls that the first comprehensive ordinances for the French army were not issued until 1732 and the first general regulations for the Austrian army did not appear until 1737, the priority of the Prussian army in this respect is evident. It was believed that these regulations gave the Prussian army a definite advantage; hence they were carefully guarded to keep them from passing into the possession of foreigners. Only the commissioned officers had copies of them, and when new regulations were issued the old copies were carefully collected and destroyed. Fassmann states that any officer who permitted a foreigner to read the regulations or who even communicated them orally was, if discovered, immediately sentenced to imprisonment for life.[8]

But the Prussian advantage did not remain merely a theoretical one. By dint of endless drilling the Prussian troops attained a degree of rapidity, uniformity, and precision hitherto unknown in the execution of military maneuvers. The greatest importance was put on quick loading and fir-

[8] *Leben und Thaten Friedrich Wilhelms I*, p. 739.

ing. Gradually the Prussian troops grew so skilled in this respect that they were far superior to the troops of other nations. In general the Prussian infantry reached such a degree of perfection that Old Dessauer himself wrote to the king: "Friend and foe admire Your Majesty's infantry; friends see it as the wonder of the world, and enemies regard it with trembling." [9] The adventurer Pöllnitz who had seen most of the armies of Europe wrote: "I never saw troops march with more order and state; it seemed as if they were all moved by one spring." [10] Count Seckendorf, the imperial representative at Berlin, wrote to Prince Eugene, commander of the imperial forces: "It is certain that one cannot see troops of such good appearance, order, and correctness anywhere else in the world." [11]

Much less efficient was the development of the cavalry. Both Frederick William and Leopold of Dessau had considerable knowledge of matters pertaining to infantry, but they seemed to lack the proper understanding of the nature of cavalry. Preferring tall soldiers to those of small stature, the Prussian monarch put too much emphasis on the size of his cavalrymen. This necessitated the use of large horses, which made the cavalry less mobile. Count Seckendorf, after viewing the Prussian cavalry, expressed doubts in a letter to Prince Eugene regarding the ability of "the terribly large horses, some of which are nineteen hands high, to withstand the rigors of a severe campaign." [12] Furthermore, Frederick William's sense of economy caused him to spare the horses too much, with the result that the cavalrymen were poor horsemen. Frederick II said of his father's cavalrymen: "They were giants on elephants and could neither move freely nor fight well. There was not a review during which

[9] *Briefe Friedrich Wilhelms an Leopold zu Anhalt-Dessau*, p. 319.
[10] Pöllnitz, *Mémoires*, I, 21.
[11] Förster, *Urkundenbuch*, II, 41.   [12] *Ibid.*, p. 38.

riders, because of their clumsiness, did not fall off their horses. They were not masters of their horses, and their officers had no idea of the meaning of cavalry service." [13]

The discipline which Frederick William established in the Prussian army was of a severity unknown since Roman times. It demanded absolute subordination in every respect. The regulations of 1726, for example, state: "When one takes the oath to the flag one renounces oneself and surrenders entirely, even one's life and all, to the monarch, in order to fulfill the Lord's will; and through this blind obedience one receives the grace and the confirmation of the title of soldier." [14] This obedience was required in small details as well as in important matters. "Order and punctuality," Varnhagen von Ense wrote, "were extended with implacable severity to the most insignificant matters . . . The difference between the great and the small, the essential and the unessential, disappeared entirely. A uniform regularity governed everything and was enforced by an ubiquitous and terrible discipline." [15] The chief means of enforcing the iron discipline was the cudgel. It was hard for Frederick William to understand how there could be any discipline without it. Upon reviewing the Hanoverian troops he wrote to Leopold of Dessau: "I find that the soldiers lack the proper subordination because they cannot be thrashed without incurring the king's displeasure. Despite the fact that the common soldiers know this, there is order; that puzzles me most." [16] A large proportion of the Prussian recruits, drawn from the peasantry, were so raw and unwieldy, it is true, that they would respond only to a caning. Many of the peasants, in fact, were accustomed to being beaten by their masters, while others,

[13] *Œuvres*, I, 221.
[14] Frederick William I, *Erlasse und Briefe*, p. 24.
[15] *Biographische Denkmale*, p. 275.
[16] *Briefe an Leopold zu Anhalt-Dessau*, p. 293.

having been forcibly enlisted, disliked the military life and could be kept in order only by the sternest discipline.

Thus the tone of the army was harsh, even cruel, according to more modern standards. The common soldier was often cudgeled severely for the slightest infraction of the rules. "Every accident was punished as if it were a crime. A slip in the manual exercises, an improperly-polished button on the uniform, or water spots on the spatterdashes would draw down a severe caning. Caning, in fact, became so common that it was regarded as part of the service, and no drill passed without one." [17] Any form of insubordination was visited with more severe punishments. The regulations issued in 1713 state that any soldier "who resists, be it with words or reasoning, is to run the gauntlet thirty times. Whoever draws his sword or takes up a weapon for purposes of resistance shall be shot." [18] Such punishments as caning and running the gauntlet were pronounced by the company commander; more severe punishments, including imprisonment and death, were imposed by a court martial. In cases of capital punishment the criminal was broken on the wheel, hanged, or burned if he had committed a "common" crime; otherwise he was decapitated or shot. Drunkenness, except in line of duty, was not punished. Gambling, on the other hand, either with cards or with dice, was forbidden under punishment of running the gauntlet.

Frederick William himself, with the eye of a martinet, saw that the regulations he had drawn up were observed with the utmost punctiliousness. Hardly a day passed on which he did not appear on the parade grounds in Berlin or Potsdam to inspect or to drill his troops. In addition there were regular reviews of the troops stationed in other parts of his territo-

[17] Varnhagen von Ense, *Biographische Denkmale*, p. 275.
[18] *Corp. const.*, III (Part 1), 338.

ries. No drillmaster in the kingdom could approach him in exactitude. So carefully did he watch the movements of the troops that he would immediately detect the slightest irregularities. Woe to the battalion which did not execute every movement perfectly, for the king's wrath would descend upon it with all fury. If, however, he found everything in order, he would manifest a paternal friendliness toward his "blue boys," as he familiarly called his soldiers. The higher officers he treated as comrades; those below the rank of captain and the enlisted men he regarded as his children. Often when he met one of the latter on his travels he would address him as "my son" and ask him such questions as: "How long have you been in my service? How do you like being in my service? Have you received your rightful dues?" [19] All soldiers had free access to the king, who would listen to their complaints with great patience. If one of them accosted him on the street with a petition he would often settle the matter then and there. In court a soldier could expect prompt justice, his case taking precedence over those of civilians.

The king's paternal solicitude notwithstanding, the number of deserters from the Prussian army was large. The causes of these desertions were the severity and harshness of the discipline and the fact that many soldiers had been forcibly enlisted. In 1714 no less than 3,471 infantrymen and 70 artillerymen absconded. The total for the entire reign was 30,216, the lowest number in any one year being 401 in 1739.[20] Time and again Frederick William issued decrees

[19] Fassmann, *Leben und Thaten Friedrich Wilhelms I*, p. 740; Beneckendorf, *Karakterzüge aus dem Leben König Friedrich Wilhelms I*, IV, 53.

[20] See Jany, *Geschichte der königlichen-preussischen Armee*, I, 680; also "Mittheilungen aus dem Archiv des königlichen Kriegsministeriums," *Militär-Wochenblatt*, LXXVI (1891), 1031–1036.

which stated that all apprehended deserters would be hanged without mercy.[21] Nevertheless the desertions continued. How ineffective the king's threats were is shown by the fact that in 1721 he offered a general pardon to all deserters who would return within two months. More than this, he offered them bonuses ranging from ten to thirty taler for coming back.[22]

As Frederick William's reign progressed, however, the number of deserters gradually grew less. The decrease was due, in the main, to two factors: first, the improved morale resulting from the assignment to each regiment of a definite district from which it was to draw its recruits, thereby fostering the rise of a local feeling in the various regiments; second, greater precautions to prevent desertions. Soldiers, for example, were forbidden to go more than a quarter mile from their garrisons without a pass. No stranger was permitted to pass in or out of a city in which soldiers were quartered without a thorough examination. The watchmen of all villages were, in fact, ordered to accost every person unknown to them and to demand that he identify himself and give good reasons for being there. As most of the soldiers were quartered in private homes, each landlord was ordered to keep strict watch over them. To prevent escape he could even take away their shoes at night. If a soldier, nevertheless, succeeded in escaping, the landlord had to find a capable substitute or step into the ranks himself. Those guilty of aiding a deserter to abscond or of concealing him after he had made his escape were to be hanged on the spot.

When a deserter's absence was discovered, the alarm was immediately sounded, and horsemen, if there were some at hand, were sent in hot pursuit; otherwise a detachment of

[21] Decrees in *Corp. const.*, III (Part 1), 339 *et sqq.*
[22] *Ibid.*, pp. 413–414.

infantry was sent out. Burghers and peasants in the neighboring towns and villages were also required to join in the search and to notify all the surrounding villages that a deserter was at large. The royal decree stated that all must participate in "a careful search of the brush and the forest and, if the grain is high, of the grainfields." [23] If the inhabitants of a town failed to do their utmost to apprehend a deserter, the town was liable to a fine of two hundred taler, while a village might be compelled to pay half as much. "In case a village," a royal decree reads, "is so poor that it cannot raise the fine, the two most prominent peasants are to be sentenced to hard labor in a military fortress for a period of two months. In a poor town eight of the most prominent citizens are to be punished in a like manner." [24] The reward for the capture of a deserter was at first ten and later twelve taler. All this made it more difficult for deserters to escape, but, as already stated, failed to put an end to desertions.

It was by no means easy to find recruits in the desired numbers to replace the deserters and to augment the size of the Prussian army. The enlistment, it is true, was for life, not for a short period. Frederick William's soldier was a *miles perpetuus*. All those who entered the service were required to remain in it until dismissed by the king. Accordingly the number of those mustered out each year was not overwhelming. Nevertheless, the aged and the sick who were dismissed each year amounted to about 20 percent of the standing army. The number of recruits raised by voluntary enlistment was insufficient to replace the infirm and superannuated soldiers and the deserters and at the same time to increase the size of the army. Hence forcible methods were used to impress recruits into the service. Recruiting officers became the terror of towns, villages, and the countryside.

[23] *Ibid.*, p. 457.
[24] *Ibid.*, p. 455; see also *AB, Beh.*, III, 600 *et sqq.*

No able-bodied man was safe from their force and cunning, for they organized regular hunts on the highroads, in the villages, and in the fields. On a number of occasions they went so far as to invade congregations during divine service, and they carried off the tallest and strongest men. The result was that large numbers of young men, particularly those who lived near the frontiers, left Prussian territory to escape forcible enlistment. In some districts a regular emigration took place. So many men left the border districts of East Prussia that it was feared there would soon not be enough to cultivate the land. A report issued by the University of Königsberg in 1724 states that sixteen of its students had been enlisted by force and that twenty-eight had left the university because they feared that the recruiting agents might seize them. On February 1, 1724, for example, Georg Salewsky, a student of theology, was seized by two agents and taken to the guardhouse, where he was tortured and beaten for days before he consented to take the oath of enlistment.[25]

To Frederick William it was a matter of indifference whence and how the soldiers were recruited so long as the expense was not too great and the economic development of his territories did not suffer. But when it became apparent that agriculture, trade, and industry would be seriously curtailed if the emigration caused by the fear of forcible recruiting continued, he took a hand in the matter. Already in the first year of his reign he issued an edict which declared that every subject who crossed the border without permission would be regarded as a deserter.[26] It was to no avail; young men continued to leave the country in large numbers. Finally, in May, 1714, he sought to allay the fears of his people

[25] Bornhak, *Geschichte der preussischen Universitätsverwaltung*, p. 79.
[26] *Corp. const.*, III (Part 1), 349–352.

by ordering that in the future no man was to be forced into the service against his will.[27] But he left a large loophole for his recruiters by permitting

officials in the city and country districts to enlist disobedient burghers, peasants, and suchlike subjects who squander their substance or commit other such crimes, wherefore it is better that the city, community or village be purged of them; also of domestic servants, be they lackeys, coachmen, farm servants, or other servants, who do not serve their masters well . . . This and the like must not be styled forcible recruiting.

Accordingly forcible recruiting continued much as before. How easily the edict against seizure could be circumvented is shown by the case of a student of law at the University of Königsberg named Korn. On the 29th of April, 1729, this robust young man was seized on a street in Königsberg, plied with strong liquor until he became drunk and cursed in the presence of "witnesses," and was then enlisted as a moral delinquent.[28] One of the handwritten newspapers which circulated at the time reported in 1717 that despite the king's open prohibition of forcible recruiting he "secretly gave his officers permission to get recruits wherever they could." [29] When complaints again became widespread, Frederick William sought to still them by a new edict (February 26, 1721) against forcible recruiting.[30] But, like the former one, this edict remained a dead letter.

The efforts of the local recruiting agents were supplemented by recruiting outside the Prussian territories. Usually hundreds of agents, and at times as many as a thousand, were busy seeking recruits in the neighboring countries. But

[27] *Ibid.*, pp. 359–364.
[28] Bornhak, *Geschichte der preussischen Universitätsverwaltung*, p. 80.
[29] Friedländer, *Berliner geschriebene Zeitungen*, p. 635.
[30] *Corp. const.*, III (Part 1), 415–418.

this was both expensive and a prolific source of friction with other states. Whereas recruiting was allowed in Austria-Hungary only by special permission which few could secure, it was entirely forbidden in many of the other German states. In 1729 a quarrel arising from the activities of some Prussian recruiters in Hanover nearly brought about a war between the two states. Outside Germany the Poles resented the recruiting efforts of the Prussian agents so greatly that they threatened to hang without further ado all foreign agents caught recruiting. Hence it became increasingly difficult to obtain the requisite number of men.

To insure himself a larger number of recruits and, at the same time, to still the complaints over forcible recruiting at home, Frederick William, in 1733, adopted a system of modified conscription. By an order which he sent to the commanders of the various regiments he divided his kingdom into circles or districts, according to the number of hearths, and assigned to each regiment a specific district from which it was to fill its ranks. Each district, in turn, was subdivided into as many cantons as there were companies in the regiment to which it was allotted. Frederick William himself explained the system in an order to General von Röder.

I have resolved and found it conducive to the conservation of the army [he wrote] to assign to each regiment a district and hearths for purposes of enrollment. I am sending you this disposition to acquaint you with the hearths that have been assigned to your regiment. They number 7947, so that when divided into ten parts each company will have some 790 hearths.[31]

If the quota of a regiment was not filled by voluntary enlistment of recruits living in its district, the company could

---

[31] *Erlasse und Briefe des Königs Friedrich Wilhelm I von Preussen*, p. 28; Altmann, *Ausgewählte Urkunden*, I, 166–167.

make good the deficiency from a list of those eligible for service. The king specifically stated that "all subjects according to their natural birth and the order and command of God Almighty are obliged to serve with their goods and blood," [32] thereby laying down, as it were, the principle of universal liability to military service. Thus by a stroke of the pen the Prussian monarch changed the old obligation of serving in the militia for local defense into the new one of serving in the standing army.

But the principle of universal military service was not enforced. Liberal exemptions were made in the interests of industry, trade, agriculture, and education. Among those exempted were the nobles, the woolen workers, apprentices in a number of industries, resident owners of a house and a farm, the sons of parents possessing ten thousand taler or more, foreign servants working in Prussia, the first generation of colonists who had settled in Prussia, clergymen's sons who were studying theology, and, by special permission of the regimental commander, those who were learning to be cooks, gardeners, and artisans. In short, the nobles and practically the whole upper stratum of the bourgeoisie down to the more prosperous artisans were exempted. Many of the former, however, entered the Prussian army as officers, as shall be shown later. Thus the burden of serving in the ranks fell largely on the shoulders of the small artisans, servants, agricultural laborers, and poor peasants. It was a policy calculated to permit the growth of the army without putting obstacles in the way of the expansion of commerce and industry. How largely the Prussian army was composed of noncommercial and nonindustrial elements is indicated by Frederick the Great's boast that "he could carry on a war while Prussian merchant and manufacturer went unknow-

[32] *Corp const.*, III (Part 1), 360.

ing and undisturbed about his business." [33] But the upper middle class was exempted only at a price; it had to bear the burden of a system of taxation designed chiefly to meet the expenses of a large standing army.

All young males subject to military service were put on the regimental lists. At first many were enrolled soon after birth, but later the minimum age for enrollment was set at ten. The enrolled were not permitted to take the military oath until they had been confirmed in the Church and had partaken of the Lord's Supper, so that, as the king put it, "they would not profane the oath." Having taken the oath, they were subject to call when they were needed in the regiment. The establishment of this so-called "canton system" not only assured Frederick William a large permanent supply of recruits; it was also a long step toward making the Prussian army a national one. Recruiting abroad was still continued, but it was only supplementary. Native recruits now formed the backbone of the Prussian army. More than this, the establishment of the canton system also resulted in a definite improvement in the type of Prussian recruits. Previously the recruits had most often been habitual idlers or even criminals and generally worthless humans whom the local authorities had delivered to the army or who had been forcibly recruited. Now all members of certain classes were required to serve. Military service was no longer the result of a sudden forcible seizure by recruiting agents, but a career for which children were enrolled while they were still very young.

During peace time these native conscripts did not remain with their regiments throughout the entire year. Only during the so-called drill months, April, May, and June, were all

[33] Ford, "Boyen's Military Law," *American Historical Review*, XX (1914–1915), 531.

companies required to be at full strength. During the other months a captain could grant a furlough each month to three noncommissioned officers and thirty enlisted men, or about one-quarter of the total strength of the company. In the harvest months—July, August, and September—the number could be increased to fifty enlisted men; in other words, to about 40 percent of the total strength. There was, however, the restriction that no soldier was to be granted a furlough for more than two months each year. Later the time was extended to three months, and the number of men permitted to go on furlough during the non-harvest months was raised to fifty. In this way the native sons who were serving in the army could also be used to increase the productive capacities of the country. At first the men on furlough received half their pay (the pay of a common soldier was 2½ reichstaler per month), but later only furloughs without pay were granted. The money Frederick William saved he used for foreign recruiting. In 1740 about one-third of the enlisted men were still foreigners.

If there was still a considerable number of non-Prussians in the ranks of the Prussian army, this was not true of the officers' corps. Whereas the Great Elector had obtained officers wherever he found capable men, Frederick William chose almost all his officers from among his subjects. What is more, he drew them almost exclusively from the nobility. At the end of his reign all the generals were noblemen, and there was only one non-noble among fifty-seven colonels and two among forty-six lieutenant-colonels. Among the lower commissioned officers the number of non-nobles was slightly larger, but they were, nevertheless, the exception. Thus another step was taken toward making the Prussian army a national one. Previously many Prussian noblemen had entered the military service of such countries as France, Holland, Denmark or Poland; now they were required to enter the Prussian army. When Privy Councillor von Wallenrodt, for example, asked permission for his son to enter the French service, he received from Frederick William the curt reply: "The king of Prussia is as good as the king of France." [34] If at first some of the noble families were opposed to seeing their sons enter the king's service, Frederick William did not hesitate to send his messengers to requisition the young noblemen. As the number of noblemen in the officers' corps increased, to be an officer was regarded more and more as a privilege reserved for the nobility, and many *Junkers* eagerly adopted the military profession as a career. Through this military service Junkerdom, which had formerly been hostile to the throne, became its chief support.

This mobilization of the Prussian nobility for service in the Prussian army was one of the great achievements of Frederick William. In France the absolute monarchy had broken the power of the nobles, but had not integrated them into the new system. In Prussia, Frederick William achieved what Louis XIV had failed to do. After the Great Elector had deprived the *Junkers* of most of their power his grandson forced them into the Prussian uniform and taught them to regard the king's service as the most honorable and most natural profession. As a reward for their service he constituted his commissioned officers a special class, the preservation of which was carefully guarded. They were sharply separated from the noncommissioned officers and enlisted men. Whereas the regulations had previously been the same for all the men of the army, separate regulations were drawn up in 1726 for the commissioned officers. This sharp distinction between officers and men was of practical value because it facilitated the maintenance of that strict discipline which

[34] *AB, Beh.,* IV (Part 2), 6.

Frederick William had made a characteristic of the Prussian system. But the Prussian monarch not only constituted his officers a separate class; he also gave them the foremost place in the state and in society. In other words, they became, as Frederick the Great put it, *le premier état dans le royaume* (the first class in the kingdom)." [35] It was a higher position than that enjoyed by the military officers of any other country. The king regarded himself only as "the first officer" of his country and, as previously stated, treated all officers above the rank of captain as his comrades.

All officers from the ensign up were appointed by the king himself, and the basis of promotion was, at least theoretically, competency or merit. When Old Dessauer himself requested that his son be made commander of a regiment, Frederick William told his best friend that the son must first prove himself worthy of the position. This high conception of promotion, though the king did not always adhere to it, was extraordinary at a time when the important superior positions in the Austrian, French, and British armies were obtained by purchase, court favor, or high birth, and the higher officers filled the subordinate positions as they pleased. In choosing his officers the king preferred the sons of the lesser nobility, because the wealthy nobles often wanted to serve only for a limited time. But the heirs of the wealthier families as well as those of the poorer ones were expected to consecrate themselves to the king's service. Accordingly, Frederick William advised his son to raise all young noblemen for his service from their youth, "so that they will know no lord but God and the king of Prussia." [36] To make sure that his officers would be properly trained he

[35] Cited in Hoven, *Der preussische Offizier des 18. Jahrhunderts*, p. 7.
[36] *AB, Beh.*, III, 451.

opened cadet schools in which the young nobles were instructed at state expense. This training not only made for a better-educated nobility; it also provided careers for the sons of poor noblemen whose interests had been wholly agrarian. As most of the Prussian aristocrats were Protestant, they did not, like the French nobles, have the Roman Catholic Church as an outlet for their younger sons.

Although Frederick William probably had the finest troops in Europe, he made little use of them. His army was always ready to take the field upon short notice, but it seldom left its quarters except for grand reviews and extensive maneuvers. He would threaten, scold, bluster, and brandish the sword; yet as soon as action was impending, he returned the blade to its scabbard. On two occasions only did his troops march to war. Early in his reign he helped the Danes take Stralsund from the Swedes, and later, in the War of the Polish Succession, he sent an auxiliary corps of ten thousand men to Prince Eugene of Savoy, the commander of the imperial troops. In the latter case, however, peace was concluded between France and the Holy Roman Empire before a sanguinary encounter took place.

Frederick William's reluctance to use his troops for actual fighting must not be taken to mean that he himself lacked the true military ardor; quite the contrary. His statement that he "loved nothing better than war" was in all essentials a true one. As crown prince he had proved his mettle by exposing himself to the heavy fire of the French in the battle of Malplaquet. His coolness and bravery on this occasion evoked the admiration of tried generals, among them Prince Eugene himself. His reluctance to use his army in actual warfare was founded on other motives, one of which was his love for his "blue boys." As the Austrian representative put it in his report, "He loves his soldiers so much that he is real childish about it." [37] Like a miser who takes his gold out of the coffers to feast his eyes on it, but cannot bring himself to spend it, Frederick William liked to drill his soldiers and to review them, but could not bear the thought of sending them into battle. Then there was the expense of a war, an expense which the Prussian monarch felt must be avoided. Finally, Frederick William's conscience would not permit him to start a war unless he was firmly convinced that it was a just one. In the instructions for his successor he wrote:

I beg you, my dear successor, not to start an unjust war. If you do not, God will give you and your armies His constant blessing and courage. . . . Read history and you will see that unjust wars do not turn out well, for which you have King Louis XIV of France, King Augustus of Poland, and the Elector of Bavaria as examples. . . . You are indeed a great ruler on earth, but you must give account to God for all unrighteous wars and bloodshed, and that is a difficult matter.[38]

This is not to say that Frederick William had no territorial acquisitions in view. There were the unsettled claims to Jülich and Berg, Courland, the rest of Pomerania, and to parts of Silesia. But he decided to leave the final settlement of these claims to his son and successor. It was enough for him to have organized the industrial and military strength of Prussia. As early as 1722 he wrote in the instructions for his successor:

The Elector Frederick William gave prestige and prosperity to our House; my father obtained the royal dignity; and I have put the country and the army on a good footing. It is up to you, my dear successor, to continue what your forbears started and to obtain for us those territories which belong to our House through God and our right. Therefore I beseech you, for God's

---

[37] *AB, Beh.*, I, 441.   [38] *Ibid.*, III, 462.

sake, to keep up the army and to strengthen it more and more, and to make it more formidable.[39]

Certainly in this respect Frederick II carried out the wishes of his father. With the veteran material Frederick William had collected he won for himself the title of "the Great" and raised Prussia to the rank of a great power in Europe. Carlyle's statement regarding the battle of Mollwitz, "It is a victory which must in reality be ascribed to Frederick William and to old Dessauer who are far away," applies to a greater or lesser extent to all of Frederick's victories in the War of the Austrian Succession.

But Frederick William's influence did not stop here. The principle he laid down in the statement, "If one wishes to decide anything in this world, it cannot be done with the pen if it is not supported by the power of the sword," became the inspiration for others. Emperor William II, for example, said of Frederick William: "He maintained peace, but it was nevertheless he who wrote that everlastingly true sentence: 'If one wishes to decide anything in this world, it cannot be done with the pen if it is not supported by the power of the sword.' " [40] Again, in a speech of January 1, 1900, after declaring that he would "carry through the work of reorganizing the navy" in the same spirit in which his grandfather had strengthened the army, William II said: "With the two united I hope, with a firm trust in God's guidance, to be in a position to prove the truth of the statement of Frederick William I: 'If one wishes to decide anything in this world, it cannot be done with the pen if it is not supported by the power of the sword.' " [41]

[39] *Ibid.*, p. 461.   [40] William II, *Meine Vorfahren*, p. 90.
[41] *Die Reden Kaiser Wilhelms II*, II, 183–184.

CHAPTER SIX

The Regiment of Giants

IN BUILDING UP the Prussian army Frederick William manifested an almost pathological love for tall soldiers. This was perhaps the oddest of his idiosyncrasies, his weakness of weaknesses. It was a passion which cost him vast sums, involved him in international difficulties, and made him the jest of the civilized world. As a boy he had evinced a liking for tall soldiers. At Wusterhausen, the royal hunting seat, he collected a squad of tall peasants and spent much time in drilling them. Later, when his father gave him the command of a regiment which was stationed at Wusterhausen, he replaced the small men in its ranks with giant rustics, using for this purpose a large part of his allowance, as the *Account of My Ducats* shows. Since his father did not share his passion for tall men, the crown prince, it is reported, had to conceal his stalwarts in stables and haylofts when the old king came to Wusterhausen. After Frederick William became king he gave free reign to his passion. He believed, it appears, that tall soldiers have greater strength and greater endurance than those of small stature. This idea gradually took such firm hold on his mind that size often became the basic criterion in judging both officers and enlisted men. Thus an officer of small stature, though a man of extraordinary ability, had little chance of being promoted. Moreover, toward the end of his reign he was usually ready to overlook irregularities if a number of tall soldiers had been added to a regiment since the previous inspection; if not, everything about the regiment would displease him.

Since Frederick William's judgment of a company or regiment was greatly influenced by the number of tall recruits found in it, a contest resulted between the companies and regiments to see which could get the largest number of young giants. Every nook and corner of Prussian territory was carefully combed by the recruiting agents. When they found a young man of impressive inches they would stop at nothing to put him in a uniform. If they failed to induce him to enlist by persuasion or craft, the recruiting agents or officers could obtain written permission from the king to employ force. In the regulations he issued in 1718 Frederick William stated that "if a captain knows of a tall handsome flugleman (leader of a file) whom he cannot get in the regular manner he is to report the fact to the commander of his regiment, who is to write His Majesty in detail and then await orders as to whether the captain is to take the recruit by force or not." [1] No wonder the Prussian mothers admonished their sons: "Stop growing or the recruiting agents will get you." [2] The converse idea was stated by Frederick William in an order of May 1, 1733: "That which has no growth is not to be enrolled." [3] If the king himself met a fine-looking man of uncommon stature on his walks or travels, he would try to enlist him. On a number of occasions when the

[1] Lehmann, "Werbung, Wehrpflicht und Beurlaubung unter Friedrich Wilhelm I," *Historische Zeitschrift*, LXVII (1891), 265.

[2] Bernay, *Das deutsche Heer*, p. 46.

[3] Document published in Courbière, *Geschichte der brandenburgisch-preussischen Heeresverfassung*, p. 89 *et sqq.*

desired recruit showed no readiness the king simply had him taken to the guardhouse until he changed his mind. When money was required to obtain a young giant, Frederick William, otherwise so close-fisted, spared no expense. The price paid for a man a little more than six feet tall was usually seven hundred to one thousand taler; more if he was taller.

Another way in which Frederick William obtained tall recruits was by barter. When the Saxon Field-Marshal von Flemming wanted a skilled Prussian bassoon player for his private band, he succeeded in getting him in return for a tall and handsome Saxon soldier, despite the fact that the bassoon player was a great favorite of the queen of Prussia. Count von Wackerbarth, also a Saxon, who wanted a blooded Spanish stallion which King Frederick I had purchased shortly before his death, was able to get it for nothing less than thirty tall recruits. When the king of Denmark sought to procure the extradition from Prussian territory of the murderer of Count von Rantzau, he was compelled to give Frederick William twelve tall recruits in exchange. In 1735 the Prussian ruler gave the bishop of Vilna permission to take refuge in Prussia in return for the promise of a number of tall recruits. After the peace of Vienna (October 3, 1735) the bishop attempted to return to Poland, but was held at Tilsit because he had not made good his promise. Count von Manteuffel, whose intercession in the case was requested, politely declined. "I would," Manteuffel wrote, "readily attempt to help him were he accused, for instance, of having tried to dethrone the king of Prussia or of having made an attempt upon the king's life; but to interfere in behalf of a person who has promised tall men would be exposing myself to the most unpleasant consequences without the slightest hope of success." [4]

[4] Weber, *Aus vier Jahrhunderten*, II, 200 *et sqq.*

The surest way of ingratiating oneself with Frederick William was to make him a present of tall recruits. La Chétardie, the French minister at Berlin, reported Frederick William as saying, "The most beautiful girl or woman in the world would be a matter of indifference to me, but (tall) soldiers—they are my weakness. He who sends them to me can lead me wherever he will." [5] Not infrequently the gift of tall recruits won for the donor some much-coveted office, the command of a regiment, or some other emolument or honor. As the knowledge of Frederick William's fondness for tall soldiers circulated throughout Europe, the rulers of other states and diplomatic representatives frequently presented the Prussian monarch with giant recruits as a means of courting his favor. In thanking for the recruits Frederick William would usually say: "I take them as a mark of your true friendship." As early as 1714 Peter the Great of Russia sent him eighty tall Muscovites. Later, after a visit, the tsar sent 150 of the tallest men to be found in Russia. Thereafter contingents from Russia arrived in Prussia almost every year. The gift of tall soldiers was repeatedly used by Count Seckendorf, the Austrian envoy, in his efforts to bind Prussia to Austria. "I am convinced," he wrote to Prince Eugene (October, 1726), "that the best thing to do in this matter is to give the king himself twenty-four of the finest, tallest, and youngest men that can be found in Hungary, Croatia, and Bohemia. I could achieve more with such a present than with the most powerful arguments." [6] The conclusion of the secret treaty of Wusterhausen in 1729 is the best proof of the efficacy of his gifts.

When such gifts arrived, all was sunshine about the king. Thus, when his son-in-law, the margrave of Bayreuth,

[5] Cited in Lavisse, *La Jeunesse du Grand Frédéric*, pp. 71–72.
[6] Förster, *Urkundenbuch*, II, 179.

brought him a gift of eight towering recruits, tears of joy stood in his eyes. He embraced the margrave repeatedly and said again and again, "Mon dieu! What pleasure you give me!" A professor of the Joachimsthal Gymnasium who sought the king's favor, but had no tall soldiers to give him, wrote an essay in which he tried to prove that man's possibilities for perfection are in direct proportion to his height. After he had published the essay his friends pointed out to him that the king himself was only of medium height, a fact which caused the "learned" professor to destroy the printed essays as quickly as possible.[7]

But the tall recruits he received as presents added to those he gained by barter and by recruiting within Prussia did not satisfy the gigantomania of Frederick William. Each acquisition only stimulated his appetite for more. To get as many as possible he made Europe his private hunting ground. At times as many as eight hundred to a thousand Prussian agents were busy trying to glean Europe's tall men. Wherever there was a young man whose head protruded above the crowd there one of these agents would appear sooner or later. For Saxony the Prussian agents had a list in which every man a few inches above the average height was entered. If the price of tall Prussians was high, that of tall foreigners was much higher. Count von Manteuffel states that an Austrian nobleman "sold" his son, who was extraordinarily tall, to a Prussian agent for four thousand taler in cash and a monthly pension of ten taler. In 1732 General Schmettau sold a flugelman to the king for five thousand taler, and the next year Seckendorf presented to the monarch a tall Tyrolese for whom he claimed to have paid the same amount. James

[7] Krauske, "Vom Hofe Friedrich Wilhelms I," in *Hohenzollern-Jahrbuch*, V (1901), 191.

Kirkland, a colossal Irishman, who was found in London, cost Frederick William no less than 8,862 taler.[8]

A less expensive method of obtaining tall men was to induce them by some stratagem to go to Prussia and then to impress them by force. A tall young gentleman from Courland, having come to Germany to continue his studies, soon attracted the attention of a Prussian recruiting officer, who befriended him and invited him to come to Berlin as his guest. When they arrived in Berlin the officer immediately turned his victim over to the guard, declaring him to be a recruit. Compelled to enlist, the young student was consoled with the promise that he would be a noncommissioned officer within a year and an ensign in three years. A favorite method of entrapping unwary Englishmen and Irishmen of Brobdingnagian proportions was to engage them as valets or footmen for travel on the continent and then to deliver them to the Prussian king at Potsdam. Von Borcke, the Prussian ambassador to England, employed this method a number of times, and as a result became so unpopular in England that the English government asked Frederick William to recall him. One of Von Borcke's victims was William Willis, a young man of about twenty-three, six feet and four inches tall, of Barford in Bedfordshire. Having been informed of the whereabouts of this young giant, Von Borcke sent a certain Hugh Montgomery to kidnap him if possible. Montgomery made the acquaintance of Willis, invited him to drink at a neighboring inn, and then told him that his master, an Irish lord, had directed him to procure a tall man to serve as valet during extensive travels on the continent. The annual wage of twenty pounds, with an additional fourteen shillings

---

[8] Förster, *Friedrich Wilhelm I*, II, 297 *et sqq.;* Weber, *Aus vier Jahrhunderten*, II, 209.

a week for board, which Montgomery said his lord would pay, proved so attractive that the unsuspecting youth accompanied him to London. There they were told that the Irish lord had departed for Holland, but had left funds with a friend (Von Borcke) for the traveling expenses of the new servant. As Willis was unaccustomed to travel, Von Borcke obligingly sent his own valet along as company. Upon their arrival at The Hague they were told that the Irish lord had started on his journey and was already in Germany. By this time Willis was ready to return home, but he was finally persuaded to go as far as Potsdam, where he was immediately measured for a uniform.[9]

All other methods failing, the Prussian agents, wherever they could do so with any degree of safety, would take sizable recruits by force even in foreign countries. In Hanover, for example, Prussian recruiters laid an ambush on the road between Harburg and Lüneburg for a postillion who had resisted their persuasions. When he arrived they seized him and carried him off, permitting the horse with the letter bag to go forward. Agents went as far afield as the Italian Tyrol to seize a tall recruit. They did not even stop at invading a monastery in Rome to kidnap a friar of gigantic stature. Not all such crimping expeditions ended successfully, however. When in 1732 the crown prince, as a means of ingratiating himself with his father, reported that there was a tall shepherd in Anhalt-Cöthen, only three miles from the Prussian frontier, the king wrote in the margin of the report: "We must, if possible, gain possession of the man. If it can be done in no other way, he must be enticed to come to the border and must then be quietly seized." After all induce-

[9] Weber, *Aus vier Jahrhunderten*, II, 191; Cotton, "English Captives in Potsdam in the Eighteenth Century," *National Review*, LXX (1918), 487.

ments to get him to enter the Prussian service had failed, the Prussian recruiters managed to seize him, but before they could cross the border he made a dash for freedom. Seeing that any pursuit would be useless, the Prussian officer took his pistol and killed the shepherd, whereupon the recruiters quickly escaped by crossing into Prussian territory. An equally tragic incident is reported to have taken place in the duchy of Jülich. A certain Baron Hompesch, who was one of Frederick William's agents, ordered from a tall master joiner a cupboard as long and broad as the artisan himself. Upon examining the finished product Hompesch declared it to be too short. When the joiner got into the cupboard to show that it was of the correct height, the baron suddenly fastened the door and ordered his attendants to take the cupboard across the border. Later, when it was opened, the tall man was found to have suffocated.[10]

Such man-hunting excesses stirred angry reclamations in many states. The Elector of Cologne, from whose territories Prussian agents had carried off several men, seized an equal number of Prussians and held them until Frederick William released his subjects. Hanover, the Palatinate, and Hesse-Cassel went so far as to form an alliance to combat the activities of the Prussian recruiters after a series of seizures in Hanover had nearly caused a war between the two states. Three Prussian officers imprisoned in Hungary for recruiting in 1722 were released only through the intervention of Frederick William himself. A few years later a Prussian agent was sentenced to five years' imprisonment at hard labor.[11] In 1726 the emperor, as a means of drawing Frederick

[10] Weber, *Aus vier Jahrhunderten*, II, 193 *et sqq.*; Förster, *Friedrich Wilhelm I*, II, 305 *et sqq.*

[11] Lukinich, "Preussische Werbungen in Ungarn," *Ungarische Jahrbücher*, VI (1926), 20 *et sqq.*

William into an alliance, gave Prussia special permission to enlist tall recruits in his territories, but the excesses perpetrated by the recruiters forced him to retract that permission in 1736. In Holland, too, great bitterness was aroused by the recruiting activities. After repeated representations to the Prussian court had proved ineffectual, a Prussian noncommissioned officer was shot and a Prussian agent hanged in Maestricht. When the excesses still did not cease, a Prussian officer was hanged in full uniform at Lüttich. A Prussian recruiting officer arrested in Saxony and sentenced to be hanged was saved only after Frederick William firmly told Von Suhm, the Saxon envoy at Berlin, that "he would have to answer in person" if the sentence were carried out.

When the recruiting activities continued, earnest protestations against them were sent to Frederick William from all quarters; so many that Count Seckendorf wrote to Prince Eugene: "It is feared that this passion for recruiting will yet cause trouble all around." [12] Attempts were made to arouse the King's religious sentiments against the system by the citation of such Bible passages as: "And he that stealeth a man and selleth him, or if he be found in his hand he shall surely be put to death" (Exodus 21:16) and "If a man be found stealing any of his brethren of the children of Israel and maketh merchandise of him or selleth him, then that thief shall die" (Deuteronomy 24:7). Moreover, many rulers earnestly begged the Prussian king to stop the excesses of his agents. In 1732, for example, Count von Wackerbarth wrote to the Saxon Marshal von Flemming: "I know that the empress as well as Prince Eugene has made serious representations to His Prussian Majesty on his passion for tall men and the means he employs and the expense he incurs

[12] Förster, *Urkundenbuch*, II, 38.

to get hold of them; and it is believed that this remonstrance has made an impression on his mind." [13]

If Count von Wackerbarth seriously believed that the recruiting would cease, he was deluding himself. The search for Goliaths and its concomitant excesses continued despite all the protestations, clamors, and reprisals. When the complaints became particularly loud and the demands for reparations became insistent, Frederick William would deny that any excesses had ever been perpetrated, averring that the stories were invented by those who hated his officers. The forcible enlistment of tall men stirred few if any scruples in his mind. According to Morgenstern, who was in a position to know, the Prussian autocrat believed that he had a God-given mortgage on all the tall fellows in Europe. "Regarding the enlistment of tall recruits," Morgenstern wrote, "he was convinced that those who refused him permission to do so were wronging him; that God had, so to speak, empowered him to take the tall men because he knew how to prize and cherish them." [14] To prove that God had expressly countenanced the kidnapping of tall men Frederick William would cite such Bible passages as: "He will take your menservants, and your maidservants, and your goodliest young men, and your asses, and put them to his work" (I Samuel 8:6) and "When Saul saw any strong man and valiant man, he took him unto him" (I Samuel 14:52).

Accordingly Frederick William continued to spur on his recruiting agents to bring in more tall recruits. A captain who had no new "long fellows" from abroad when the king inspected the company would call down upon himself the royal wrath. Thus General von Forcade begged Marshal

[13] Weber, *Aus vier Jahrhunderten*, II, 204–207.
[14] *Ueber Friedrich Wilhelm I*, p. 203.

von Flemming to send him a few tall recruits, because "the king has declared," he wrote, "that the man who has no good recruits will be broken like a glass." [15] If the report of Count von Manteuffel is reliable, the Prussian ruler sent a major to the military prison at Spandau for a period of six years because he had no tall recruits to present to the king. Rothe, the secretary of the Saxon legation in Berlin, wrote on June 16, 1739: "His Majesty has broken, in front of their companies, two majors, one named Katt, of Glasenapp's regiment; the other of the regiment of Prince Charles. No other reason can be alleged than that they had not a sufficient number of tall recruits." [16]

The tallest of the tall men his agents collected or that he received as gifts Frederick William added to the Potsdam Giant Regiment. It was a collection of giants such as the world had not seen before; nor has there been any similar collection since. Composed at first of two battalions of six hundred men each, the regiment grew until it reached a maximum of almost three thousand. No man was admitted to the regiment unless he was over six feet, some of the tallest members being nearly eight feet. To make them appear even taller, the Prussian monarch had them wear tall miter-shaped hats, which added some twelve to fifteen inches to the stature of each grenadier. In his instructions to his captains and to the recruiting agents the king had repeatedly stated that the tall recruits "must not be corpulent, have weak legs, disagreeable faces, short noses, or short legs." [17] But if we can believe Baron Bielfeld, who saw the regiment of giants in 1739, the recruiters were not too successful in carrying out the king's instructions.

[15] Weber, *Aus vier Jahrhunderten*, II, 208.
[16] *Ibid.*, p. 209.
[17] See Linnebach, *König Friedrich Wilhelm I und Fürst Leopold zu Anhalt-Dessau*, p. 29 et sqq.

The sight of this troop [Bielfeld wrote] more astonished than pleased me. They appear to me like so many walking colossi; but nature seems to have been entirely preoccupied with giving them an uncommon stature, for they have little proportion of figure, being for the most part either ugly, bow-legged, or ill-made in some part of their bodies, so that the regiment in general is more marvelous than fine.[18]

This collection of "walking colossi" was one of the great curiosities of Europe. From far and wide visitors came to see it. But it was also an object of ridicule, particularly in the foreign newssheets of the day. The *Dutch Courant*, for example, reported the death of a tall grenadier and added that when his body was opened it was found to contain two stomachs, but no heart. Upon reading the account Frederick William sent a letter to the paper in which he stated that the account was quite correct, but that the editor had omitted to mention that the deceased was a Dutchman.

Frederick William himself was the colonel of the regiment of giants. Shouting staccato commands in his gruff voice, he would drill these sons of Anak for hours on end. It was one of his greatest delights. So that he might watch them drill when affairs of state prevented him from drilling them himself, he chose for his workroom at Potsdam a room overlooking the parade grounds. He knew most of his grenadiers by name and regarded them much as a sentimental father does his children. When confined to his apartments because of illness in 1734 he had about two hundred of the tallest grenadiers march past his bed. The sight of his "blue boys" was a better tonic than any medicine his physician could have prescribed. He who otherwise insisted that the laws of the land be carried out to the very letter on one occasion caned the members of an entire military court be-

[18] *Letters of Baron Bielfeld*, III, 66.

cause they had condemned one of his tall grenadiers to death for the theft of six thousand taler, though that was the punishment provided by law. His love for his giants was, in fact, so great that he could not bring himself to refuse a petition presented to him by one of them. So many lawyers took advantage of this weakness to settle cases for their clients that it became imperative to stop this mode of presenting petitions to the king. When Chancellor von Cocceji inquired of Frederick William what the punishment for presenting a petition through the intervention of a giant grenadier was to be, the king drew on the petition a sketch of a gallows on which a lawyer and a dog were hanging side by side. Cocceji, taking the king's answer seriously, published an edict which declared that a lawyer who was found guilty of using a member of the Potsdam Giant Regiment to expedite settlement of a case was to be hanged together with a dog. It is doubtful, however, whether the king was in earnest. More than anything else he probably sought to frighten the lawyers. There is no case on record in which the punishment was carried out.[19]

The Potsdam grenadiers were given the best of care. Physicians carefully watched over their health, and chaplains ministered to the needs of their souls. Church attendance on Sunday was as much a part of their discipline as drill during the rest of the week. At regular intervals the entire regiment was bled, because the king believed that bleeding had a beneficial effect. To set a good example he went so far as to have himself bled in full view of the regiment. Each year every grenadier received a new uniform consisting of a blue jacket embroidered with gold and lined with red, with cuffs

[19] Beneckendorf, *Karakterzüge aus dem Leben König Friedrich Wilhelms I*, I, 113–117, and VII, 32 *et sqq.*; Förster, *Friedrich Wilhelm I*, II, 263, 270.

of scarlet. The waistcoat and breeches were straw-colored, and the whole was set off by white spatterdashes and the high miters. For reasons of economy the jackets were very short and the breeches tight, so that any grenadier who tried to stoop courted disaster. Frederick William was so proud of the general appearance of his Potsdam Regiment that he had life-size portraits of the tallest members painted, which he hung in the halls of the royal palaces. As a special mark of his favor he permitted some of the grenadiers to carry on trades or to keep shops of various kinds; upon others he bestowed lands or sinecures. If they were married, he gave them cottages; if not, he often found wives for them in the hope that they would be more contented with their lives. He was particularly pleased when such couples chose him as godfather for their children.

Despite the many favors that were heaped upon them there was much discontent among the giant grenadiers. Many, having been forcibly impressed, hated their oppressors; while others, who had joined willingly, became homesick. To prevent desertions the king was forced to exercise perpetual vigilance. In 1730 there was discovered a plot by eighty-seven Hungarians, Poles, and Wallachians, who had planned to set fire to Potsdam and desert in the confusion. Another plot to escape involved more than twenty grenadiers, mostly Frenchmen. Upon hearing of it, Frederick William had the accused arrested and brought before him. According to an eyewitness the ringleader, when questioned by the king, "put his hat on his head *á la morbleu*, stemmed his fists in his side, and said that he could stand it no longer; that he was heartily tired of his life, and the sooner the king had him hung the better." The king, instead of having him hung, sentenced him to have his ears and nose cut off and sent him to Spandau condemned to hard labor for life. The others were flogged and returned to the ranks. But in spite of all precautions attempts at escape were successful now and then. When one of his tall "blue boys" succeeded in escaping, Frederick William's gaiety and good humor would vanish for days. Count von Manteuffel reports that when a sergeant arrived one evening, while Frederick William was in his Tobacco Parliament, to report that a tall Bohemian of the Potsdam regiment had succeeded in escaping, the king turned pale, put down his pipe, and did not speak again during the rest of the evening.[20]

In the British Museum there is a curious petition, addressed to Viscount Torrington, in which nineteen giant Englishmen beg to be freed from the Prussian service. It reads in part:

May It Please Your Grace,—Wether to sit down tamely under our Cruel Bondage, and dwindle our Lives away in Chagrin and dispair, or boldly to risque all in the noble pursuit of Liberty, is the Question. The first methinks seems too Temid and mean for an English soul to Comply with, and the latter has its train of dangers. Tho', when we consider that death for the unhappy has nothing in it frightfull, this does Incourage us to trust the flattering Gipsy once more, and we do firmly believe that could our miserable bondage but reach the Ears of such noble Patrons as your Grace, whose Chiefest Care is the Interest and tranquillity of your Country, you would not suffer our Calamity to be much longer Lived, and, to be plain, the strings of our Outragious Fate, together with Ruminating on our never to be forgotten Liberty, was Sufficient, had not hope Intercepted to force us to shorten our days. This has been the fate of numbers, who, unwilling longer to Bear the Oppressor's wrongs, have plunged themselves into Uncertainty.—Such fatal Consequences must undoubtedly follow an unrestrained unlimited Power join'd with a Malicious will and a Brutall dispo-

---

[20] Weber, *Aus vier Jahrhunderten*, II, 219 *et sqq.*

sition to mischief,—And I Vow that the unnatural Action here
in force is far above the Conception of either Humanity or
Reason: for what man Can Bear, and more especially he that's
born free, The Cruel Inhumane strokes of Brutal sway, the Insulting Insolence of Knavish Officers? and this impos'd upon
him for Life, after useing the most Enormous and the most
Diabolical methods to devest him of his tranquillity— But may
it please your Grace, thanks to honesty undaunted, we are a
Number of whome I will Give Your Grace a List, that do retain
some tinctures of our Native Bravery, as Our Glorious Struggles
here for our Liberty, and the honour of our Nation, Can well
witness, and not withstanding the difficulty hitherto has Caus'd
us Unnumerable Inhumane Stripes, These Loyal sufferings can
never Prevent our Noble pursuit of Bravery.

A. Peter Friendly	George Watson	Stephen Ramsden
William Willis	Thomas Spendlow	John Mayhew
George Wilkins	Edward Bevan	Robert Clifford
John Evans	Alexander Gordon	James Dickson
Christopher Weathreal	Joseph Earl	John Jopp
Antony Best	John Mussendine	James Cavell

This, May It Please Your Grace, I don't doubt is sufficient to
Convince you what heavy burdens we lye under, and hope it
will so potently move your Compassion to our Aid that we
may reap the long struggled for Benefit, which Glorious Action
will draw the Blessings of God and the prayers of Men Upon
You and Consequently redound to Your Never Dying Name.

[Signed] Curtius [21]

But the petition was in vain. Once a tall recruit had entered
the service of Frederick William, there was little chance of
his being released. Thus, when the parents of the Chevalier
d'Argentera, an unusually tall young man who had been
tricked into accompanying a recruiting agent to Prussia,
became apprehensive concerning his safety because they received no answers to their letters, they appealed to Rothe,

[21] Cotton, "English Captives in Potsdam in the Eighteenth Century," *National Review*, LXX (1918), 486–487.

the secretary of the Saxon legation in Berlin, for news of their son. After a search Rothe finally found the young man a prisoner in the Prussian guardhouse, where he had been sent for refusing to enlist as a grenadier. To the parents Rothe could offer no better consolation than this: "It seems to me that he will have no better chance of escape than the other foreign marquises, counts, and barons who have been brought here through great promises and after all were put into the ranks." [22] Guy Dickens, the English ambassador to Prussia, wrote after vainly trying to secure the release of the aforesaid William Willis:

They laugh at me when I mention the thing and ask me, half in jest, half in earnest, how I can urge such a matter seriously or think it possible they can part with a man who has six feet four inches. I should be less unreasonable if I demanded a province or two . . . Release! They had no such word in their dictionary, and it was to be wished that the English would strike it out of theirs. They might hang as many Prussian recruiters as they could ketch but as for the tall men in question the only way to get them off was to come and fetch them with one hundred thousand men.[23]

Having an eye for the future, the king was not satisfied with merely recruiting men of large stature; he also attempted to perpetuate them in Prussia by marrying his giants to woman of large stature. Little, however, appears to have come from his experiments. When in 1725 it was reported that an extraordinarily large child had been born in Cleves of one of these unions, Frederick William was so overjoyed that he could not see it soon enough. Although the season was midwinter and the roads were hardly passable, he ordered the child brought to Berlin immediately. Finally, however, he consented to a postponement on ac-

[22] Weber, *Aus vier Jahrhunderten*, II, 191–192.
[23] Cited in Hutchinson, *Romance of a Regiment*, pp. 140–141.

count of the weather. But when it was March he could no longer restrain his impatience and sent the order: "Make haste! The weather is good now." Whether the child grew up to be a giant the records do not state.[24] A favorite story of contemporaries concerned Frederick William and a Saxon girl. It was said that one day while he was traveling from Potsdam to Berlin the king met along the way a well-proportioned girl of gigantic stature. Learning that she was single and that to return to her home in Saxony after having marketed in Berlin she would pass through Potsdam, the king decided on the spot that she would make a good wife for one of his huge grenadiers, an Irishman named Macdoll. When the girl consented to deliver a message to the commandant at Berlin, he took paper and pencil and wrote: "The bearer is to be married without delay to Macdoll, the big Irishman. Don't listen to objections." Then he gave the girl a taler for her pains and went his way. But the plan miscarried. Either the girl could read or she suspected a trick. Whatever the case, she did not deliver it herself, but gave it to an old crone she found begging at the gates of Potsdam. One may imagine the surprise of the commandant upon opening the note and finding it a positive command to marry the bearer immediately to the grenadier Macdoll. As for the grenadier, his consternation and repugnance were so great that he was prevailed upon only by threats and promises to submit to the will of the king. When Frederick William learned that he had been imposed upon and that his newly-married giant was disconsolate, he ordered an immediate annulment.[25]

Toward the end of his life Frederick William appears to have recognized the folly of collecting giants. It is reported

[24] Beneckendorf, *Karakterzüge aus dem Leben König Friedrich Wilhelms I*, VIII, 29–30.
[25] Förster, *Friedrich Wilhelm I*, II, 300–301.

that shortly before his death he told his son Frederick that he had been wrong "in making the (Potsdam) regiment his hobby and spending more than 700,000 taler on it." [26] He also declared that he should have broken up the regiment long before had not his false pride prevented it. To this statement he added the hope that Frederick would act more wisely on succeeding him. Whether by his father's advice or not, Frederick the Great did disband the regiment soon after his accession.

[26] Weber, *Aus vier Jahrhunderten*, II, 223–224.

CHAPTER SEVEN

Frederick William Creates the Prussian Bureaucracy

SOON AFTER he became king Frederick William took up the task of reorganizing the administration of his territories. Basically the task was one of joining the scattered provinces in a closely-knit administrative system centering in the king. The immediate object of this reorganization was to insure to the crown a maximum income so that it could meet the increasing financial needs of the army. According to a German historian: "All the endeavors of the king with regard to administration and political economy had the ultimate purpose of procuring the necessary means for the support and augmentation of the army." [1] At Frederick William's accession the administration of the Hohenzollern territories was still organized largely on a provincial basis, each province having its own laws and institutions. This aggregation of provinces was a unit only for purposes of war and foreign policy. Nor was there any desire on the part of the inhabitants or the Estates to fuse the provincial organizations into one unified administration. Much of the

[1] Braubach, "Der Aufstieg Brandenburg-Preussens 1640 bis 1815," in Geschichte der führenden Völker, XV, 237.

administration was still in the hands of the old feudal and territorial officials, who sought in every way known to them to perpetuate the particularism they represented. The Great Elector had taken an important step toward the creation of a unified central administration by putting the management of the military revenues under the direction of a minister of war in Berlin. But this was only a beginning. Frederick William I was to do the major part of the work of centralizing the administration, and his successors were to complete the task.

In the first year of his reign Frederick William put greater order into the government by merging the separate administrations of the domains, the mint, the postal service, and the customs duties in a general board of finance (*Generalfinanzdirektorium*) and by subordinating many of the hitherto independent local officials to this board. But in addition to this board there was the War Commissariat (*Oberkriegskommissariat*) which had charge of all funds collected for the army, including the excise taxes in the cities and the direct taxes on land in the country. Functioning side by side, these two boards often came into collision, causing much confusion and red tape. Frederick William himself stated a few years later that he knew of more than a thousand instances in which the interests of the two boards had clashed. Finally, in 1722, he decided, probably at the suggestion of Leopold of Dessau, to amalgamate the dual system into one supreme board of finance, war, and domains (*Ober-Finanz, Kriegs und Domänen Direktorium*), called, in brief, the General Directory. After turning the idea over in his mind for some time, he withdrew to the palace at Schönebeck, and there with his own hand drew up the instructions for the new administrative body. His private secretary then "translated" the king's jargon into intelligible

German, and on the nineteenth of January, 1723, the instructions were put into force.

The General Directory was, as Frederick William put it, "a supreme board right behind the king." [2] Its supreme duty, as the Prussian monarch repeatedly and energetically impressed upon it, was to see that the revenues were collected promptly and to the last pfennig, which was necessary if Prussia was to support its large army without foreign subsidies.[3] But its functions were not limited to the collection of revenues. It also had charge of the activities which produced the revenues. These included, besides the royal domains, the mint and the postal system, also the salt monopoly, the royal mills, mines and breweries, and in general the industries in the towns and cities. In fact, it supervised the entire internal administration, excepting justice, education and religious affairs. In its organization the General Directory was divided into four departments, each department having charge of the administration in several provinces. A minister presided over each department and had a number of councillors as his assistants. But the departments were not separate divisions. Each minister was dependent upon the others for decisions on matters in his department, and all decisions were signed by the ministers as a group. If the ministers could not agree, they notified the king and he then made the decision. All the decisions of the General Directory were, of course, subject to ratification by Frederick William, who characteristically had made himself president of the board. He did not, however, occupy the presidential chair. His presidency

[2] *AB, Beh.*, IV (Part 2), 140.

[3] *Ibid.*, III, 591, 667. Even after the establishment of the General Directory the funds collected for the army remained separate from the revenues originally designated for court and administrative purposes. Frederick William, it appears, feared that if the two did not remain separate a luxury-loving successor might spend most of the total income on the court and thus neglect the army.

was merely a symbol that the final authority reposed in the king. Even if he had wished to attend the meetings, the press of his duties would have prevented him from doing so.

In drawing up the instructions Frederick William, with his passion for detail, regulated most minutely the entire range of General Directory's activity.[4] He directed that it was to meet on Monday, Wednesday, Thursday, and Friday of each week, in the summer at seven A. M. and in the winter at eight. Each department was assigned a particular day of the week on which it submitted its reports and accounts for discussion. No member was to leave the session "until every matter has been settled for the department whose special day it is, so that not one bit of the work is left undone." [5] If a session lasted later than two in the afternoon, the members were to be served with "four good dishes" from the royal kitchens, "together with an adequate quantity of beer and wine." The instructions went so far as to state that only half the members were to eat at one time; the others were to continue working until those who were eating had finished and were again at work. Frederick William even decreed that the meal should be served by a single servant so that the room would not be crowded with servants.

From Berlin the General Directory extended its jurisdiction into the provinces by the appointment of provincial chambers (*Kriegs und Domänenkammern*), which were, so to speak, the counterpart of the intendants in France. They had, however, less freedom of action and fewer opportunities for the exercise of personal judgment than the intendants. Elaborate written instructions, which could not be disregarded without punishment, minutely regulated all ordinary activities of the provincial chambers. Any unusual matters

[4] Instructions in Förster, *Urkundenbuch*, II, 173–255, and *AB, Beh.*, III, 533–653.
[5] *AB, Beh.*, III, 583.

had to be referred to the General Directory, whose decisions were in turn submitted to the king.

Under the provincial chambers all local authorities were subordinated in such a way as to demolish the last shreds of local autonomy. It was the final victory of royal absolutism over the old local and feudal authorities. Thus the royal officials absorbed the administrative functions of the local diets, the members of which retained only their social standing. Even the control of the municipal governments was transferred to the royal officials from the oligarchies, which had excluded most of the citizens from any part in the government. Thereafter the tax commissary (*Steuerrat*), without whose consent little could be done, became the real ruler of the municipalities.[6] He superintended all activities which in any way contributed to, or could be detrimental to, the royal finances. In other words, he had a hand in everything. Thus there was in Frederick William's new system an unprecedented measure of state penetration into local government. So all-embracing was the control of the central government that certain historians have styled it state socialism.[7]

This reorganization completely delocalized the entire administration. Whereas the Great Elector had been forced to promise that he would appoint as officials of a province only those who were native to that province, Frederick William ordered the chambers "not to recommend people who were born in the provinces in which there is a vacant office to be filled."[8] In this way he succeeded in breaking the power

[6] He himself being without independent competence had to report all matters to the provincial chamber.

[7] Spengler, *Preussentum und Sozialismus*, p. 31; *Cambridge Modern History*, VI, 224.

[8] Schmoller, "Der preussische Beamtenstand unter Friedrich Wilhelm I," *Preussische Jahrbücher*, XXVI (1870), 159.

of local families and family cliques. At the death of Frederick William, it has been said, the Prussian administration functioned like the works of a clock, with the king himself as the main spring. But the simile must not be taken too literally. Frederick William had indeed established a certain administrative unity, yet the unification was not complete. There were still many cogs missing, and others were slipping.

In an autocracy such as Frederick William had established it was but natural that the appointment of all important civil officials should be in the hands of the sovereign. The Great Elector had, by and large, gained the right to appoint most of the higher officials in his various provinces. But his choice, as already stated, had still been somewhat restricted in that he was required in Prussia, for example, to appoint only local noblemen of the Lutheran persuasion to the higher offices. During the reign of Frederick I the right of appointing subordinate officials was largely assumed by the leading ministers. Frederick William, however, claimed the sole right of appointment. "No one," he stated soon after his accession, "shall be appointed to any office unless I do it myself." [9] This right he asserted throughout his reign.

Having gained the right to appoint all officials, Frederick William adopted measures calculated to raise the general standard of efficiency. The Great Elector had already introduced considerable improvement in this respect by trying to choose only able officials. But it was merely a beginning, and much that he accomplished was undone during the succeeding reign. Upon taking up the reins of government Frederick William decreed that officials must have the proper training for the office to which they are appointed.

[9] *AB, Beh.,* II, 29.

At various times during his reign he issued decrees regarding certain officials. He decreed, for instance, that those aspiring to become judges, lawyers, and procurators must take a specified course in a Prussian university.[10] For other offices a prescribed course of study was not a primary requisite, but the king did demand a certain type of practical training. To demonstrate his fitness a candidate had to undergo a thorough examination. As the number of officials was large and vacancies were frequent, Frederick William had his boards draw up lists of eligibles for the various offices. Only "the most able, faithful, and upright" young men, he told the boards repeatedly, were to be placed on these lists.[11]

But Frederick William himself was not always guided solely by a candidate's fitness for office. If an applicant had "special virtues" in the eyes of the king, he might be appointed even though he had not passed the examinations in a satisfactory manner. To be a soldier or an ex-soldier was such a virtue. Among the lower officials the collectors of the excise, the mounted policemen, and others were almost all invalid or superannuated soldiers. In addition, the king, as stated earlier, also appointed military men to higher offices without much regard for their fitness. General von Blankensee, for example, was appointed to a high office in Pomerania, though his ability to write was largely limited to signing his own name. Another "special virtue" was the offer of an applicant to furnish a tall recruit or to donate a certain sum to the recruiting fund. The Great Elector had introduced the practice of withholding half, later only a quarter, of the first year's salary of his officials for the benefit of the marine fund. This practice was discontinued

[10] Ibid., IV (Part 2), 310, 352.
[11] Ibid., I, 620; III, 577; IV (Part 1), 163.

by Frederick William, but he was pleased when applicants for an office expressed their willingness to donate a certain sum to the recruiting fund. Often the king would reply when a high official asked him who was to be appointed to a certain office: "He that gives most." [12] Frederick William would even barter with an applicant over the size of the donation. When on one occasion he was offered two hundred reichstaler, he wrote in the margin of the application: "He has money. Must pay 1,000 taler." [13] In 1733 the provincial chamber of Cleves recommended to the king that a certain Türck be appointed mayor of Duisberg. This city, the board reported, already had two mayors, but added that both lacked the proper education for the office. Türck, on the other hand, not only had the proper training but was also willing to pay three hundred taler into the recruiting fund. In answer Frederick William wrote: "So those who have not studied are idiots. Then I am also an idiot." But the offer to donate a sum to the recruiting fund was another matter; hence he added: "If Türck pays 1,200 reichstaler to the recruiting fund, you may appoint him; otherwise the offer is flatly refused." [14] In justice to Frederick William it must be stated that he did not invariably chose the applicant who offered to donate the largest sum.

Once in the Prussian civil service, an official became subject to a discipline no less stern than that of the Prussian army. Such a discipline Frederick William regarded as the highest form of order, as the apex of efficiency. He stated the requirements of office in no uncertain terms. To two officials who resisted transfer to Tilsit he wrote: "You must serve your master with body and soul, with goods and chat-

[12] See Förster, *Urkundenbuch*, I, 60.
[13] *AB, Beh.*, IV (Part 1), 550; V (Part 1), 740.
[14] *Ibid.*, V (Part 1), 543.

tels, with honor and conscience, and stake upon this service everything but your salvation." [15] What he specially demanded of his officials was untiring diligence, the utmost efficiency, incorruptible fidelity to duty, and above all prompt and absolute obedience. As a means of preventing bribery and corruption he who did not hesitate to accept cash or tall recruits from candidates for office forbade his officials to accept gifts in any form whatever. The oath required of the privy councillors, for example, included the promise: "I will not accept or receive gifts, gratuities, presents, pensions, or promises of any nature or character whatsoever, either from foreigners or native-born persons, from high or low, through myself or through others, be they members of my immediate family, servants, relatives, or strangers." [16] Every effort was made to encourage and strengthen an active Christianity among the officials. "Whosoever is not faithful to God," Frederick William stated, "will be so much less faithful to me, a mere man." [17] The cultivation of such virtues as honesty and uprightness was particularly stressed. In the instructions for the General Directory he ordered the members of that body "always to tell me the truth and not to come before me with untruths." [18] But he also told them that if the country was ever visited by a disaster they were "either to hide the truth from the people or at least to minimize the disaster as much as possible." [19]

More than anything else Frederick William demanded prompt and unquestioning obedience of his officials. As he put it in a letter to Leopold of Dessau: "There must be subordination; that is the most important thing in the entire

---

[15] *AB, Beh.*, II, 128; see also III, 651, 658, 666.
[16] *Ibid.*, I, 325.   [17] *Ibid.*, III, 311.
[18] *Ibid.*, p. 573.   [19] *Ibid.*, p. 256.

service." [20] His slogan from the first was: "Don't argue!"
"Everyone," he stated, "must do his duty without arguing
and must render complete obedience to the printed and
written regulations and orders." [21] Nothing irritated him
more than argument or contradiction on the part of his
officials. To the members of the General Directory he said
emphatically: "I hope you will not demand that I be like
the emperor who can say no more than his boards permit
him to say, and if it pleases them the emperor must be in
the wrong. I will never stand for anything like that, but
will prove that I am able to rule." [22] At the slightest suspicion
of insubordination Frederick William would shower his civil
officials with such threats as the following:

They shall dance to my music or the devil take me. Like the
Tsar I will hang and roast, and treat them as rebels. They will
be amazed that I can be so severe. But what can I do? These
things must be done or I am no longer master. When I give
orders to a military officer, they are obeyed. But these accursed
scoundrels think they are better and will not obey me. I will
singe and burn and treat them in a tyrannical manner. I have
command of my army and shall not have command of these
sacramental scoundrels. If I permitted that I would be a
cowardly rascal. [23]

On the other hand, he promised those who would serve him
"with unsullied fidelity and untiring diligence" that "they
can be firmly confident that I shall support them against the
whole world and permit no intrigues except such as purpose to improve the civil service. I shall condemn no one before I have personally examined him in the presence of the
informers." [24]

[20] *Briefe an Leopold zu Anhalt-Dessau*, p. 185.
[21] *AB, Beh.*, V (Part 1), 565; see also II, 167; III, 295, 573, 651,
655, 699; IV (Part 1), 244, 674, 731.
[22] Droysen, *Geschichte der preussischen Politik*, IV, 353.
[23] *AB, Beh.*, II, 130.   [24] *Ibid.*, III, 651.

To prevent laxness and malfeasance Frederick William kept a perpetual vigilance over his officials. His opinion of their trustworthiness was very low, if his statements can be accepted at their face value. For example, he answered an application for a position with the statement: "I can now appoint no more officials. I have enough thieves."[25] As previously indicated he frequently called the officials as a whole "scoundrels" (*Blackisten* or *Blackscheisser*). He believed that he must be continually "on their necks" to keep them orderly and honest.[26] Consequently he regularly visited even his most distant provinces. To the Königsberg board, which he could not visit as frequently as he desired, the king sent his portrait with the request that it be put in a prominent place so that it might serve as a perpetual reminder of his orders.[27] The officials and boards stationed in Berlin and Potsdam could not tell at what moment the king might walk in and demand an accounting. The result was that a "fear of the never-resting eye of the king pervaded the entire administration." "God has given me eyes," Frederick William stated, "so that I can immediately see whether my rules and orders are given prompt attention."[28] Count Manteuffel reported that Frederick William, on one of his early morning walks in Potsdam, saw a post coach arrive at the post house when it was still closed. When the vigorous knocking of the passengers failed to roust out the postmaster, the king himself entered the house by a rear door and finding the postmaster in bed gave him a sound thrashing. "Such incidents," Manteuffel adds, "serve to make everyone quick and prompt."[29]

As the king could not be everywhere or see everything,

[25] *Ibid.*, II, 245.   [26] *Ibid.*, V (Part 2), 537.
[27] *Ibid.*, p. 246.   [28] *Ibid.*, V (Part 1), 675.
[29] *Ibid.*, I, 381 *et sqq.*; *Briefe und Erlasse Friedrich Wilhelms I*, p. 22; Weber, *Aus vier Jahrhunderten*, I, 98.

tried officials assisted him in keeping watch over their fellow officials. Their duty, as the king stated it, was to inform him "how everything is and who is an honorable man and who is untrustworthy." [30] Some functioned openly as inspectors and others worked in secret. Both sent detailed reports of their findings to the king. In addition to the individual inspectors and spies appointed by the king there was also an official body called the "Fiscalate," organized to establish a complete system of espionage in all the Prussian provinces. All officials from the highest to the lowest were under its supervision. In secret instructions to Von Katsch, the minister of justice and chief of the Fiscalate, Frederick stated:

If he discovers anything that is contrary to my instructions or interest, Von Katsch must immediately report it to me, for if he does not, he will be held responsible for it. Von Katsch is to spare no one, even though it be my brother. [N.B. Frederick William had no brother.] It is self-evident that he should carefully watch for every kind of thievery. If he does all this conscientiously, without sparing anyone, he may be assured that I will energetically support him against everyone.[31]

Frederick William's mistrust was such that he probably instructed others to spy on Von Katsch.

Many of the members of the Fiscalate appear to have been anything but upright themselves. The Fiscalate was so dreaded and detested that, if we can believe contemporary statements, honest men seldom sought appointment to this office; those who were honest seldom remained honest long after their appointment. The members of the Fiscalate, it appears, readily reported the delinquencies and irregularities of the poorer officials to the king; but when the "malefactor" was wealthy, they sought to obtain bribes from him for suppressing the accusation. For this reason they

[30] *AB, Beh.,* IV (Part 2), 231.
[31] *AB, Beh.,* III, 667.

watched wealthy officials much more closely. The most trivial circumstances often served as bases for accusations. Thus Baron Geuder, member of the provincial chamber at Halberstadt, who lived near a church, was discovered one day by a "fiscal" drinking coffee in the church with a friend while they were listening to organ music. The fiscal immediately accused the baron of desecrating the temple of God and, when the latter refused to take the accusation seriously, reported him to the king. But there was still a way of avoiding a trial—the donation of a certain sum to the recruiting fund, which the baron immediately did. "The baron," a contemporary wrote, "did not deem it advisable on account of the extraordinary zeal which Frederick William had often manifested in religious matters to defend himself against this unexpected charge, but quietly paid the sum of a thousand taler demanded from him and his guest." [32] Even military officers of high rank were not safe from the accusations of the fiscals. Lieutenant-General Wreech, for example, upon being accused by the Fiscalate of saying uncomplimentary things about the local board, hastily acknowledged his shortcomings to the king and paid 1,000 taler into the recruiting fund. Insults against his person the king did not take too seriously. On a report which stated that a certain preacher had made insulting remarks about him and was also a Socinian the king wrote: "What he has said against me, I forgive him; but if he is a Socinian, he is to be immured." [33] When the consistory testified to the orthodoxy of the preacher, he went unpunished.

A further device of the king for preventing irregularities and negligences was that of making every official responsible for his subordinates. The discipline was, in fact, carried so

[32] Beneckendorf, *Karakterzüge aus dem Leben König Friedrich Wilhelms I*, VII, 56; Förster, *Friedrich Wilhelm I*, II, 268.
[33] *Ibid.*

far that every official was responsible not only for his own actions and for those of his subordinates but also for those of his colleagues. It was, as Frederick William stated it, the principle of "one for all and all for one." [34] He decreed, for example, that in case of malfeasance "the entire board will be held responsible. Hence the members must watch diligently in order to insure their own safety." [35] This system left few loopholes for malpractice.

Severe penalties were unhesitatingly meted out for negligence or any transgression of the prescribed rules. The welfare of his state, Frederick William believed, demanded exemplary punishment. In the instructions for the General Directory he stated: "Those who do not obey these instructions in every respect will be punished in an exemplary manner such as has hitherto not been seen in Germany." [36] Negligence of a minor nature was subject to monetary fines. Thus a collector of revenue whose accounts were not up to the minute had to pay a month's salary to the fund for invalid soldiers.[37] The same punishment was visited on clerks for misaddressing letters.[38] Even more severe was the punishment of higher officials. Regarding the members of the General Directory the king decreed: "Whoever is an hour late and has no written permission from the king must pay a hundred ducats. Whoever is absent without permission of the king and is not ill must spend six months in the fortress of Spandau on bread and water. His salary for that period is to be paid into the fund for invalids." [39] Repeated absence was to be punished with dismissal *cum infamia*, "for," the king added, "we pay our officials to work." Other negligences were to be punished with imprisonment at hard labor in the fortresses of Spandau, Wesel, Cüstrin, or Fried-

[34] *AB, Beh.*, III, 687.
[35] *Ibid.*
[36] *AB, Beh.*, III, 574.
[37] *Ibid.*, IV (Part 2), 154.
[38] *Ibid.*, V (Part 2), 656.
[39] *Ibid.*, III, 574.

richsburg. The imposition of this punishment, it appears, was not infrequent.[40] One official, for example, was imprisoned in the fortress of Friedrichsburg for telling the king that he would rather resign his office than be transferred to the province of Lithuania.[41] As early as April 23, 1713, the Saxon representative in Berlin wrote: "The good days are over; now there is talk of imprisonment at hard labor if it is believed—and it is frequently believed—that this or that one is not doing his duty." [42]

Officials guilty of embezzlement or any financial irregularities drew down the fiercest anger of the king and were punished in summary fashion. "Whosoever steals ten reichstaler," the king decreed, "is to be hanged in chains on an iron gallows and a collar of tin ducats is to be placed about his neck." [43] This sentence was carried out in a number of cases. In 1720 the ministry reported to the king that a deficit of three thousand taler had been found in the accounts of Commissary Berger in Memel, but in extenuation of the crime stated that Berger had not been able to support his family on his monthly salary of twelve taler and that he had offered his house as security for the repayment of the deficit. Upon receiving the report Frederick William wrote in the margin: "I forgive him the debt, but he is to be hanged." [44] Even more sad was the fate of Adam Friedrich Hesse, tax commissioner in the province of Prussia, who was sentenced by a criminal court to four years in prison for being unable to explain a deficit of four thousand taler in his accounts. When the sentence was submitted to the king for his confirmation, he wrote in the margin: "Hesse has stolen four thousand taler from me; hence he must hang." The sentence

---

[40] See Friedländer, *Berliner geschriebene Zeitungen*, p. 308; Stenzel, *Geschichte des preussischen Staats*, III, 303.

[41] *AB, Beh.*, II, 129.   [42] *Ibid.*, I, 322.

[43] *Ibid.*, V (Part 1), 454.   [44] Förster, *Urkundenbuch*, I, 51.

was accordingly executed in Berlin, but later it was discovered that certain items had been wrongly charged to the accounts and that there was no deficiency whatever.[45] When a deficit of 1,215 taler was found in the accounts of the tax collector Ungar upon his death, the ministry reported that the official had left just enough property to cover the deficit, but that the confiscation of the property would leave the widow penniless. It suggested that in view of the fact that the official had served the government for thirteen years the widow be permitted to keep two hundred taler. After reading the report the king wrote upon it: "They must not remit a pfennig. Everything that he left in goods, chattels, and houses is to be taken." [46]

An even more striking case of the severity of the punishment which the king inflicted is that of Herr von Schlubhut, Councillor of War and Domains at Königsberg. The Criminal Court at Berlin, having found him guilty of purloining funds from the accounts of East Prussia, sentenced him to imprisonment for several years. But the king regarded the sentence as altogether too mild and refused to confirm it before he had personally interviewed the recreant. When they met, Frederick William flayed Schlubhut soundly for betraying his trust; he even went so far as to threaten the nobleman with the gallows. Schlubhut, instead of admitting his guilt and asking the royal pardon, haughtily remarked that he intended to reimburse the treasury and that in Prussia it was not customary to hang noblemen. This proud and unrepentant stand so exasperated the king that he arbitrarily condemned Schlubhut to die by the hands of the common hangman. The sentence naturally aroused a storm of protest. Many powerful families sought to dissuade the king

[45] *AB, Beh.*, V (Part 1), 452–456; V (Part 2), 657–658; Förster, *Friedrich Wilhelm I*, II, 269–270.
[46] Förster, *Urkundenbuch*, I, 52.

from carrying out the sentence. On the day before the execution the court preacher delivered a sermon on the text, "Be merciful and ye shall obtain mercy," which brought tears to the royal eyes, but Frederick William adhered inflexibly to what he regarded as his duty. "I believe," he said, "it will have a good effect in deterring others." So that the lesson might prove more impressive all the members of the Chamber of War and Domains were compelled to witness the execution.[47]

Though the requirements were high, the remuneration was so low as to make the expression *travailler pour le roi de Prusse* (to work for the king of Prussia) almost synonymous with poor stipend. Some of the higher officials, it is true, could live well, but the majority of the civil officials were paid so poorly that they found it difficult, and at times impossible, to subsist on their salaries. Only very rarely did the king grant an official a raise; when he did, it was a special mark of distinction.[48] He would often ignore requests for salary increases. If he did answer them he would either advise the petitioners to resign if they were dissatisfied, or he would write upon the petition statements like the following: "The times are growing worse from day to day, and the country or my treasuries are to be burdened with an increase of salaries. That wont do!"[49] To one official who complained that his salary was insufficient to meet the ordinary living expenses the king retorted: "You must follow my maxims and limit your expenses to your income."[50] Officials, he declared, must serve rather for the honor of participating in the government than for the salaries they receive. But if the salaries the Prussian monarch paid his officials were small,

[47] *AB, Beh.,* V (Part 1), 917; Fassmann, *Leben und Thaten Friedrich Wilhelms I,* p. 422 *et sqq.*

[48] *Ibid.,* IV (Part 1), 213-214.

[49] *Ibid.,* IV (Part 1), 213-214.   [50] *Ibid.,* V (Part 1), 600.

he did see to it that they were paid promptly, which had not always been done in the reign of his predecessor.[51] Frederick William knew that certain payment of the salaries, even though they were small, was a means of sustaining honesty and zeal among his officials. He also impressed upon his son that he should pay the salaries of his officials promptly, "so that they need not wait." [52]

What prospects for old age had these hard-working officials whose meager salaries hardly permitted them to live—much less to put something aside? For many the prospects were not rosy. The granting of a pension by Frederick William was a rare exception. In this respect both the Great Elector and Frederick I had been much more liberal. Not only did Frederick William grant fewer pensions than his predecessors had; he even withdrew pensions from many who had been pensioned by his father.[53] Nevertheless, the prospects of a penniless old age were not so certain as they may appear. Many of the officials who were in fair health retained their offices and their salaries to the end. As they grew older the burden of their work was eased, younger men taking part of it upon their shoulders. Infinitely worse were the prospects for widows and orphans. Whether or not they received a small pension depended largely upon the mood of the king at the time he received the request. When in 1725 the widow of a royal collector of rents asked for a pension of eighty taler a year to help her support her four children and the one that was about to be born, Frederick William wrote on the petition: "This is not Spain, where everyone gets a pension. She is still very young. She must work and earn her bread in an honorable manner." [54]

[51] *Ibid.*, I, 155 *et sqq.*
[52] *Ibid.*, III, 456.
[53] See, for example, *AB, Beh.*, I, 578.
[54] Cited in Bornhak, *Geschichte der preussischen Universitätsverwaltung*, p. 118.

He even refused the plea of a widow who asked that her husband's salary be continued during the so-called three months of grace (*Gnadenvierteljahr*), although the General Directory proposed that it be paid. "When an officer is killed," Frederick William wrote, "his heirs do not receive a month of grace, but they do receive the salary for the month in which he was killed. Hence it should be the same for the civil servants." [55] There are even cases on record in which the king refused to pay to the heirs money which the state owed the deceased. He would write upon the application: "He's dead" and declare the matter closed.[56]

In summary, Frederick William coördinated the various branches of the civil administration into one supreme board, the General Directory. This board supervised and controlled, with but few exceptions, the comprehensive activities of the Prussian state. All the local authorities, including the provincial chambers, the rural and local commissaries, and the municipal magistrates, were responsible to it. But even the General Directory had no independent competence. So all-embracing was the royal autocracy that the decisions of this "supreme board" were invalid without the king's approval. The higher officials of this centralized bureaucracy were chosen from both the nobility and the middle class. "In a profounder sense than was true of the army, the Prussian bureaucracy served as a loadstone which attracted and absorbed into the service of the monarchy the most industrious and intelligent section of the population, thus binding their interests closely to those of the state." [57] By means of a severe discipline Frederick William succeeded in raising his officials to a standard of industry and honesty unrivaled in his day.

[55] *Ibid.*, II, 1.   [56] See, for example, *AB, Beh.*, IV (Part 1), 706.
[57] Dorn, "The Prussian Bureaucracy in the Eighteenth Century," *Political Science Quarterly*, XLVI (1931), 406.

The military spirit which under Frederick William permeated the whole of Prussia [Isaacsohn writes] [58] was particularly strong among the officials and gave the entire state the military character it has ever since retained. . . . Ministers of state, like generals and colonels, obeyed unquestioningly and carried out orders with military precision and punctuality. . . . Every minister, even though he might be easygoing and softhearted, was compelled in his own interest to maintain in his department the same rigid spirit of order, punctuality and speed which the king enforced on his own ministers, and from the minister's room the spirit of order and efficiency spread throughout all the departments and throughout all ranks down to the humblest officials. . . . Never before had it been impressed upon the officials so urgently and so unceasingly that they were personally responsible, and never before had personal responsibility been so sternly enforced.

Frederick William's achievement becomes striking in the light of a comparison of his officials with those of the preceding reign. The Great Elector had appointed many able officials, but after the accession of Frederick I "most of the honorable persons were forced out of the higher offices." [59] The holding of a high civil office became, by and large, a means of enriching oneself by graft of various kinds. When Frederick William took the reins of government in hand he kept most of the old officials, but established a new discipline. Shortly after the opening of his reign he said that faithful civil servants were "so rare that one must seek them with a light during the day." [60] There are, however, no such recorded statements for the latter part of his reign. Though he did not achieve his ideal, his desire for able, diligent, and faithful officials was in the main fulfilled. His officials complained and grumbled under the yoke of the stern military

[58] *Geschichte des preussischen Beamtenthums*, III, 201 et sqq.
[59] Schmoller, "Der preussische Beamtenstand unter Friedrich Wilhelm I," *Preussische Jahrbücher*, XXVI (1870), 150.
[60] *AB, Beh.*, II, 121.

discipline, giving vent to their feelings in statements such as: "He is worse than the tsar and Charles XII"; but, and this was of primary importance to Frederick William, they did produce the revenues necessary to support his standing army. It was no small achievement, for the army was that of a first-rate power, while the resources from which the officials gathered the revenues were those of a third-rate state. Moreover, they collected enough so that the king, after paying the expenses of his army, was able to accumulate a large fund for war purposes. There were many complaints from the taxpayers about high taxes. Actually, however, the taxes were no higher than those of Austria, and they were less than those of France.[61]

[61] Schmoller, "Historische Betrachtungen über Staatenbildung und Finanzentwicklung," *Jahrbuch für Gesetzgebung und Verwaltung,* XXXIII (1909), 1–64.

CHAPTER EIGHT

Frederick William's Attempts at Judicial Reform

BY THE establishment of the General Directory, Frederick William had, as already stated, centralized most phases of the internal administration. One of the exceptions was the administration of justice. The process of unification and centralization in this branch of the administration lagged because it was of secondary interest to a government intent above all on obtaining sufficient funds to build and support a large army. Hence the provincial, feudal, and municipal authorities were permitted to exercise their judicial functions longer than those functions more immediately related to financial and military affairs. At the accession of Frederick William justice was still largely organized on a local or at best on a provincial basis. Not only were the officials who administered the law local or provincial officials; the law itself and also the mode of judicial procedure differed in the various provinces. There was, in fact, considerable legal confusion within the provinces themselves. Furthermore, there was no high court of appeal for all the provinces, except the king in his *ex officio* capacity. Whereas the *Kammergericht* at Berlin was the highest court of appeal for Brandenburg,

East Prussia had its own special court of appeal in Königsberg. The rest of the provinces, excepting Ravensburg, were under the jurisdiction of the High Court of Appeal (*Oberappellationsgericht*) in Berlin. Even then the jurisdiction of these courts was limited to civil cases. The administration of criminal justice was entirely separate, the highest court of appeal in criminal cases, next to the king himself, being the Privy Council. In addition there was also a third division of the administration of justice for the adjudication of ecclesiastical questions. Thus the administration of justice was anything but unified; nor was it centralized except in the person of the king.

In the courts of civil justice the conditions were deplorable indeed when Frederick William succeeded his father to the throne in 1713. The confusion of the laws, the incompetence and corruption of the judges, and the protraction of the legal processes made it difficult, if not impossible, to obtain justice in the higher as well as in the lower courts. The salaries of the judges were on the whole so low that many were forced to supplement them from other sources. To what extent this was possible can be seen from the fact that of the twenty to twenty-two councillors in the *Kammergericht* only six shared in the fees; nevertheless applicants were willing to pay large sums to the recruiting fund in order to be appointed councillors in this court. In all courts the number of judges and especially of lawyers and procurators was excessive, and only a minority of them had a legal education. The commission appointed by Frederick William in the first year of his reign to survey the state of judicial affairs reported that "very few of the excessive number of lawyers and procurators have even an elementary knowledge of law." [1] Among them were many persons of

[1] *AB, Beh.,* I, 531.

the lowest moral type, who served as the channels through which the judges were bribed. Most of the lawyers and procurators, the report stated, are

good-for-nothing individuals, born to become a burden to society [who], not having learned an honorable and useful trade in their youth and having failed in everything else, are compelled by dire necessity to seek strife and contention or even to instigate them, to incite subjects against the government and against peace-loving individuals, and everywhere to stoke the fires of strife and contention.

This host of hungry advocates would draw out legal processes as long as possible in order to collect larger fees and would often demand their fees before the case was decided. Hence the widespread complaints that the legal fees were too high, the processes too protracted, and the possibility of obtaining justice too uncertain. These complaints were especially loud among the peasants, many of whom were unable to obtain justice after their holdings were taken from them by the nobility. Ordinary lawsuits often lasted twenty to thirty years, and no less than three to five decisions were necessary in cases involving as little as ten taler. The expenses of such lawsuits too often spelled economic ruin for the peasant seeking justice. Little wonder, then, that the officials reported that "the present state of justice is ruining the peasantry."

Although plans had been drawn up during the reign of Frederick I for a thorough-going reform, nothing had been done toward carrying them out. But Frederick William was more determined than his predecessor. To him the elimination of confusion and corruption from the administration of justice was a matter both of conscience and of political and economic policy. Besides regarding drastic judicial reform as his sacred duty, he also saw that an orderly, inexpensive, and speedy justice, particularly in civil matters, would be an invaluable adjunct to the development of commerce and industry. Shortly after his accession he wrote to Bartholdi, whom Frederick I had made minister of justice:

Among the most important affairs to which we turn our attention upon occupying the royal throne is this, that in all the provinces under our rule justice is administered speedily, impartially, with clean hands and without any prejudice or discrimination, to poor and rich, high and low. We hearby most graciously command you to take up this matter without the slightest delay and, with the aid of a number of honorable and capable members of the board of justice, to draw up regulations which will eliminate existing disorders, abuses, and weaknesses from the administration of justice, shorten all trials as much as possible, and, if it can be done, settle each case within the period of a year; which will also introduce such changes as are necessary to make justice flourish in our provinces, so that everyone who is compelled to have recourse to the courts will obtain prompt justice.[2]

When Bartholdi took his time in drawing up the scheme for reform, Frederick William became impatient. At the end of a month he wrote to his minister: "One month has already passed, and there are only eleven more, at the end of which time the code of law for the entire country must be ready. . . . It is necessary for me to speak sharply, for the state of judicial affairs is so bad that it cries aloud to heaven, and if I do not remedy it, I shall draw the responsibility upon myself." [3] These words spurred Bartholdi and his assistants to draw up the regulations within a short time. Upon receiving them the king sent copies to all the higher civil courts in the Prussian state together with the royal command that they "must be observed and enforced completely and rigidly." So that everyone would be conversant

[2] *Ibid.*, I, 520–521.   [3] *Ibid.*, p. 522.

with them, the higher officials were instructed to give a copy
to every subordinate official; copies were also to be posted
where they could easily be seen, and "one copy was to lie
perpetually on the table of every court." These regulations
were still a far cry from the code which Frederick William
desired; in fact, in this respect the achievements of his reign
fell short of the goal he had set. The changes which the new
regulations introduced into the administration of justice only
prepared the way for the much-needed codification of the
laws in the Prussian state. The actual task of compiling such
a code was not taken up until after Frederick William's
death and was not completed until near the end of the century. Nevertheless, it is worthwhile to remember that the
minister who was to direct this task during a large part of
the succeeding reign was Samuel von Cocceji, whom
Frederick William appointed *Ministre Chef de Justice* in
1737.

The regulations which Bartholdi and his associates drew
up in 1713 purposed to eliminate the worst abuses from the
administration of civil justice.[4] They prescribed that lawsuits be concluded as soon as possible; that only as many
lawyers and procurators be permitted in each court as the
work of that court required; and that all classes receive equal
treatment in matters of justice. Furthermore, judges were
ordered under threat of dismissal and even of flogging and
imprisonment, to pronounce only honest verdicts. Gifts and
also promises of gifts to judges were strictly forbidden.
Finally, the regulations insisted on the fitness and honesty of
all officials of justice. Only such judges were to be appointed,
the regulations stated, as have a proper knowledge of the law
and have demonstrated their fitness for the office. Those

[4] There is a condensation of the regulations in *AB, Beh.*, I, 525–
533. The full text is to be found in *Corp. const.*, II (Part 1), 517–550.

aspiring to be lawyers were ordered to present testimonials regarding their studies, their experience, and their character. Later, special courses of training in Prussian universities were required of all who desired to become officials of justice.[5]

Frederick William's efforts at reform did raise the educational standard of the officials of justice, and they also reduced the excessive number of judges, lawyers, and procurators. In other respects, however, the results were meager. Bribery and corruption continued to be widespread, and lawsuits were still drawn out much as before. Frederick William himself stated in the instructions for his successor, which he wrote in 1722: "Regarding the administration of justice in my kingdom, I have tried everything to make it honest and speedy, but have failed to do so."[6] Time and again during the remainder of his reign he issued decrees which demanded prompt and impartial justice for all.[7] Nevertheless, in 1735 conditions in the courts were still so bad that the king was moved to write: "The administration of justice is worse here and in Poland than in any other place in the world."[8] Finally, in 1737, feeling that he would not live much longer, Frederick William made a more determined effort to get at the root of the evils with which the administration of civil justice was beset. He appointed a commission, with Samuel von Cocceji at its head as *Ministre Chef de Justice*, to make a careful survey of conditions and to suggest remedies for their improvement. On the basis of the reports the king issued a whole series of edicts during the last years of his reign. Some of the edicts, particularly

[5] *Corp. const.*, II (Part 1), 735–738.   [6] *AB, Beh.*, III, 457.
[7] *AB, Beh.*, II, 226, 537, 539–540, 579; IV (Part 1), 18, 713; IV (Part 2), 92, 353; V (Part 1), 208–212; V (Part 2), 63–65; *Corp. const.*, II (Part 1), 597–603, 645–656, 717–720, 737–740, 821–838.
[8] *AB, Beh.*, V (Part 1), 819.

those regarding the training of the officials, did effect some improvement; but others were ineffectual. At least one actually put obstacles in the way of reform—the decree of 1738 which curtailed the fees of the officials of justice still further.[9]

One of the principal reasons for Frederick William's failure to effect the desired reforms was his unwillingness to pay his officials of justice adequate salaries. His statement with regard to his officials that "we pay them to work" did not apply to the officials of justice. Salaries were still no higher than they had been in the reign of the Great Elector, although both the cost of living and the amount of work each official was expected to do had increased considerably since that time. Frederick William, seeking to save every possible pfennig of the national revenue for the army, was determined that the expenses for judicial affairs must not exceed the sum his grandfather had spent for the same purpose. In a number of instances he even reduced salaries or abolished them entirely. "In each court," a German historian writes, "there were very few salaried positions, and they were mostly held by older officials who were no longer able to do much work. One can therefore say that most of the work in the courts was at that time done by unsalaried officials." [10] Hence most of the officials had to depend for a living upon whatever fees or incidental sums they could collect in one way or another. Such a state of affairs did not tend toward raising the standards of honesty and of efficiency. On the contrary, it caused the officials to draw out the lawsuits as a means of collecting larger fees. Even more disastrous to the moral standard was the reduction of the fees at

[9] *Corp. const. continuatio*, I, 161–172, 199–210.
[10] Hintze, in Introduction, *AB, Beh.*, VI (Part 1), 208.

various times during Frederick William's reign, which purposed to make lawsuits less expensive to the clients.[11] According to Hintze, "no honest man could any longer earn his bread" after the general reduction of fees in 1738.[12]

In reducing both the salaries and the fees Frederick William was motivated in part by his antipathy to the officials of justice. At the time of his accession he already had a low opinion of them, regarding them as "the most good-for-nothing people in the world." When in the course of his reign it became evident that his efforts to reform the administration of civil justice were not achieving the desired results, his feelings toward them turned into downright hatred. On one occasion, when he was asked in which branch of the administration a certain applicant was to be placed, he answered: "Find out whether he has sense and a good head. If he has put him into the chamber of the Electoral Mark and let him work hard; if he is a stupid devil make him a councillor of justice in Cleves—for that he is good enough." [13] Lawyers and procurators he regarded as leeches and parasites on the body of society.[14] So that "one can recognize the scoundrels," as the king put it, he ordered them to wear a distinctive garb. Lawyers were to dress in black with a cloak that reached to the knees and a scarf designed by the king himself; while procurators were to wear a black coat with facings on the lapels.[15] A lawyer or procurator who appeared on the street in any other garb was to be impressed into the army at once. When Cocceji later proposed that lawyers who had demonstrated their honesty be per-

[11] *Corp. const.*, IV (Part 2), 58–59, 370, 458–459.
[12] *AB, Beh.*, VI (Part 1), 211.
[13] *Ibid.*, IV (Part 1), 392–393.
[14] See *Ibid.*, IV (Part 2), 93; VI (Part 1), 210.
[15] *Ibid.*, I, 382; V (Part 2), 397.

mitted to dispense with this garb, the king curtly rejected the proposal. The distinctive garb remained and therewith the low regard of the public for the wearers.

More successful were Frederick William's efforts to reform criminal justice. When he became king, criminal justice was still exercised largely by more-or-less independent feudal and municipal courts. In other words, those who conducted the investigations, presided over the trials, pronounced the verdicts, and inflicted the punishments were not royal officials. Frequently they were lawyers to whom these functions had been delegated by feudal lords or municipalities. In the Hohenzollern provinces, as well as in the other states of Germany, criminal justice was still regulated in the main by the statutes adopted at the Diet of Regensburg in 1532 and collectively called the "Carolina." The complex and protracted modes of criminal procedure prescribed by the Carolina had during the course of the seventeenth century become even more complex and protracted because of the addition of various local customs and laws of criminal procedure. The result was that the criminal investigations and trials became so lengthy that the fines from which the feudal and municipal authorities had formerly reaped a financial harvest no longer sufficed to meet the expenses of the local courts. Hence many justices would agree to a smaller fine if the accused confessed voluntarily, thereby saving the courts the expense of investigations and trials. The poor were often beaten until they confessed, after which they were beaten again as punishment and then turned loose. This was so common that it gave rise to the saying: "The cudgel is not only the *corpus juris* but also the Carolina." Thus the two crying needs of criminal justice in the Prussian state were a common penal code and a set of regulations to expedite criminal procedure. "It is plain," a German historian writes, "that the lack of a penal code and a common mode of criminal procedure, since the Carolina was becoming more and more useless, everywhere made for uncertainty in the execution of criminal justice; everywhere chance and the will, or even the mood, of the officials, not the law, was the deciding factor." [16]

Frederick William's efforts to give his provinces a common penal code were not, as already stated, crowned with success; but he did manage to establish a common mode of criminal procedure in the Prussian state. The first step in this direction was the *Criminal-Ordnung* (rules of criminal procedure) published in 1717 to regulate the administration of criminal justice in Brandenburg.[17] Not only did these regulations simplify greatly the mode of criminal procedure prescribed in the Carolina; they also put all courts having criminal jurisdiction under the supervision of the royal officials. Criminal investigations and inquisitions were thenceforth to be conducted by officials under the supervision of the councillors of criminal justice (*Criminalräte*) in the provincial chambers. The records of all criminal investigations and trials were ordered sent to them, and usually they pronounced the verdict. Thus the feudal and municipal courts of Brandenburg lost most of the authority they still exercised in matters of criminal jurisdiction. In 1721 the *Criminal-Ordnung* was made effective also in Pomerania, Magdeburg, and with some slight modifications in Cleves and Mark. In the same year Cocceji drew up a similar set of regulations for East Prussia, thereby making the mode of criminal procedure uniform in all the larger provinces. All the officials of justice in these provinces had to promise on oath strictly to observe all the provisions of the *Criminal-*

[16] Holtze, *Strafrechtspflege unter König Friedrich Wilhelm I*, p. 3.
[17] *Corp. const.*, II (Part 3), 62–110.

Ordnung; the task of seeing that they were observed was intrusted to the Fiscalate.

Although the administration of criminal justice was still organized on a provincial basis, it was centralized in the person of the king. He was at once the highest court of appeal and the supreme judge. As such he rarely interfered in matters of civil justice; in fact, toward the end of his reign he issued a cabinet order which directed that all inquiries in matters of civil justice be sent to the minister of justice. "His Majesty," the order stated, "desires to be free of such inquiries because the burdensome tasks of government leave him no time for such matters." [18] On the other hand, he decreed that the verdicts in all major criminal cases be sent to him for confirmation.[19] These included all cases in which punishment by death or by expulsion from the country was imposed; also all cases of treason, witchcraft, and dueling; and, finally, all cases in which the king's officials were defendants. Often when he believed that the ends of justice were not being served he would overrule the sentences of the courts. Usually the punishment was made more severe; only rarely did he mitigate it. This arbitrary conduct on the part of the king was motivated by a desire to establish a common standard of justice in his provinces. He endeavored to make certain that criminals did not escape punishment either through bribery or their social influence and also that no one was punished unjustly. His motto, as he stated it himself, was: "Fiat justitia et pereat mundus! (Let justice be done, even if the earth perish)." [20] Laudable in some respects, this zeal for justice became so excessive that on some occasions it defeated its own ends. One such case, that of

[18] *AB, Beh.,* V (Part 1), 37.
[19] *Corp. const.,* II (Part 3), 57–58, 109–112, 121–122; *AB, Beh.,* III, 525–526; IV (Part 1), 613–614.
[20] Preuss, *Friedrich der Grosse,* I, 43.

the Tax Commissioner Hesse, who after being hanged by order of the king was found to be innocent, has already been mentioned. At another time a Jew who was accused of theft steadfastly declared his innocence even under torture. Upon receiving a report of the case Frederick William declared he would take the matter on his own conscience, and he ordered the man to be hanged.[21] In his eagerness to make justice speedy and certain Frederick William frequently failed to accord to the accused the right of a trial before a criminal court. Upon receiving reports of crimes he would sometimes pass judgment on the accused without awaiting the verdict of the courts. He would decide a case by simply writing a few words in the margin of the report; not infrequently the words would be: "Is to be hanged."

In the Hohenzollern provinces, as in most European countries, the punishments for criminal offenses were still very severe. The humanitarian tendencies which later in the eighteenth century brought about a more humane treatment of criminals were not yet visible in the criminal justice of Frederick William's reign. Criminals were still branded, pinched with glowing tongs, broken on the wheel, and drawn and quartered. Those guilty of treason, for instance, were flogged, pinched with glowing tongs, beheaded and quartered, after which the remains were exposed on the place of execution. Even for lesser crimes the punishments were very severe. For example, a person found guilty of carrying a weapon of any kind while attempting unlawful entry was to be broken on the wheel. The punishment (1720) for breaking the glass in a street lantern was a severe scourging, a fine of two hundred taler and banishment from the country for ten years; and in 1732 branding was added to the list of punishments. A business man found guilty of

[21] Fassmann, *Leben und Thaten Friedrich Wilhelms I*, p. 1074.

borrowing money after he realized that he was insolvent
was to be hanged (1723). The lending of money to minors
was punishable with confiscation of property and imprisonment for life (1730).[22] More than this, the use of torture
was still permitted as a means of forcing a confession from
an accused person. Although vigorous protests against this
barbarous practice had been launched by Christian Thomasius and other disciples of the German Enlightenment, the
Prussian government continued the use of torture, endeavoring to justify itself by claiming that torture was used only
when the evidence strongly indicated the guilt of the accused. Even if the accused maintained his innocence under
torture, he was not freed. The court would then proceed
against him on the basis of the evidence it had previously
collected. Frederick William, it is true, did try to curb the
use of torture,[23] but he took no steps to abolish it, fearing
that if he did, crime would run rampant in his territories.
It remained for Frederick the Great, shortly after his accession to the throne, to abolish the use of torture in all
cases except treason and murder.[24]

Frederick William even made the punishment of certain
crimes more severe in an effort to reduce their number. An
edict of 1735, for example, stated that "any thief who
breaks open a box, door, or cupboard to steal something, be
it of great value or small, whether the goods are restored or
not, is to be hanged in front of the house in which the
theft was committed. If a thief without forcible entry steals

[22] *Corp. const.*, II (Part 3), 179–184; Roscher, *Geschichte der
National-Oekonomik*, p. 362.

[23] See, for example, *AB, Beh.*, V (Part 2), 22, 772.

[24] See Koser, "Die Abschaffung der Tortur durch Friedrich den
Grossen," *Forschungen zur brandenburgischen und preussischen
Geschichte*, VI (1893), 575–581. Even Frederick the Great did not
publish his cabinet order because he feared that the abolition of torture might result in a crime wave.

anything of a value greater than 50 reichstaler, he is to be hanged in the same manner." [25] There are only two recorded instances in which this sentence was carried out in Berlin. Hanging a thief before the house in which the theft was committed appears to have been discontinued because such a house thereafter was called a *Galgenhaus* (gallows house) and it was considered a disgrace to live in it.[26] Again, to reduce the number of child murders Frederick William decreed that women guilty of infanticide were to be drowned in a leather sack which they were compelled to make with their own hands.[27] When he was later informed that certain judges had taken the liberty of commuting the sentence for infanticide to decapitation, he upbraided them and forbade any such leniency in the future.[28]

The numerous cases of infanticide [a German historian writes] were in large measure the result of the military conditions of the time. In order to get the soldiers to settle down and thereby to keep them from deserting, they were encouraged to enter into all kinds of alliances, with servant girls and others, in which the strict form of marriage played only a modest role. If the military friend expressed his displeasure over the expected arrival of a child or even threatened to leave, it was excusable if the mother did away with the child at birth or soon thereafter. If the deed was discovered the mother was "sacked" and the father went in search of another sweetheart. In like manner a woman who aided a deserter by lending him her clothes was hanged, while the deserter himself usually suffered no more severe punishment than being compelled to run the gauntlet. These were the serious consequences of a system of recruiting which took a terrible toll in blood from the women of the lower classes.[29]

---

[25] *Corp. const.*, II (Part 3), 179–184.
[26] See Holtze, *Geschichte der Stadt Berlin*, p. 70.
[27] *Corp. const.*, II (Part 3), 121–124.   [28] *Ibid.*, pp. 131–134.
[29] Holtze, *Strafrechtspflege unter König Friedrich Wilhelm I*, pp. 82–83.

The severe punishments prescribed by the Prussian laws were not merely prescribed, they were actually carried out, particularly if the perpetrators of the crimes were poor. Thus, for example, the Castellan Runck, after having been found guilty of theft, was pinched with glowing tongs and then broken on the wheel. On March 22, 1736, according to a contemporary record, six thieves were taken to the gallows. Of these, three were first hanged and then taken down and broken on the wheel. Two others were decapitated, and their bodies were then tied to the wheel, while the sixth, who had confessed immediately, thereby facilitating the conviction of the others, was sentenced to imprisonment for life.[30] Women as well as men were broken on the wheel, as is illustrated by the execution of a tailor and his wife on January 3, 1736.[31]

A wealthy person could atone for a crime by making a large donation to the recruiting fund, and a tall young man could escape punishment by declaring his willingness to shoulder a musket; but this was possible only if no blood had been shed. In cases of bloodshed the sentence was carried out even on grenadiers who had cost the king large sums, for he believed it to be his God-given duty to enforce literally the words of Genesis (9:6): "Whosoever sheddeth man's blood by man shall his blood be shed." In the instructions for his successor he stated emphatically: "When one sheds blood, his blood must be shed, so that no blood remains on the land to draw down divine vengeance upon it." [32] Accordingly, even a high officer in the army who was guilty of killing a person in a duel could expect no mercy. When, for example, Count Seckendorf, the king's bosom friend, interceded in behalf of a certain Major von

[30] Holtze, ed., "Chronistische Aufzeichnungen eines Berliners," in *Schriften des Vereins für die Geschichte Berlins*, XXXVI (1899), 68.
[31] *Ibid.*   [32] *AB, Beh.*, III, 457.

Damitz who had killed a fellow officer in a duel, the king answered: "It would give me great pleasure to grant your request, if human blood had not been shed, for which I neither can nor will pardon anyone in the world." [33] When another officer fled the country after killing a fellow officer in a duel, Frederick William had his property confiscated and his portrait suspended from the gallows. The officer entered the service of Augustus of Saxony and soon rose to an important position. On one of Frederick William's visits to Saxony the fugitive appeared before him to ask his forgiveness. The Prussian king, however, would not forgive the man who had shed blood, even though Augustus urged him to forgive and forget. He offered to restore the officer's property, but stated firmly that if the latter ever returned to Prussian territory he would be compelled to hang him.[34]

But in at least one respect the government of Frederick William gave evidence of a humanitarian tendency, that is, in the punishment of those accused of witchcraft. During the sixteenth and the seventeenth centuries the belief in witchcraft had flared up anew in most of the countries of Europe, resulting in a frenzy of witch-finding and witch-burning. Both Protestants and Catholics showed an equal zeal in hunting down those who were supposed to be witches. Those found guilty of practicing witchcraft were burned at the stake, in justification of which severity the witch-hunters quoted the words from Exodus (22:18) "Thou shalt not suffer a witch to live." Since those accused of witchcraft were most often tortured until they stated that they were guilty, the accusation was almost tantamount to a death sentence. Under torture the victims were forced to confess, for example, that they had spread

[33] Förster, *Urkundenbuch*, III, 239.
[34] Beneckendorf, *Karakterzüge aus dem Leben König Friedrich Wilhelms I*, I, 61.

epidemics or cattle pests; caused barrenness in man, woman, or beast; raised hail, tempests, lightning, or thunder; traveled through the air on broomsticks to the Blocksberg; or entered into various other pacts with Satan, signing them in their own blood. A frequent accusation leveled against a woman suspected of witchcraft was that she had entered into a marriage pact with Satan. Some were even accused of having borne children to him. By the end of the seventeenth century the witch mania had spent some of its fury. The last of the great burnings, it appears, were those in Salzburg where 97 persons were burned at the stake in 1686. But individual cases of witch trials and burnings were still numerous.

Prominent among those who sought to dispel the witch superstition during the early years of the eighteenth century was Christian Thomasius, the father of German journalism and professor of law at the University of Halle. Thomasius did not deny the existence of witches, lest the witch-hunters quote the Bible in contradiction, but he did cast ridicule upon the idea that a hoofed, horned, and tailed devil whisked poor wretches through the air to the Blocksberg, where he was supposed to make the pacts upon which the accusations of witchcraft rested. Though his statements were roundly denounced by many, he also had his supporters. Among those whose ideas were influenced by the statements of Thomasius was Frederick William. The Prussian monarch did not immediately abolish witchcraft trials, but, soon after his accession, he did decree that all sentences in cases of witchcraft be sent to him for confirmation. That he did not intend to confirm a death sentence is indicated by the fact that he ordered to be removed all stakes at which witches had been burned. Only in two instances, it appears, were witch trials instituted during his reign. The first involved the wife of a shoemaker at Nauen who was accused of having sold butter which changed into cow dung over night. When Frederick William was informed of the trial, he immediately ordered that the charges be dropped. In 1728 the board which had charge of criminal affairs in Berlin reported to the king that a young woman had confessed entering into a marriage compact with the devil and living with him as his wife. The report stated that the woman deserved death by fire, but, since it was possible that she was insane, suggested confinement in the workhouse at Spandau for life. This sentence was confirmed by the king.[35]

In summing up Frederick William's achievements the German legal historian Stölzel writes:

All the plans which Frederick William's great son followed in his reforms of justice had their roots in the efforts and aims of the father; hardly a single new idea appeared under Frederick II. What Frederick William had started was continued without a break during the reign of his successor, naturally in a spirit different from that of the first decades of the century. The very official (Samuel von Cocceji), his *Ministre Chef de Justice*, whom Frederick William had trained, even though he often misunderstood him, carried to completion as Frederick II's Lord High Chancellor that which Frederick William had set as a goal for himself.[36]

---

[35] See Holtze, *Strafrechtspflege*, p. 21.

[36] *Brandenburg-Preussens Rechtsverwaltung und Rechtsverfassung*, II, 138.

CHAPTER NINE

Education and Toleration

BUSY AS he was with his many other tasks and reforming activities, Frederick William also found time to give some attention to the spread of popular education. In September, 1717, he published the following edict:

We have noticed with displeasure, and inspectors and clergymen have also complained to us at various times, that parents, particularly in the country, are very negligent about sending their children to school, allowing them to grow up grossly ignorant of reading, writing, and arithmetic, as well as of the knowledge of those things that are most necessary for their welfare and eternal salvation.

In order to abolish this most pernicious evil we have resolved to publish this edict and in it most graciously and earnestly to enjoin that parents living in localities where there are schools should henceforth be compelled, under penalty of two *Dreier* (one *Dreier*, two pence) weekly for each child, to send their children to school daily in the winter; in the summer, when they are needed for work in the fields, they are to be sent at least once or twice each week, so that they will not forget entirely what they learned in the winter.[1]

Because of this edict Frederick William has been styled "the father of the German elementary school" and "the

[1] *Corp. const.*, I (Part 1), 527–530.

originator of the idea of compulsory education." Such statements, however, are not founded on historical facts. Compulsory education was repeatedly advocated by both Catholic and Protestant reformers as far back as the sixteenth century. Luther, for example, said: "If the government can compel those who are fitted for it to carry spears and guns, to scale walls, and to do other things in preparation for war, how much more can and must it compel its subjects to keep their children in school." [2] Compulsory attendance at school had even been decreed in at least one German state long before Frederick William isued his edict. A decree promulgated in Gotha in 1642 reads: "All children, both boys and girls, living in villages as well as in cities must as soon as they have reached the age of five be sent to school both in summer and in winter." [3] Moreover, the edict of Frederick William did not decree compulsory education for all the children in the Prussian state. As the edict plainly states, it applied only to those children living in places where "there are schools." Even then the edict was not enforced, for Frederick William found it necessary to renew the same in 1736. "Our salutary edict," he stated, "has not been carried out, and consequently the young are grossly ignorant of reading, writing, and arithmetic, as well as of those things that are necessary for their souls and salvation." [4]

Another point, often overlooked, is that Frederick William was interested in religious rather than in secular education. His real concern was the religious welfare of his subjects, secular education being merely ancillary to this purpose. Like the reformers of the sixteenth century and the Pietists of his time, he regarded the school as the annex of

[2] Lehmann, *Historische Aufsätze und Reden*, p. 111.
[3] Schmid, *Geschichte der Erziehung*, IV (Part 1), 37.
[4] *Corp. const.*, I (Part 2), 267–268.

the Church. Thus he wrote in the instructions for his successor: "Build churches and schools wherever they are lacking, so that God's Holy Word may be disseminated more and more under your rule." [5] Those desiring to teach in the Prussian schools, he decreed, must be proficient in reading, writing, and arithmetic, but above all must demonstrate their ability to teach the children "the basic principles of Christianity." The idea was expressed even more forcibly on another occasion, when he said: "What good is there in cultivating and improving my country, if I make no Christians." [6] Accordingly, he added this order to the decree of 1717: "We desire and earnestly command that henceforth all clergymen, especially those in the country districts, instruct their congregations in the elementary truths of religion each Sunday afternoon without fail." Besides the eternal salvation of his subjects, Frederick William had another reason for insisting upon religious instruction for everyone. By making them God-fearing he would create in his subjects the proper obedience and submission to the government "established by God." In other words, religious instruction was useful in inculcating in the Prussian people an absolute obedience to Hohenzollern authority. Thus both the Church and the school were made part of the bureaucratic apparatus with which the Prussian monarch ruled his territories.

Frederick William, it is true, did more to promote elementary education than any previous Hohenzollern or than any contemporary sovereign. Even the large and wealthy states of that period did little or nothing for the education of the masses. But the Prussian ruler's achievements in this respect have been greatly exaggerated by Droysen,

[5] *AB, Beh.,* III, 457.
[6] Stolze, "Friedrich Wilhelm I und die Volksschule," *Historische Zeitschrift,* CVII (1911), 83.

Treitschke, and other Prussian historians. Beyond publishing the edict of 1717 he gave little actual aid to the spread of elementary education before 1732. During the last years of his reign he contributed materials for the building of schools, almost all of which were built in East Prussia. The total number of schools built during his reign was about 1,100, but most of them were of such flimsy construction that they were soon in a state of disrepair.[7] The underlying reasons for this activity in Prussia were: (1) the provinces of East Prussia were the most backward with regard to education; (2) a large part of the population of East Prussia was non-German and therefore needed to be Germanized, as the king saw it; (3) Frederick William had promised the Salzburgers churches and schools if they would come to East Prussia. In educational matters, as in other things, the king's thrift was evident. On the whole he saved every possible pfennig for the army. Much is made by Prussian historians of the fund of fifty thousand taler, called *mons pietatis* (bank of piety), which Frederick William established toward the end of his reign for purposes of elementary education. Such a sum, however, was very little for a ruler who had an annual income of almost seven million taler and who annually spent tens of thousands for tall recruits. The reason for his "generosity" in establishing the fund of fifty thousand taler was that he desired to make a "thank-offering" upon his recovery from a serious illness.

At the end of Frederick William's reign the standard of elementary education was still very low in the Hohenzollern provinces. Most of the village schools had neither proper school buildings nor trained teachers. A large number of the buildings were in such a state of dilapidation that

[7] See Schmoller, "Die Verwaltung Ostpreussens unter Friedrich Wilhelm I," *Historische Zeitschrift*, XXX (1871), 67.

classes had to be dismissed during severe weather. Nor did Frederick William make provisions for the training of teachers. Beyond the ability to read religious books, he thought that his subjects had little need for education. Moreover, the income from teaching in the villages was so small that few teachers could live on it. According to the decree of 1717 parents were to pay two *Dreier* tuition per child each week. Had the teachers received this sum promptly, they might have been able to live on it, at least during the school months. However, some peasants were unable and others were unwilling to pay the tuition. Hence most village teachers depended upon supplementary work. In most villages the teachers were really artisans, particularly blacksmiths, wheelwrights, linen weavers, carpenters, and, more often, tailors who could read and write. Such teachers would usually use their workshop as a schoolroom, or the school building would serve as both a workshop and a school. To these artisans Frederick William added another type of teacher, the old or invalid soldier. He decreed that among the applicants for teaching vacancies "the old soldier should be given preference over all others, whoever they may be." [8] In this way the old soldiers were in a measure provided for without any cost to the king.

Nowhere except in a few cities was there a systematic or standardized program of instruction. The central factor in elementary education was religion. Instruction consisted mainly of the laborious reading of Bible stories, the memorizing of the catechism and of Bible verses, and the singing of hymns. Because of the limited knowledge of most village teachers, writing and arithmetic were still regarded unusual achievements as late as 1754. The period of instruction was limited largely to the winter months, for as soon

[8] Cited in Lehmann, *Historische Aufsätze und Reden*, p. 127.

as the weather became warmer in the spring the village children were needed for work in the fields. Even then not all the children attended or had the opportunity to attend school during the winter months. According to the report of a government commission in 1732 only 10 percent of the children in East Prussia had any kind of instruction whatsoever.[9] In the other Prussian provinces the proportion of those attending school was much higher, and even in East Prussia there was considerable improvement before the end of Frederick William's reign. But in none of the provinces did school attendance become general. Many thousands of children continued to grow up without any schooling. In 1763 Councillor Süssmilch could still write: "There are many villages where there is hardly one who can write or read handwriting."[10] Of course this did not apply only to Prussia; it was true of many parts of Germany. In some states conditions were worse than in the Hohenzollern territories; in others they were better.

If Frederick William's reign shows considerable progress in the spread of elementary education, this was not true of higher education in general. During the early decades of the eighteenth century the Pietists did establish a number of teachers' seminaries in the Hohenzollern provinces, but for the universities the reign of Frederick William was on the whole a period of decline. The atmosphere created by the philistinism and militarism of the "Royal Drill Sergeant" was not conducive to the advancement of higher learning. As previously stated, Frederick William regarded as a waste of time any learning that could not be put to practical use. "Christianity, reading, writing, and arithmetic," he

[9] Reicke, *Die Schulreorganisation Friedrich Wilhelms I in den samländischen Hauptämtern Fischhausen und Schaaken*, p. 6.
[10] Cited in Lehmann, *Historische Aufsätze und Reden*, p. 130.

said, "is enough; everything else is tomfoolery." [11] During
the early part of his reign he had little use for the universities except insofar as they taught Protestant theology and
ethics. Thus he ordered that "all students be well-grounded
in Christianity," so that "they may arrive at a true piety." [12]
At Halle, the most important of the Prussian universities, a
narrow Pietistic spirit reigned supreme. It was the Pietist
members of the Halle faculty who denounced Wolff's ra-
tionalism, causing Frederick William to banish him from
the Hohenzollern territories. However, the Prussian autocrat changed his attitude near the end of his reign. Not only
did he invite Wolff to return; he also ordered all students
of theology to study the philosophy he had formerly regarded as so much "hot air." "They must," he wrote, "be
thoroughly grounded in philosophy and in a sound logic,
after the example of Professor Wolff." [13] As a means of
promoting the economic development of his territories he
further established during the later years of his reign chairs
for the teaching of cameralism, both at Halle and at Frankfurt. But it was not until the reign of Frederick the Great
that a freer spirit began to prevail in the Prussian universities.

With regard to religion Frederick William was more tolerant than most rulers of his age. His was a tolerance rooted
in the desire to build a strong army and to make his state
prosperous. Essentially his ideas on toleration were those of
his predecessors, but he was in some respects more tolerant
than they had been. In choosing officials the Great Elector
had given open preference to the adherents of the Re-

[11] Cited in Balk, *Die Friedrich-Wilhelms-Universität*, p. 30.
[12] *Corp. const.*, I (Part 2), 229 *et sqq.*
[13] Cited in Bornhak, *Geschichte der preussischen Universitätsverwaltung*, p. 158.

formed confession and had also advised his successor to appoint "such qualified and capable subjects of the Reformed religion as are at hand." [14] Frederick I still favored the Reformed rather than the Lutherans when both were equally capable. But Frederick William did not distinguish between the two groups in choosing his officials. He saw no essential difference between the Lutheran and the Reformed confessions. In the instructions for his successor he did declare himself a Calvinist, but he hastened to add that "a Lutheran who lives a godly life may be saved equally as well." [15] "The difference," he continued, "exists solely in the squabbles of the clergy; therefore hold the Reformed and the Lutherans in equal respect, treat both religions well, and do not distinguish between them." In fact, Frederick William cherished the hope of uniting the two evangelical groups. To this end he built a number of churches in which the adherents of both were to worship in common. When the Lutheran clergyman Rolof objected to the joint worship, Frederick William wrote to him: "I regard both religions as one and find no difference between them; hence I demand that my order be carried out." [16] Another time he wrote: "May God forgive all clergymen, since they will have to give account before the judgment seat of God for having stirred up strife and for having caused division in His work." [17]

The same desire which motivated his efforts to bring about a union of the Lutheran and the Reformed churches also caused him to oppose the smaller Protestant sects. It was his desire for religious unity in his state. He regarded the two major Protestant confessions as sufficient for the religious needs of all Protestants. Those who tried to form

[14] Testament in Ranke, *Sämmtliche Werke*, XXVI, 501 *et sqq.*
[15] *AB, Beh.*, III, 457.
[16] Förster, *Friedrich Wilhelm I*, II, 339.   [17] *Ibid.*

further religious groups were in his opinion guilty of causing division in his kingdom. Hence he tried to discourage the growth of special sects. It was only against the Mennonites, however, that he adopted severe measures; and then only because they were opposed to military service. In 1732 he issued an edict which ordered all Mennonites to leave East Prussia at once under the threat of imprisonment and hard labor. After expelling these thrifty and hardworking people, he requested the provincial chamber to populate the land they had vacated with "good Christians who do not abhor the profession of arms." [18]

In the same manner in which he ordered such affairs in the State as agriculture, industry, and commerce, Frederick William also regulated religious matters. Clergymen were ordered to mention in every sermon the duties of the subject toward the government, particularly the duty of paying taxes promptly. But the sermons were not to be too long. In 1714 he issued an edict which stated that "the sermons, excepting the singing and the prayers, are never to last longer than an hour, under punishment of two *taler*." [19] When this order was not strictly observed, he renewed it, adding that the church wardens would also be fined if they did not compel the preachers to observe the royal edict.[20] In general, despite Frederick William's religiosity he ruled the clergy with a firm hand. At no time did he permit them to interfere in political affairs. In his testament of 1722 he wrote:

My dear successor must give the consistories strict orders to keep a careful watch that the sermons in the pulpits of the land as well as those preached before the regiments contain no attacks

---

[18] See Baczko, *Geschichte Preussens*, VI, 427; Lehmann, *Preussen und die katholische Kirche*, I, 405.

[19] *Corp. const.*, I (Part 1), 513–514.   [20] *Ibid.*, pp. 527–528.

on the authority of the ruler. If a clergyman attacks the government either directly or indirectly, he is to be dismissed at once. My dear successor, this point is important.[21]

That a ruler who had such a high conception of his royal absolutism and was such an ardent Protestant should have but little sympathy for the Roman Catholic Church is easily understandable. In the instructions for the education of his son he put the Roman Catholic religion on the same level with "the atheistic, Arian, and Socinian sects," requesting the tutors to instil a distaste for it in young Frederick's mind.[22] But he did grant freedom of conscience to all Roman Catholics, and in localities where there were many he permitted the holding of Catholic worship under certain restrictions. In the instructions for his sucessor he wrote: "As regards the Catholic religion, you must tolerate it according to the provisions of the peace of Westphalia and the pact of Wehlau."[23] Despite the opposition of many higher officials and Protestant clergymen he granted the Roman Catholics permission to worship publicly in Berlin, and he even purchased a house and engaged a priest for that purpose. In the peace of Utrecht (1713) he was given Gelderland, the population of which was entirely Roman Catholic, on condition that the status of the Roman Catholic religion remain the same and the bishop of Roermonde continue to exercise his diocesan authority. Frederick William accepted the condition without hesitation and fulfilled it to the letter. In 1717 he also granted the Roman Catholics of the province of Lingen permission to hold worship, after they had represented to him that in being compelled to journey to a neighboring state to worship they took time

[21] AB, Beh., III, 457.

[22] Cramer, *Zur Geschichte Friedrich Wilhelms I und Friedrichs II,* p. 3.

[23] AB, Beh., III, 457.

from their work and also spent money outside the country. When a Protestant zealot asked him why he permitted Roman Catholic worship in his provinces, Frederick William replied: "Because there are so many Roman Catholic people." [24] The basic reason was that he wanted to keep them satisfied and happy, so that they would not leave his provinces. It was his purpose, as he stated it, to populate—not to depopulate—his territories.

In the army Catholic recruits were welcomed as warmly as Protestants, Frederick William's agents being as zealous in gathering recruits in Roman Catholic as in Protestant countries. Not only did he himself appoint Roman Catholic priests to minister to the needs of the Roman Catholic soldiers, but he also urged his successor to do likewise. "In your regiments," he wrote, "there are many Roman Catholics whom you must grant the freedom of holding Roman Catholic worship, and you must also permit the priests to visit the regiments each month." [25] Fassmann probably exaggerates when he states that one-fourth of the soldiers in Frederick William's army were Roman Catholic. The number was, however, so large that in such cities as Potsdam, Spandau, Frankfurt, Stettin, Magdeburg, Stendal and Halle, Roman Catholic congregations of soldiers were formed and houses were established in which they could worship, subject to certain restrictions. On one point Frederick William, like his grandfather, was most emphatic: he refused to tolerate the Jesuits. In his drastic fashion he styled them "birds who make room for satan and expand his kingdom." [26] "Jesuits you must not tolerate in your country," he wrote to his successor; "they are devils who are capable of much evil and will harm you, your country, and your

[24] Cited in Lehmann, *Preussen und die katholische Kirche*, I, 407.
[25] *AB, Beh.*, III, 457.   [26] Förster, *Urkundenbuch*, III, 249.

people. Hence you must not tolerate them in your country under any pretext whatsoever." [27]

As for the Jews, they were tolerated after a fashion, but there was no question of granting them equal rights with the Christians. It was the Great Elector who permitted a limited number to return after a period during which they were forbidden to reside in Brandenburg. In 1670 two families, exiled from Vienna by the Emperor Leopold, were granted permission to settle in Berlin, and in the following year the Elector signed a decree which allowed fifty Jewish families to reside in Brandenburg for a period of twenty years.[28] Others, who had no residence permits, filtered in during the subsequent decades, so that by the middle of the reign of Frederick William I the number of Jews living in the territories of Prussia reached a total of about six thousand. The Great Elector's reasons for permitting Jews to settle in Brandenburg were purely economic. He believed that with their acute knowledge of commerce, their long experience in business matters, and their spirit of enterprise they would infuse a vigorous life into the commerce of his territories. Moreover, he hoped that their example would excite his stolid and self-satisfied subjects to greater commercial and industrial activity. Although allowed to practice only the trades which were not controlled by the guilds, they were granted considerable freedom in commerce. They were specifically forbidden to lend money at a higher rate than that set by the government and also to export sound specie or to import debased coinage. But they were permitted to open shops and to have booths and stalls at fairs and markets. The decree of 1671 mentioned particularly that they could buy and sell houses, old and new clothes, wool, spices, and meat. For this right each Jew was

[27] *AB, Beh.*, III, 458.   [28] *Corp. const.*, V (Part 5), 120–126.

required to pay to the government an annual *Schutzgeld* (protection tax) of eight taler, only gravediggers, midwives, and teachers being exempt. When certain merchants objected to the presence of the Jews on the ground that they were ruining the commerce of Brandenburg, the Great Elector replied: "The Jews and their commerce, far from being detrimental to the country, are decidedly beneficial to it." [29]

This policy of tolerating the Jews and taxing them lightly because they were active in expanding the commerce of Brandenburg was continued during the early years of the next reign, but the policy changed when the ministers trained under the Great Elector were gradually replaced by those who were interested in raising funds to meet the immediate expenses of the royal court more than in a far-sighted plan for the development of commerce. As they found it increasingly difficult to gather sufficient taxes to pay for the royal ostentation and extravagance, they inflicted more and more taxes and levies on the Jews. In 1700 the protection tax was doubled and the Jews were ordered to pay three thousand taler annually as a group.[30] Other levies imposed upon them included a tax at the birth of a child and another when a person died. Before he was permitted to marry, each young Jewish male had to pay to the government a tax which varied according to his wealth. Such "privileges" as the opening of a synagogue or the ownership of a cemetery had to be purchased from the government. Beyond this the government, on some pretext or other, frequently exacted large sums from the Jews. Thus, in 1689 it demanded sixteen thousand taler from the Jews as a whole, declaring that anyone refusing to pay his share

[29] Cited in Stern-Täubler, *Der preussische Staat und die Juden,* p. 49.

[30] *Corp. const.,* V (Part 5), 131–146.

would be expelled from the country at once. In 1701 the government sought to collect a tax on the total possessions of each Jew, but accepted the offer of the Jews to pay a lump sum of twenty thousand taler in place of the tax.[31]

Another method adopted by the state for exploiting the Jews financially was to impose fines upon them on any possible excuse that could be trumped up. In 1700 the Jewish community of Berlin, for example, was fined ten thousand ducats for "malversations and criminal disobedience." The greater the need of the government for money, the more fantastic did the pretexts for fining the Jews become. When, for instance, the royal seal disappeared in 1704, the government demanded six hundred reichstaler from the Jews of East Prussia, because, it concluded, the thief must have been a Jew. Jews who did not pay their various taxes and their share of the levies and fines promptly were treated very harshly. "More and more frequently," writes a German historian, "was the punishment of execution pronounced on dilatory taxpayers, more and more arbitrarily were even the poorest forced to pay contributions, more and more pitilessly were those who had no letters of protection expelled from the country, thrown into prison, or sentenced to hard labor." [32] But, while the government was increasing the taxes and levies, it was also restricting the economic opportunities of the Jews. Already, in 1696, because of complaints by Christian merchants, the government ordered the Jews to close all shops and booths which had been opened since 1690. Thereafter new shops and booths could be opened only by special permission.[33] The next year they were forbidden to purchase real estate of any kind without special permission; also, the privilege of

[31] See Stern-Täubler, *Der preussische Staat und die Juden*, pp. 76 *et sqq.*
[32] *Ibid.*, p. 88.   [33] *Corp. const.*, V (Part 5), 127–130.

selling meat was withdrawn.[34] Despite all this the Jewish population in Brandenburg-Prussia continued to increase during the reign of Frederick I.

Upon taking up the reins of government Frederick William turned again to the policy of the Great Elector. He had strong religious prejudices against the Jews, styling them "the betrayers of Christ," but he saw in them useful instruments for the development of commerce and industry—a development which was the *sine qua non* for the establishment of a strong army. Hence in 1714 he restored to the Jews the rights and the privileges which the Great Elector had granted them, but which had been withdrawn during the reign of Frederick I.[35] These included, besides the commercial and industrial privileges, the right to buy or to build houses. In East Prussia, which was economically more backward than the other provinces, Frederick William even gave Jews plots of ground on condition that they would build houses on them and settle there. After the economic oppression of the preceding reign it appeared to the Jews as if a new and happier period was being ushered in for them. But the prospect was illusory. Soon the Christian merchants began to complain loudly and incessantly that the Jews were ruining their business by unfair competition and fraudulent practices. Such complaints were not entirely groundless. Even Jewish historians state that certain Jewish merchants overstepped the bounds of liberty granted to the Jews as a whole. And the anti-Semites were not slow to make the most of every such case, thereby giving point to the accusations against the Jewish merchants as a whole.

The result was that the king gradually came to believe that the Jews were detrimental to his country in many ways. Only the fact that they were a prolific source of

[34] *Ibid.*, pp. 129–130.   [35] *Ibid.*, pp. 157–166.

revenue moved him to permit them to remain in his provinces. In 1722 he wrote in the instructions for his successor: "The Jews are the locusts of a country and ruin Christians. I beg you, do not give new letters of protection even though they do offer you much money, for it will cause you great harm and will ruin your subjects." [36] Years before this he had already begun to restrict the economic activity of the Jews. In 1718 he decreed that all Jewish shops which had been opened since 1690 were to be closed at once and that no new shops were to be opened without special permission. The next year he deprived the Jews of the right to buy or to build houses, stating that they must "everywhere live only in rented houses." [37] During the rest of the reign more and more restrictive measures were taken. In 1727 the king forbade the Jewish merchants to sell wool, because, as he alleged, they had circumvented the prohibition on the export of wool.[38] The same year, upon receiving numerous complaints from Christian manufacturers of woolen goods that the competition of the Jewish manufacturers was ruining their business, the government also forbade the Jews to manufacture woolen goods.[39] The actual cause of the business depression which evoked the complaints of the Christian manufacturers was, not the Jewish manufacturers themselves, but the fact that more woolen cloth was being made than the country could use or could be sold outside. In such economic crises the king again and again compelled the Jews to purchase the surplus woolen cloth and to sell it as best they could.

[36] *AB, Beh.*, III, 459.   [37] *Corp. const.*, V (Part 5), 179–180.
[38] *Ibid.*, V (Part 2), 369–370.
[39] *Ibid.*, pp. 365–370. This decree was not strictly enforced. In a number of cases the king himself gave Jews permission to open textile factories on condition that they operate a certain number of looms in them.

Continued complaints by Christian merchants impelled Frederick William in 1730 to issue for all Jews residing within the Prussian state a series of regulations which forced their economic activity into limits that were narrower than those imposed upon them during the preceding reign.[40] His reasons for doing this, as he stated them in the regulations, were that the Jews have "to the great harm of Christian merchants, extended their activities beyond the limits the government set for them in trade and industry and that, contrary to our most gracious intention, Jews without letters of protection have managed to sneak in." Jewish merchants were forbidden to trade in groceries, spices, untanned hides, and foreign woolens; native woolens and linens they were allowed to sell only by special permission. "The rest of the Jews," the regulations state, "must content themselves with the sale of old clothes or with the trade in knick-knacks and second-hand goods. The Jews may also engage in money-changing and horse-trading." As for those Jews who were not merchants, not only agriculture but also all the regular trades, excepting the engraving of seals were closed to them. Furthermore, they were also forbidden to brew beer, distill spirits, and to slaughter cattle for the purpose of selling meat to Christians.

But while the economic opportunities were becoming more limited, the exactions of the government were gradually increasing. "If you need money," Frederick William advised his son, "levy the sum of 20,000 or 30,000 taler upon the entire Jewry, and do that every three or four years, and this above the protection tax." [41] He himself followed this advice religiously. In 1720 he had already raised the annual protection tax for the Jews as a whole to twenty thousand taler; in addition he collected forty-eight hun-

[40] *Corp. const.*, V (Part 5), 193–200.   [41] *AB, Beh.*, III, 459.

dred taler from the Jews each year for exempting them from military service.[42] Other taxes were also raised and upon every possible excuse new levies were exacted from them. When the Jewish congregation of Berlin requested the king to remit the burial tax for poor Jews, he answered curtly that if the tax were not paid the hangman would take the body and bury it under the gallows. Another method of exploiting the Jews was to compel them to buy surplus manufactures. In 1722, for example, the king decreed that the Jews living in the New Mark must buy ten thousand taler worth of woolen cloth each year from the royal factory (*Lagerhaus*) in Berlin.[43] Thenceforth it became almost a regular policy to unload the surplus products of the Prussian manufactories onto the Jews. This the king did not regard as an injustice, "for the Jews," he stated in a rescript to the General Directory, "are tolerated in our country for the very reason that they should do this, and they would otherwise not be tolerated in the country solely because of the small protection tax they pay." [44] When commerce and industry began to flourish the king decided it would be a better country if there were no Jews in it. Accordingly he decreed in 1728 that when a Jew dies his letter of protection cannot be sold to another,[45] an order which, if it had been carried out, would have caused the Jews to die out. Toward the end of his reign he was restrained only with great difficulty from expelling all Jews from his territories after several Jews were found to have

[42] See Rachel, "Die Juden im Berliner Wirtschaftsleben," *Zeitschrift für die Geschichte der Juden in Deutschland*, II (1930), 181.

[43] See Stern-Täubler, "Die Juden in der Handelspolitik Friedrich Wilhelms I," *Zeitschrift für die Geschichte der Juden in Deutschland*, V (1935), 214.

[44] AB, *Die Wollindustrie in Preussen unter Friedrich Wilhelm I*, p. 335.

[45] *Corp. const.*, V (Part 5), 191–194.

participated in a robbery.[46] As it was, he did order the number of Jews in Berlin reduced from 234 to 120 families. However, the order was carried out only in part; only a few of the poorer Jews were expelled. The result was that after 1737 there were only ten Jews in Berlin whose possessions had a value of less than one thousand taler. In general, despite all restrictions and exactions, the number of Jews in the Prussian provinces was larger at the end of Frederick William's reign than it had been at the beginning.[47]

[46] *AB, Handels, Zoll, und Akzisepolitik,* II (Part 1), 136.
[47] See Rachel, "Die Juden im Berliner Wirtschaftsleben," *Zeitschrift für die Geschichte der Juden in Deutschland,* II (1930), 182.

Frederick William the Mercantilist

IN HIS economic policies Frederick William was a mercantilist. Mercantilism was not a definite system of thought; it was rather a tendency. Insofar as it can be defined, it was the sum total of the means employed by the statesmen of the period from the end of the fifteenth to the second half of the eighteenth century to create strong commercial and industrial states. Their aim included, first, the transformation of a local economy into a national economy; in other words, the concentration of all economic life under the direction of a powerful central government. This phase of Frederick William's activities is discussed in an earlier chapter. More important to the mercantilists was the development of the strength of their respective states over against that of other states. The best means of making a state strong, they decided, was the accumulation of wealth, particularly in the form of precious metals. Being the general medium of exchange, gold and silver could easily be converted into the commodities desired. This was of special importance in times of war, which the mercantilists were always anticipating. As the saying, so frequently repeated in mercantilist writings, had it: "Money is the sinews of war." It was believed that the nation which possessed gold and silver "hath courage, hath men, and all other instruments to defend itself."

The means employed by the mercantilists to acquire a supply of precious metals varied in the different countries according to time and circumstances. While the Spaniards were fortunate enough to discover rich mines in the new world which enabled the Spanish rulers to make their state influential in Europe, the other nations, having no mines, looked to trade and industry as a means of increasing their national wealth. The dominating objective was to establish a so-called "balance of trade." In other words, as much as possible was to be exported, and as little as possible imported—the difference between exports and imports flowing into the country in the form of precious metals. To make the balance as large as possible, only raw materials were to be imported; and after they had gone through the process of manufacture the finished product was again to be exported. The price received abroad for the finished product above the cost of the raw materials was considered clear gain. If the raw materials were produced at home, the gain was regarded as 100 percent. So that the volume of export might be as large as possible, considerable attention was given to development of home industries. Not only were the old industries expanded, new ones were also established, often with the aid of state subsidies. To protect the home markets from being flooded by foreign goods, tariff barriers were raised against the outside world. Some states also gave considerable attention to the development of agriculture. While England paid export premiums on grain in order to raise its price for the benefit of the landowners, other nations put restrictions on the export of grain as a means of insuring cheaper food to the industrial work-

ers. But as much as the means may have differed, the goal
was always the same: the increase of wealth in the mother
country.

Frederick William, as previously stated, wanted wealth
primarily because it was the *sine qua non* for building a
large standing army and for supporting it in times of war.
There was nothing new in this. The Great Elector had
sought wealth for the same reason. But the policies of the
two men differed concerning the means they employed.
The Great Elector, believing that the country could best
become prosperous through the export and the carrying
trade, made the development of trade the central feature of
his economic policy. Frederick William I was not, of
course, opposed to the expansion of foreign trade; on the
contrary, he did much to promote it. It was, however, of
secondary importance to him. His economic policy was
based on the conviction that prosperity was to be had,
above all, through the development of the native industries
and of agriculture. To him, not merchants and traders, but
manufacturers and peasants were the real productive agents.
If the native industries could supply the home markets, the
importation of foreign products would become unnecessary and much of the wealth that was annually sent abroad
for foreign products would remain in the country.

The underlying purpose of the development of industry
and agriculture was to make the Prussian subjects more
prosperous so that they could carry a heavier burden of
taxes. In other words, Frederick William sought to increase
his revenues. These revenues were derived from various
sources, one important source being the royal domains discussed in an earlier chapter. Then there were the customs
duties which annually yielded a considerable sum. But the
taxes which yielded the largest revenues were the *Kontri-*

bution and the *Akzise* (excise tax). The *Kontribution* was levied only in the agricultural districts. It was not a land tax, but one based on the ability of an individual to pay. In this respect it was like the *taille* in France. The principal tax of the Prussian cities was the *Akzise*. Besides being levied on such articles of consumption as food, drink, and clothing, it was also levied on city property and on certain industries according to the number of employees. Neither the *Kontribution* nor the *Akzise* was uniform in all the Prussian provinces; both varied in each province according to local conditions. At the opening of Frederick William's reign the latter was not yet levied in some of the Prussian provinces. First imposed in Brandenburg on beer in the fifteenth century, it had been extended to other articles by the Great Elector in 1641. Thereafter it was changed and extended a number of times before Frederick William, in the first year of his reign, took up the work of introducing it into those provinces in which it did not yet exist [1] and also of making it more uniform in all the Prussian provinces.

The policy of trying to make his subjects prosperous so that they could pay more taxes was, of course, not original with Frederick William. In a rudimentary form it had already been initiated by the Great Elector. During the succeeding reign, however, but little progress had been made in developing it. It remained for Frederick William to take up the policy, with his characteristic vigor and determination. In carrying it out he proceeded in such an independent manner that he may well be regarded as the creator of Prussian mercantilism. He distinguished himself principally in four respects. First, he did his utmost to spur all his sub-

[1] The one exception was Gelderland. Special rights accorded to it in the treaty of Utrecht prevented the introduction of the *Akzise* into this province.

jects to work diligently. Secondly, he promoted the expansion of the old Prussian industries and also established new ones. Thirdly, he founded a system of industrial and agrarian protection which is often compared with that established by Colbert in France.[2] Fourthly, he continued the policy of attracting colonists, thereby greatly increasing the population and the productive powers of his territories.

From the first day of his reign to the last Frederick William tried to arouse his subjects to the advantages of unremitting industry. Regarding indolence as "one of the worst of all vices," he sought to make diligence the first virtue of the land. Everyone, he insisted, must engage in productive work of some kind. His demands included even the Berlin market women who were waiting for customers. An edict which he issued in 1723 reads: "The huckstresses and other saleswomen on the streets and in the markets are not to sit with open mouths, but are to spin wool and flax, knit, or sew—under punishment of losing their concessions."[3] All beggars and vagabonds were to be turned over to the military authorities if they were fit for military service; otherwise they were to be sent to a workhouse. The reason Frederick William despised lawyers, philosophers, actors, and dancing masters was because he thought that their work was not productive. This also explains in part the severe decrees he issued regarding gypsies. Because they lived, as he said, solely by robbery and theft, producing nothing, all gypsies found on Prussian territory were to be scourged, branded, and expelled from the country. When this did not rid his provinces of them, he ordered that every gypsy over eighteen who was apprehended was to be

[2] Frederick William, it seems, borrowed many of the mercantilist principles he established in Prussia from Colbert. See Ranke, *Neun Bücher preussischer Geschichte*, I, 148.

[3] *Corp. const.*, V (Part 2), 355-358.

hanged immediately, while those under eighteen were to be sent to homes for orphans. Officials who failed to carry out this decree were to be dismissed from office and in addition required to pay a fine of a thousand taler.[4]

In addition to issuing edicts the king, in his daily intercourse with the people, was wont emphatically to discourage any signs of idleness. If he met idlers on the street, he would roundly berate them, order them to "go and do something," and then send them on their way with a sound thrashing. In applying the cane he showed little favoritism; all and sundry were caned if he believed their behavior warranted it. The king would, for example, tell a clergyman whom he found staring at the soldiers to go home and pray or a woman to go home and mind her brats, always emphasizing with his cudgel whatever advice he might give. Frederick William's habit of indiscriminate caning caused his subjects to avoid him whenever they could. This nettled him, for he desired to hold the love of his people. Yet, even in this matter he tried by force to obtain what he deemed his just due as a sovereign. It is reported that one day a boy saw the king approaching and obviously tried to avoid meeting him. Frederick William had his pages overtake the boy. "Why do you run away?" he asked the trembling lad. "Because I am afraid," was the reply. "You must not be afraid, you must love me," Frederick William blustered, at the same time raining blows on the back of the frightened youth.[5] Paradoxically, he who invariably carried his cane with him and seldom hesitated to use it wrote concerning his peasants: "They must not suffer themselves to be treated like slaves with whips and blows, but when any

[4] *Ibid.*, II (Part 3), 141–144; *Corp. const., continuatio,* I, 299–302.
[5] Förster, *Friedrich Wilhelm I*, I, 238.

such treatment is inflicted on them they should complain immediately to the proper authorities." [6]

In his efforts to build up the industries in his territories Frederick William devoted most of his attention to the textile industries, particularly to those engaged in the manufacture of woolens. Each year large sums were being sent to other countries for textiles which were used by the army as well as by civilians. To discourage the importation of French clothing by civilians, he dressed the executioners and the court fools in the latest French styles. Everyone was urged to use only native cloths. The queen and the princesses were required to set an example by wearing only dresses of the plainest kind made of woolen cloth manufactured in Prussia. But the decree which gave new life to the Prussian textile industries was that of June 3, 1713, which ordered all regimental commanders to purchase only domestic cloth for the army.[7] Frederick I had already issued such an order, but it had been largely disregarded. Frederick William was more determined. Only a few weeks after the first decree he issued a second one, which definitely regulated the purchase of clothing for the army.[8] Any officer found guilty of purchasing foreign clothing for himself or his men, except by royal permission, was to pay a fine of a hundred ducats to the fund for invalid soldiers. The king even went so far as to forbid merchants and contractors to sell foreign products to army officers without permission. Since not all articles of clothing needed by the army were manufactured in the Prussian provinces, he did at first permit the use of some foreign products. But at the same time he commissioned Privy Councillor von Kraut to

[6] *Ibid.*, II, 275.   [7] *Corp. const.*, V (Part 2), 459–464.
[8] *Ibid.*, III (Part 1), 333–336.

establish as soon as possible such industries as were necessary to supply all the demands of the army. Thus the army
which was putting such heavy tax burdens on Prussian subjects became to many a means of subsistence.

As a center for the manufacture of woolens he founded
the Berlin *Lagerhaus* (1714), which he hoped would restore the prosperity that had been destroyed by the abolition of luxury articles. The *Lagerhaus* was, on the one
hand, a kind of warehouse, or, better, a series of warehouses,
in which the wool produced in the Prussian provinces was
collected and then distributed to artisans and manufacturers
for cash or partly on credit. But it was more than a mere
warehouse, for various grades of woolen cloth were made
in it, the art of weaving some of the finer cloths having been
introduced by French refugees. Some kinds were made entirely in the *Lagerhaus*, while others were roughly woven
in the homes of artisans and finished in the *Lagerhaus*. Insofar as possible Frederick William sought to employ artisans who had previously lived on charity and workers who
were members of a soldier's family. The wages which the
king paid his cloth weavers in 1726 were 25 percent higher
than those paid by private manufacturers. As early as 1716
the woolen cloth produced by the *Lagerhaus* together with
that made by other native manufacturers was sufficient for
the needs of the army. Only linen for underwear and gaiters
still had to be imported from Silesia.⁹

It was not enough that the king set a high standard of
workmanship in the *Lagerhaus*. Before the domestic cloths
could compete successfully with foreign cloths, both in
the home and in foreign markets, it was necessary for them
to be of a uniformly high quality. The quality of the cloth

⁹ See AB, *Die Wollindustrie in Preussen unter Friedrich Wilhelm I*, pp. 20 et sqq.

made by many clothmakers in the Hohenzollern territories was still very low. The Great Elector had already tried to standardize the quality of native cloths by issuing a decree (March 30, 1680) which provided for the appointment of inspectors to examine all the cloth made in Brandenburg in order to make sure that it measured up to certain standards.[10] These standards, however, were not new; they were the old ones set by the guilds. Nor was the basic purpose of the Great Elector anything but the enforcement of the old guild statutes, and during the reign of Frederick I even these were not enforced. Frederick William, with his characteristic vigor, not only insisted that the old standards be met but also set new ones for many types of cloth. The most important edict of the first part of his reign was that of January 30, 1723, which was effective in Brandenburg, Pomerania, Magdeburg, and Halberstadt.[11] While this decree did not directly limit the autonomy of the guilds, it did so indirectly by setting up uniform technical regulations for the manufacture and sale of woolen cloths. Its detailed prescriptions regulated every step in the manufacture of cloth, including the preparation of the wool for spinning as well as the spinning, weaving, fulling, and dyeing. It also provided for the appointment of special technical supervisors who were to see that the prescriptions were faithfully carried out. All cloth was to be examined three times before it could be sold. Immediately after it was taken from the loom the inspectors were to ascertain if it was of the proper weight, thickness, length, and breadth; if it contained the requisite number of threads; and if it had any such flaws as "sacks," "pockets," broken threads, or knots. Cloth that was up to the standard was marked with a clover leaf; and only cloth so marked could be accepted for full-

[10] *Corp. const.*, V (Part 2), 249–254.   [11] *Ibid.*, pp. 335–354.

ing. After the fulling it was again inspected to confirm its length and breadth; also to see if the quality of the wool was uniform in the entire piece of cloth and if the fulling was well done. This time, if it passed inspection, a lead marker was attached to it, bearing on one side the arms of the city in which the cloth was made and on the other a notation of the length of the cloth. Finally the cloth was examined again after it had been dyed to see if the color was even—not streaked or spotted. Cloths which satisfied the final inspector were marked according to their quality: three clover leaves for prime, two for mediocre, and one for ordinary cloth. Both merchants and tailors were forbidden to buy unmarked cloths, under punishment of one hundred reichstaler. In addition to judging the quality of the finished cloth the inspectors had another duty. The edict further stipulated that to keep the prices from fluctuating too much they should annually designate the price a clothmaker could ask for his cloth.

By promulgating the edict of 1723 Frederick William told the guilds and the cities, as it were, that it would henceforth be the function of the central government to see that the goods produced in the Prussian provinces are of a high quality. In short, the control of industry was being absorbed by the central government. A decisive change, however, was introduced only in connection with the imperial law (*Reichspatent*) of 1731, which was drawn up largely at the instigation of the Prussian government.[12] This law, styled by one historian "the first concerted legislative measure of the empire for centuries," [13] theoretically terminated the autonomy of the guilds in the Holy Roman Empire. First, it declared all the existing guild statutes

[12] *Ibid.*, pp. 765–782.
[13] AB, *Die Wollindustrie in Preussen unter Friedrich Wilhelm I,* p. 313.

"null, void, and invalid." Thenceforth the guilds were to
pass only such regulations as had previously been "sanc-
tioned, approved, and confirmed" by the "proper government authorities." In other words, the exclusive right to
prescribe regulations was reserved to the imperial and provincial governments. Secondly, guild meetings were thenceforth to be held only in the presence of a deputy appointed
by the "proper government authorities." Thirdly, it forbade the guilds thenceforth to exclude, because of their
connection with "despised" trades, any applicants except
knackers. Nor was any distinction to be made between
legitimate and illegitimate children. Fourthly, it greatly restricted the right of punishment which the guilds had previously exercised. At no time was any master, journeyman,
or apprentice to be punished without the knowledge of the
supervisor appointed by the government. Finally, the law
threatened to abolish the guilds entirely if their members
did not "suppress their wantonness, malice, and obstinacy"
and "strive to live more properly and peaceably."

The emperor signed the *Reichspatent* in June, 1731, but
months passed before it was published. Finally it was proclaimed in Austria only as a provincial, not as an imperial,
law. In the Prussian state, however, the law was promptly
published, and a thoroughgoing reform inaugurated on the
basis of it. Since it abolished the old guild statutes, the Prussian government could now draw up for each trade regulations that were uniform in the entire state, for which task
the king appointed a commission in 1732. The first thing
this commission did was to lay down a number of guiding
principles as a basis for individual regulations. Among them
were the following: First, only guilds which made goods
solely for local consumption—as, for example, the bakers,
butchers, tailors, barbers, and shoemakers—were thence-

forth to be permitted to limit the number of their masters in accordance with the demand for their products.[14] Secondly, masters who manufactured goods for a wider market —as, for example, the clothmakers and linen weavers— were to have the right to employ as many journeymen and to operate as many looms as they desired. Thirdly, the supervisors of the guilds were to be chosen from among the assistants of the municipal magistrates. Thus the guilds were put under the direct supervision of the royal officials. After these principles had been approved by the General Directory and by the king the commission proceeded with the task of drawing up new regulations for each trade, the total number of trades in Brandenburg being sixty-three. When the commission had finished its work, the regulations were declared effective in all the provinces under Frederick William's rule except East Prussia, which was outside the Holy Roman Empire and therefore not subject to imperial legislation. On June 10, 1733, Frederick William issued special regulations for East Prussia, which were practically the same as those for other provinces.[15] Most of the regulations the commission drew up remained in force for many decades. Frederick the Great made certain changes in them, but not until the nineteenth century were they subjected to a thoroughgoing revision.

Besides trying to improve the quality of the woolen goods made in his provinces, Frederick William also sought to protect the domestic cloths against foreign competition by imposing high import duties on such foreign textiles as might compete with them. Not that this was a new departure. In 1686 the Great Elector had put a duty of 10 percent on woolen and silk goods, including cloths, tapes-

[14] See Meyer, *Die Handwerkerpolitik König Friedrich Wilhelms I*, pp. 82 *et sqq.*

[15] Regulations, *ibid.*, pp. 329–354.

tries, hats, and stockings imported into Brandenburg, and in 1701 the duty on some of these imports was increased. No sooner had Frederick William seated himself upon the throne than he raised considerably the duties on woolens and linens, on some articles as much as 25 percent. The edict of November 1, 1718, further increased the duties on certain woolens, and, what is more important, it imposed duties on goods imported into Pomerania, Magdeburg, and Halberstadt, as well as into Brandenburg.[16]

When many of his subjects, particularly the nobles, continued to use foreign woolen goods despite the high tariffs, Frederick William inaugurated a policy of forbidding them to use foreign products that offered competition to domestic woolen goods. The first general edict, effective in all the provinces under his rule, was issued in Berlin on April 26, 1718. It stated that

since fine red and blue cloths and fabrics of Spanish, Polish, and other good wool are made in this and other cities in sufficient quantities of good quality, we decree that three months after the day of publication none of our officials, vassals, or subjects may use foreign red or blue cloths and fabrics for new clothing and cloaks or for upholstering carriages and chaises on punishment of ten reichstaler for each ell; they are to use the red and blue cloths and fabrics made in our country for these purposes.[17]

The decree stated further that

none of our officials, vassals, and subjects who give their servants liveries or clothing may henceforth use foreign cloths of whatever color they may be for this purpose, but they are to clothe them in domestic flannels, serges, rashes, stockings, and hats under punishment of ten reichstaler for each ell of foreign goods, each pair of stockings, or each hat.

---

[16] *Corp. const.*, IV (Part 3), 241–244, 261–266.
[17] *Ibid.*, V (Part 2), 313–316.

As a means of enforcing the decree the king specified that all clothing for servants must be made by the tailors in the cities; then he forbade all tailors to use foreign materials in making this clothing. A tailor who knowingly used foreign materials was to lose his trade rights for a year. Finally the king also expressed the desire that all his subjects follow his example and clothe themselves exclusively in domestic fabrics. A year later (May 1, 1719) this desire was made law, when all subjects were forbidden under the threat of severe punishment to use foreign fabrics "of whatever price, color, or mixture they may be" for clothing themselves and their servants or for upholstering carriages.[18] Not that there was a surplus of woolen products in the Prussian provinces, the fact was that woolen goods were not yet manufactured in sufficient quantities to meet the needs of the home markets. It was the purpose of this edict, as well as of the preceding one and of those that were to follow, to bring about an expansion of the Prussian industries so that they could supply the needs of the native population.

To insure the native artisans and manufacturers an adequate supply of wool at moderate prices Frederick William forbade its export from certain of his provinces. He feared that a scarcity of wool might not only destroy some of the newly-founded industries but that it would also cause a rise in the price of wool and therefore in the price of the finished cloth. This, in turn, would greatly increase the price of the uniforms for the army. "Since our military budget is regulated down to the smallest detail," the royal decree stated, "such an augmentation would necessarily become a burden to all our subjects." [19] An edict issued by the Great

18 *Ibid.*, pp. 317–320.
19 *AB, Handels, Zoll, und Akzisepolitik,* II (Part 2), 47–50.

Elector in 1687 had already forbidden the export of a certain type of wool (*Bündelwolle*) from Brandenburg and in the succeeding years its export from Magdeburg and Pomerania was also prohibited.[20] It appears, however, that no serious attempt was made during the reign of Frederick I to enforce the prohibitions. When Frederick William became king his first step was to enforce the decrees his predecessors had issued; then on May 28, 1714, he took the next step by issuing an edict which gave to the woolworkers the right of preëmption to all wool presented for sale in the Prussian markets.[21] In 1718 the export of every kind of wool from Brandenburg, Pomerania and Camin was forbidden for a period of eighteen months and the next year this prohibition was made permanent.[22] There was as yet no thought of forbidding the export of wool from those provinces which, like East Prussia, were still predominantly agricultural.

The immediate result of the export prohibition was a temporary drop in the price of wool which evoked loud complaints from the landowners and leaseholders. Many even threatened to stop raising sheep if the prohibition were not lifted. This, however, had little effect on the king, for he knew that they needed the sheep manure for their lands as well as the income from the sale of the wool for their budgets. The landowners and leaseholders also told the king that the native industries could not use all the wool produced in the said provinces, an assertion which contained an element of truth. Even this did not make the king relent. He hoped the export prohibition would promote the expansion of the woolen industries to a point where they

---

[20] *Corp. const.*, V (Part 2), 237–250, 255–263.
[21] *Ibid.*, V (Part 2), 41–44, 279–280, 285–288.
[22] *Ibid.*, pp. 319–322.

could use all the wool that was produced locally. Actually the unsold remainder in the provinces from which export was forbidden was small compared to the total consumed by the manufacturers. To still the complaints of the nobles in the newly acquired Hither Pomerania Frederick William did during two years permit the export of whatever wool was still unsold on May 1st. But when the nobles asked for the annulment of the decree prohibiting the export of wool he wrote on the petition: "Flatly refused under punishment of hanging and confiscation of goods if one stone of wool is taken out of the country." [23] Later he restated the punishment in the instructions for the General Directory. "You are to forbid the exportation of wool," he wrote, "under punishment of hanging for anyone who exports one stone of wool." [24] Despite these threats much wool was smuggled out of the country. The king himself acknowledged this when he stated in a royal edict of 1721: "We perceive with the greatest displeasure that there are some nobles and officials, also wool merchants and Jews, who are not obeying my earnest edict." [25] In his efforts to stop the illicit trade he went so far as to threaten those who were hired to transport the wool out of the country with confiscation of property and imprisonment for life.

Meanwhile Frederick William also sought to increase the home consumption of wool so that there would be no surplus. Among other measures he extended the import prohibitions to textiles made partly of wool and to such as competed with the lighter woolen goods made in the Prussian provinces. Thus an edict of May 10, 1721, prohibited the use of camlet (camels' hair mixed with wool); on March 13, 1722, all foreign fabrics made of a mixture of

[23] *AB, Die Wollindustrie in Preussen unter Friedrich Wilhelm I*, p. 44.
[24] *AB, Beh.*, III, 561, 596.   [25] *Corp. const.*, V (Part 2), 329–330.

wool, linen, and cotton were put on the forbidden list; and the next year all fabrics made of silk and wool were added.[26] Worthy of particular mention is the edict of November 18, 1721, which sought to promote the sale of the lighter domestic woolen fabrics, and also those made of linen, by forbidding the use for clothing of imported printed and painted chintzes and calicoes "of whatever kind they may be" under penalty of a fine of one hundred reichstaler or three days in irons.[27] Within a period of eight months all articles of clothing made of the forbidden materials, even to night caps, dressing gowns, handkerchiefs, and aprons, were to be discarded. The king, it is true, later extended the "period of grace" by several months, but he also made the decree more comprehensive by forbidding the use of imported cottons for bedding, curtains, and furniture covers. When those of his subjects who had previously used the imported chintzes and calicoes substituted imported printed flannels for them, the government also forbade the use of the latter on March 22, 1723. Another edict which purposed to increase the consumption of wool was that of November 6, 1731, forbidding all maidservants and women of low estate to wear silk dresses, camisoles, or pinafores. For a time the king and his ministers, in their eagerness to expand the manufacture of woolens, even seriously entertained the idea of adopting the English law which stipulated that the dead must be buried in woolen shrouds.[28]

The strict enforcement of the foregoing edicts was, of course, impossible. It is to be noticed that, not the importation, but only the use of certain fabrics was forbidden.

---

[26] See *AB, Handels, Zoll, und Akzisepolitik*, II (Part 1), 322.

[27] *Corp. const.*, V (Part 1), 197–198.

[28] See *AB, Die Wollindustrie in Preussen unter Friedrich Wilhelm I*, pp. 102 *et sqq.*

Merchants could still import and sell the "forbidden" fabrics to such purchasers as could offer proof that they were not Prussian subjects, a stipulation that was often conveniently neglected by the merchants. Nevertheless, the edicts, though they were not literally obeyed, did in the main achieve their purpose. Not only did the domestic manufacturers produce light woolens and mixed woolens in great quantities but they also sought to satisfy the demand for printed calicoes by imitating the foreign calicoes as nearly as they could. Both the light woolens and the calicoes were after a time produced in such quantities that the surplus was exported to neighboring states. In general the manufacture of woolen cloth expanded greatly. In Berlin, for example, the use of wool for manufacturing purposes increased from 34,969 stones in 1720 to 81,955 in 1735. During the years from 1725 to 1738 the Russian Company of Berlin was able to supply all the cloth needed by the Russian army. It was a time of plenty for the cloth weavers. As a local commissary of Brandenburg put it in 1731: "The clothmakers of the cities are having a golden age, for they can sell as much as they can manufacture, and as a result they live well." [29] This prosperity declined somewhat when the English textiles crowded those of Prussia out of the Russian market. In 1738 the Russian Company collapsed entirely and was dissolved, but by the time of Frederick William's death in 1740 the Prussian textile industry had regained some of its former prosperity.

If Frederick William sought above all to foster and to protect the manufacture of woolens, he did not neglect the other industries. One of these to the development of which he devoted considerable attention was the manufacture of

[29] Naude, "Die merkantilistische Wirtschaftspolitik Friedrich Wilhelms I," *Historische Zeitschrift*, LIV (1903), 15.

leather goods. To insure to the artisans and the manufacturers a plentiful supply of leather he issued a decree in
1717 forbidding the export from Brandenburg of all untanned skins and hides, "because experience has shown that
the country cannot furnish nearly enough skins and hides
to meet the demand." [30] On the other hand, it was permis-
sible after 1724 to export free of duty tanned cattle and
horse hides.[31] At the request of the shoemakers of Brandenburg the use of foreign shoes was forbidden in 1719, but
the edict was not strictly enforced, despite the persistent
complaints of the shoemakers.[32] Another cause for com-
plaint on the part of the makers of leather shoes was the
manufacture of wooden shoes. Frederick I, as a special
favor, had permitted the French refugees to make, wear,
and sell wooden shoes and slippers with wooden soles.[33]
However, during the first years of Frederick William's
reign the complaints against these privileges became so insistent that the king revoked the permission in 1717, declaring that the sale of wooden shoes was harming the trade of
the shoemakers.[34] The edict may have abolished the public
sale of wooden shoes, but it did not put an end to the wearing of them; they continued to be widely used by the
poorer peasants. After the king himself on a journey
through Brandenburg in 1722 had seen numerous peasants
wearing them, he issued an order which forbade their use
as well as their sale in Brandenburg, Pomerania, Magdeburg, and Halberstadt.[35] The order notwithstanding, many
peasants continued to wear wooden shoes, so that the king
found it necessary to issue a new edict in 1726, which
threatened with imprisonment those who persisted in their

[30] *Corp. const.*, V (Part 2), 157–158.   [31] *Ibid.*, pp. 165–169.
[32] See *AB, Handels, Zoll, und Akzisepolitik*, II (Part 1), 327.
[33] *Corp. const.*, V (Part 2), 665–668.
[34] *Ibid.*, pp. 669–670.   [35] *Ibid.*, pp. 725–728.

disobedience.[36] Whether this decree finally put an end to the wearing of wooden shoes is not a matter of record.

In general Frederick William's policy was one of thoroughgoing protectionism. As early as the first year of his reign he raised considerably the duties on linens, leather, and hides, as well as on woolens.[37] The next year he increased the duties on foreign cutlery, instruments, and hardware in general. Most of the duties were raised again in 1718; on hardware, for example, as high as 75 or even 100 percent of the value of the goods.[38] At the same time the duties were made effective in Pomerania, Magdeburg, and Halberstadt, as well as in Brandenburg. In this way all imports which offered competition to native products were taxed, some of them so heavily that they were excluded. This system of protectionism was not, however, extended to East Prussia, which was still largely agricultural.

Nor did Frederick William stop at trying to protect the established industries; he also worked to found new ones which he hoped would render Prussia more and more independent of foreign manufacturers. Time and again he impressed on his ministers the necessity and the importance of establishing new industries. For example, in the instructions for the General Directory he stated: "The General Directory has full knowledge of what great importance the establishment of good and well-regulated manufactures is to us and our country. It will therefore take up the matter with the greatest diligence, so that, insofar as possible, all kinds of woolen, iron, wood, and leather manufactories and artisans, not already established in our territories, may be established in them." [39] Earlier Frederick William had issued edicts offering special privileges to specified artisans

[36] *Ibid.*, pp. 747–750. [37] *Ibid.*, IV (Part 3), 241–244.
[38] *Ibid.*, pp. 261–266. [39] *AB, Beh.*, III, 595.

who would migrate to the Prussian provinces. The edict of November 29, 1718,[40] lists the kind of artisan desired and then offers them the following inducements: (1) Free civic and master's rights. (2) Freedom from excise taxes on articles of consumption for a period of two years. (3) Freedom for five years from the quartering of soldiers and all other civic burdens. (4) Freedom from military service for themselves and their sons, and also for all journeymen they bring with them. (5) All possible assistance and aid in establishing their professions. When foreign artisans failed to come in the desired numbers, the king issued a new invitation the next year, offering more liberal terms.[41] In 1732 he issued still another invitation, which offered traveling expenses, a plot of ground, certain materials for building a house, and a sum in cash in addition to the earlier inducements.[42]

Although even after the third invitation not as many artisans came as Frederick William desired, they did come in considerable numbers. Already as a result of the first invitation many weavers had migrated to Brandenburg, Magdeburg, and other Hohenzollern provinces from non-Prussian states, particularly from Saxony and from Anhalt. These immigrants contributed in no small way to the expansion of the textile industries. Despite failures in specific endeavors such as the attempt to establish the manufacture of silk, Frederick William's industrial and protectionist policies were on the whole successful. Some idea of the industrial expansion that took place in Brandenburg may be gained from the fact that the city population of that province more than doubled during Frederick William's reign.

[40] *Corp. const.*, V (Part 2), 673–676.
[41] *Ibid.*, V (Part 1), 411–412.
[42] *Ibid.*, pp. 431–434.

Since his income was derived from both agriculture and industry, Frederick William tried to promote the development of the former no less than that of the latter. The royal domains, embracing as they did a considerable part of the total acreage of arable land in the Hohenzollern provinces, were one of the major sources of royal revenue. The only way of increasing the revenues from this source was to raise the rents. To make high rents possible it was necessary to keep the price of grain at a high level. This could be achieved only by placing restrictions upon the importation of foreign, particularly Polish, grain. Not only was the grain produced in Poland of a better quality than that of East Prussia, Pomerania, or the New Mark, but also it was to be had at lower prices. When Poland had plentiful harvests Polish grain was imported in such quantities that it threatened to devaluate Prussian grain. It became imperative to take measures to protect the Prussian landowners and peasants if they were not to be impoverished. Hence, in 1721, when the price of both Prussian wheat and Prussian rye was forced down by large imports from Poland, Frederick William decided, overruling the vigorous objections of his ministers who feared reprisals from Poland, to impose an import duty on Polish grain.[43] After raising the duty several times, in 1722 he prohibited altogether the consumption of Polish grain in Pomerania, Brandenburg, and the New Mark. The next year the prohibition was extended to East Prussia. Polish grain could still be imported into the aforementioned provinces, but only for reshipment to other countries. In the succeeding years he also turned his attention to grain imported from Saxony and Mecklenburg. At times he would forbid its consumption entirely; again he would burden it with an import duty that virtually

[43] *AB, Getreidehandelspolitik*, II, 368 et sqq.

amounted to exclusion. The purpose was always the same: to keep up the price of native grain by insuring to it the home market. This system of agrarian protectionism, in freeing native grain from foreign competition, did stimulate the development of Prussian agriculture. Frederick the Great, who saw its benefits, not only retained it but even expanded it considerably.

Besides establishing a system of agrarian protection Frederick William continued the policy, established by the Great Elector, of inviting colonists to settle in the Hohenzollern territories. The population of some of the provinces was still small. This was particularly true of East Prussia, where a pestilence had taken a high toll during the years 1708 to 1711. Stadelmann sets the number of those who fell victims to it during these years at 235,806.[44] Like his grandfather, Frederick William believed that "human beings are the best wealth." [45] Immigrants were to him a highly desirable form of wealth for a number of reasons. First, they were, as previously stated, useful for the expansion of Prussian industry. Second, he needed them to cultivate the royal domains, for untenanted holdings yield no revenues. Third, their descendants would swell the ranks of the Prussian army. Frederick William told Old Dessauer that the money he was spending on the settlement of immigrants was being well spent, because "through it the land will be cultivated and when the children (of the colonists) grow up and my son becomes involved in war, he will not lack human beings." [46] In addition, there was a religious motive for inviting certain colonists. Regarding himself as the head of German Protestantism, Frederick William felt it his duty

[44] *Friedrich Wilhelm I in seiner Tätigkeit für die Landescultur Preussens*, p. 34.
[45] *Briefe an Leopold zu Anhalt-Dessau*, p. 233.   [46] *Ibid.*

to protect such as were persecuted for their Protestant faith. By offering them a place of refuge he would be doing his religious duty and at the same time gaining material benefits.

As a means of attracting colonists to his territories the Prussian monarch held out various inducements, including traveling expenses, free land, and in some instances implements, cattle, horses, and funds or materials for building purposes. The response to his invitations exceeded his fondest hopes and expectations. Many colonists came from Switzerland, Russia, Poland, Swabia, Franconia, and Saxony. According to Ranke's estimate [47] no less than 17,000 came during the first fifteen years of the reign. The largest group during the latter part of his reign came from Salzburg. When Frederick William learned that in November, 1731, an order had been published requiring all Protestants to leave the archbishopric of Salzburg within a specified time—eight days for those who owned no land and one, two, or three months for landowners, according to the value of their property—he immediately dispatched agents to invite them to his territories. At the same time he issued a proclamation which offered the Salzburgers pecuniary assistance for the journey to Prussia; also all the rights, privileges, and immunities granted to colonists who had previously migrated to his territories.[48] "Everyone," he stated, "may obtain land, more or less, according to how much he thinks he can cultivate. The king will furnish free of charge the necessary stock of cattle, pigs, and poultry, also carts and the necessary implements for cultivation, or whatever is needed for housekeeping." Moreover, he declared all

[47] *Neun Bücher preussischer Geschichte,* I, 476.
[48] Proclamation reprinted in Hoese and Eichert, *Die Salzburger,* pp. 10–11.

those signifying their intention of migrating to Prussian territory to be Prussian citizens and threatened to demand full satisfaction for any wrong done them.

Soon many Salzburgers were on their way to the Hohenzollern territories. The first group arrived at Potsdam in the spring of 1732 and was welcomed by the king and queen in person. Frederick William, bubbling over with happiness over the arrival of the immigrants, told them again and again: "You will be well off, my children." Their final destination was East Prussia where they were soon joined by others. The total number of Salzburgers who settled there, according to an official count, was 11,989.[49] Most of these settled in the northeastern part of East Prussia, more definitely known as Prussian Lithuania, which they transformed from an unpopulated waste into a flourishing province. While he was still crown prince Frederick the Great visited East Prussia and from there wrote to Voltaire in glowing terms of his father's achievements:

He rebuilt all that the pestilence had laid desolate, and sent for some thousands of families from all parts of Europe. The lands were cleared, the county repeopled; commerce began to flourish and at present the country is more prosperous and fertile than ever. There is more wealth and fruitfulness here than in any part of Germany; for all of which it is indebted to the king alone, who not only planned but also supervised the execution of all these things.[50]

The policy of colonization was on the whole eminently successful. Among those who migrated to the various Prussian provinces there were, of course, some who had been attracted solely by the benefits Frederick William offered and who departed again at the expiration of the period of privilege. But the majority of the colonists were honest and

[49] *Ibid.*   [50] *Œuvres*, XXI, 342.

hardworking. It has been estimated that during the century from 1640 to 1740 the population of the Hohenzollern provinces increased 157 percent and that at least one-fifth of this increase was due to the incoming colonists and their offspring.[51]

Thus Frederick William firmly established that mercantilism which became traditional in the Prussian state. Not only was it carried on by Frederick the Great and his successors; it was also adopted by the government of the German Empire under Bismarck. "Modern German economic policy," Werner F. Bruck writes,[52] "is built up on mercantilism. . . . Expansionism, State protection in all great spheres of production and distribution, including State ownership of various undertakings, and general tutelage of voluntarily obedient inhabitants, marked the development of Germany and especially Prussia from absolutism through constitutionalism up to totalitarianism." More recently the National Socialist state revived the old Prussian mercantilist policy. Like Frederick William, the Nazis organized and supervised the economic life of the nation for the purpose of making Germany prosperous in times of peace and self-sufficient in times of war. It is the policy of *Wehrwirtschaft* which Walter Rathenau, the great protagonist of neo-mercantilism, expressed in the words "All politics is economic politics, or preparedness for war."[53]

[51] See Schmoller, *Umrisse und Untersuchungen*, p. 574.
[52] *Social and Economic History of Germany*, pp. 37–38.
[53] *Zur Kritik der Zeit*, p. 123.

CHAPTER ELEVEN

Frederick William as Diplomatist

FREDERICK WILLIAM'S ability to manage the internal affairs of his realm had no counterpart in his handling of foreign affairs; in fact, his foreign policy, with one exception—the acquisition of Stettin—was an utter failure. The game of diplomacy, as played then, with its cynical code of unabashed intrigue, required a subtler intelligence than that possessed by the Prussian autocrat. He could order his subjects about in his gruff voice and garbled German, but when it was a question of cleverly concealing facts, dexterously parrying verbal attacks, or of relating falsehoods as if they were the veriest truths he was a clumsy amateur. Despite his boast that he could read in a person's eyes whether that person was speaking the truth, he was the easy dupe of his own ministers and courtiers. At one time or another most of his ministers were in the pay of a foreign power, particularly of Austria or of France. When Frederick William discovered this, some curious reluctance forbade him to take action. The French ambassador reported him as saying: "I am aware that many of my people are bribed by France, and I know them all. Well and good! If France wishes to be so foolish as to give them pensions, they have but to accept them. The money will remain in the country, and they and their children will spend it. . . . But they are mistaken if they believe I am not aware of it." [1] The sole reproof he administered was in the form of such comments as these in the margin of ministerial reports: "You are too fond of guineas" or "You are too fond of louis."

The attitude of self-assurance, however, was only a pose. Actually Frederick William was fully conscious of his lack of capacity for foreign affairs, and because he did not feel himself equal to the situation he was subject to irresolution and mental indecision. The object of his foreign policy was, of course, the aggrandizement of Prussia. But he was perpetually uncertain as to the proper means of achieving this object. Neither he nor his ministers had a fixed plan. Though he was always ready to enter into an alliance if he believed it was to his advantage, his lack of self-confidence made him loath to commit himself to definite obligations. No sooner had he done so than he would repent the haste with which he had acted. If after signing a treaty he believed himself to have been duped, and he usually did, he would forthwith seek ways and means of escaping adherence to his commitments. Thus he was at best a half-hearted, fitful ally upon whom no one could depend. There was method in the quick diplomatic shifts of the Great Elector, but in the case of Frederick William they were too often the result of some momentary caprice. When he did change sides because he believed he could make a better bargain, he usually did so at the wrong moment. Hence there is considerable justification for the statement of La Chétardie, the French envoy to Prussia, that Frederick

[1] Cited in Lavisse, *La Jeunesse du Grand Frédéric*, pp. 94–95.

William was "flighty, inconstant, without respect for his commitments." [2]

Had Frederick William been fully alive to the inherent possibilities of his time, with his large army he might well have played a decisive role in foreign politics and consolidated Prussia's position. As it was, the only territorial acquisition of his reign—except for Spanish Gelderland, assigned to Prussia by the treaty of Utrecht (1713)—was the town of Stettin and the adjacent district in western Pomerania. During the Northern War Stettin had been taken from the Swedes after a short siege by a combined force of Russians and Saxons. In the hope that the transaction would draw neutral Prussia to their side, Russia and Saxony agreed to surrender the city they had taken to Frederick William on the condition that he would pay the costs of the siege. But in the next year (1714) Charles XII of Sweden, upon his return from Turkey where he had taken refuge after his disastrous defeat by the army of Peter the Great at Poltava in 1709, would hear nothing of such a transaction. This moved Frederick William to join the enemies of Sweden, and a large force of Prussians, Danes, and Saxons under the command of Leopold of Dessau immediately laid siege to Stralsund, the city in which Charles had shut himself. After a futile resistance the Swedish king fled and the Prussians occupied Swedish Pomerania with Rügen and Stralsund. In the final treaty of peace, concluded in 1720, Sweden ceded Stettin and the adjacent district to Prussia in return for the payment of two million taler.

The key to Frederick William's foreign policy after 1720, particularly to his relations with the emperor, is his

[2] *Recueil des instructions données aux ambassadeurs et ministres de France depuis les traités de Westphalie jusqu'à la Révolution Française*, XVI, lvii.

desire to obtain the duchies of Jülich and Berg for his House upon the extinction of the male line of the house of Neuburg. Jülich and Berg were part of the Cleves inheritance claimed in 1609, the year in which the duke of Cleves died childless, by both the elector of Brandenburg and the duke of Neuburg on the basis of descent from the female line. When the emperor, who wished to confiscate the territory as a vacant fief, sought to push aside the claims of both, the two claimants joined in opposing him.[3] In 1610 these claimants made a provisional settlement by which Wolfgang William of Neuburg received Jülich, Berg, and the seigniory of Ravenstein, while the elector of Brandenburg took Cleves, Mark, and Ravensburg. The final treaty, not concluded until 1666, retained the earlier division, but specified that on the extinction of either of the families the territory was to pass to the other, "to the exclusion of all collateral claims." At that time such an eventuality had appeared remote, but it was imminent in 1720. Charles Philip, the last prince of the house of Neuburg, had only one daughter. This daughter was married to the count of Sulzbach, and to him Charles Philip sought to make over the succession to the duchies of Jülich and Berg. Frederick William, on the other hand, claiming that the treaty of 1666 applied only to male descendants, asserted that the Neuburg line would legally become extinct at the death of Charles Philip. Hence he was determined to claim the duchies by what he regarded as his unquestionable right, and during the rest of his life he spared no effort to gain the support of other nations for his claim.

The second outstanding feature of his foreign policy was his attempt to perpetuate the Hohenzollern tradition of

[3] Henry IV of France was about to intervene in the dispute, when he fell under the dagger of Ravaillac.

friendship with the house of Habsburg. Although he was very careful to assert his rights as an independent sovereign, he was persuaded that the interests of Prussia and Austria were one and that he must therefore give the emperor his loyal support. It was his proud boast that he was the most dependable ally of the Habsburgs. On numerous occasions he proclaimed his loyalty to the emperor in such statements as: "All German princes who are not loyal to the emperor and to the empire are scoundrels." [4] According to Count Seckendorf, the Austrian envoy, he said:

An emperor is necessary; hence we will support the house of Austria. Whoever does not agree with this statement is not an honorable German. . . . No Englishman or Frenchman shall command us Germans. I will give my children pistols and swords in their cradles so they may help keep foreigners out. . . . If the French attack a single village in Germany, that German prince who does not oppose them to the last drop of his blood is a blackguard. [5]

In a letter to Seckendorf Frederick William himself, after avowing his "true friendship" for the emperor, went on to say:

I shall prove on all occasions how sincere my feelings toward the emperor are. For him, his house, and his cause I shall sacrifice with pleasure my blood, possessions and lands. My enemies may do what they will, I will not desert the emperor unless he repulses me with his feet; otherwise I will remain faithful to him until death. [6]

If Frederick William was ready to give the emperor his full support, he expected the emperor's support for his own aims in return. Charles VI, the Habsburg emperor, resenting as he did Frederick William's efforts to strengthen Prussia's position, was certainly of no mind to help the

[4] Förster, *Urkundenbuch*, III, 333.
[5] *Ibid.*, pp. 334–335.　　　　　[6] *Ibid.*, p. 313.

Prussian monarch acquire the duchies of Jülich and Berg. Besides political reasons he also had religious reasons for not wanting them to fall into the hands of the Hohenzollern. The population of Jülich and Berg was predominantly Roman Catholic, Düsseldorf, the capital of Jülich, being a veritable citadel of Roman Catholicism. Hence it was but natural that the emperor as the champion of the Roman Catholic religion in Germany should rather see the Roman Catholic Sulzbachs get the duchies than to have them come under the sway of the strongest Protestant state in Germany. Although the emperor tried to dissemble this fact, it was not long before Frederick William realized that notwithstanding momentary blandishments the Austrian policy was sharply and continually directed against Prussia. The result was that the relations between the two courts were strained almost constantly. The Prussian monarch complained that even in legal cases adjudged by the *Reichshofrat* (Imperial Aulic Council) the decisions were invariably against Prussia and that in many cases the decisions were made without due consideration of the evidence favoring Prussia. "All the rights of this house," Frederick William stated, "even whole provinces and territories which we do now hold, are made the subject of dispute and doubt." [7] Furthermore, Frederick William also feared that the systematic persecution of the Protestants in Poland and in the Palatinate presaged the formation of a new Roman Catholic league under the leadership of the emperor.

All this paved the way for an alliance between Prussia and Great Britain. The initiative in the matter was taken by George I and Lord Townshend, his minister. As the latter put it in a letter to Sir Robert Walpole: "A neighboring prince so nearly related, so well affected to the Protestant

[7] Ranke, *Neun Bücher preussischer Geschichte*, I, 204.

cause, who has a standing army of eighty thousand men and such an extent of dominions as the king of Prussia, is certainly worth gaining." [8] On the Prussian side Queen Sophie Dorothea was ardently in favor of a close alliance between Great Britain and Prussia; in fact she had her heart set on a double marriage alliance between the two royal houses. This latter plan she discussed with George I, her father, during the summer of 1723 while they were together in Hanover. Frederick William himself was still somewhat reluctant to enter into a treaty with the house of Hanover. Happy at first over the accession of his father-in-law to the British throne, the Prussian king had become increasingly jealous upon realizing that George I had become a more prominent and more powerful monarch than himself. But when the British ruler visited Berlin at the end of the summer of 1723 this feeling was allayed sufficiently to remove Frederick William's opposition to an alliance with Great Britain. The treaty, signed at Charlottenburg in October of the same year, was purely defensive, but in a secret article the British ruler promised to support the Prussian claims to Jülich and Berg if the male line of the house of Neuburg should become extinct.[9] There was actually nothing new in the article on Jülich and Berg; it was but a renewal of the obligations stipulated in the treaties of 1661 and 1690. Nor did the treaty make any mention of the double marriage which was so eagerly desired by the Prussian queen.

Meanwhile Emperor Charles VI had an axe of his own to grind in the matter of insuring the succession of his eldest daughter to the rule of the Habsburg dominions,

[8] Letter in *Memoirs of Sir Robert Walpole*, II, 266.

[9] Text of the treaty including the secret article is to be found in Loewe, *Preussens Staatsverträge aus der Regierungszeit König Friedrich Wilhelms I*, pp. 278 et sqq.

which included (besides Austria) Hungary, Bohemia, Silesia, Moravia, Styria, Carinthia, and the Tyrol. As he had no sons, he feared that his house, like that of the Spanish Habsburgs after the death of Charles II in 1700, would become extinct and the Habsburg territories would be divided into separate units. As early as 1713 he had informed his privy councillors and dignitaries that in default of male heirs he desired his kingdoms and territories to pass undivided to his eldest daughter. After his only son died, in 1716, and since it appeared that he would have no more children, he formally decreed the succession of his daughter in 1720. During the succeeding years this decree, called the Pragmatic Sanction, was recognized by the various Estates of the Habsburg dominions.[10] Furthermore, to decrease the likelihood that the validity of his decree would be challenged by his nieces, the daughters of the former Emperor Joseph I, he compelled the latter to renounce their claims when they married, respectively, the electors of Bavaria and of Saxony. Nevertheless, he was aware that, however sincere the renunciation of the wives, the husbands would be eager to share in a division of the Habsburg territories. Hence he decided to procure, if possible, a guarantee of the Pragmatic Sanction from each of the European states. This object soon became the center about which the foreign policy of Charles VI revolved. He was ready to pay a high price for such a guarantee of the Pragmatic Sanction and when necessary to sacrifice every other consideration to its attainment.

The first guarantor of the Pragmatic Sanction was Philip V, the successful rival of Charles VI for the Spanish throne.

---

[10] The whole complex question of the Pragmatic Sanction is ably discussed by W. Michael in *Das Original der Pragmatischen Sanktion Karls VI.*

The long war of the Spanish Succession (1700–1713) had been fought over the rival claims of the two to the Spanish throne, and even the treaty of Utrecht had failed to reconcile the claimants. On the one hand Charles VI still refused to recognize Philip as the legitimate ruler of Spain; on the other, Philip could not bring himself to sanction the transfer of so large a part of the Spanish possessions to the Habsburgs. But circumstances now drew the two monarchs together. Charles wanted support for his Pragmatic Sanction, and Philip, for his part, needed an ally. Not only was the Spanish ruler on hostile terms with Great Britain and the Dutch Netherlands, but his plans for an alliance with France had also been frustrated when the duke of Bourbon, who was then regent of France, betrothed his young ward, Louis XV, to Marie, the daughter of Stanislaus Lesczinski of Poland, thereby repudiating the Spanish Infanta. Regarding this as an insult, Philip made overtures to the emperor for an alliance, and in 1725 the two monarchs signed the treaty of Vienna. In it Charles renounced his claims to the Spanish throne and Philip guaranteed the Pragmatic Sanction; also, mutual assistance was pledged in case of war.

The news that Charles VI and Philip V, implacable enemies for a quarter century, had composed their differences and entered into an alliance startled both Great Britain and France. It was feared that with the support of Spain the house of Habsburg might again attain to the ascendancy it had enjoyed in Europe under Charles V. There were even rumors of a matrimonial alliance which might result in the reunion of the Spanish and Austrian monarchies. These apprehensions caused France and Great Britain to form an alliance to counteract that of Vienna and then to set about trying to gain the support of the smaller nations of Europe, particularly of Prussia, for it. The task of drawing Prussia into the alliance was assigned to Great Britain. Negotiations were opened in the summer of 1725, when George I, together with Lord Townshend, conferred with Frederick William and Sophie Dorothea at Hanover. The Prussian queen, whose eagerness to join the two houses by a double marriage has already been mentioned, hoped this time to obtain from her father a positive promise. But also Frederick William had a number of reasons for lending a willing ear to the enemies of the imperial house. Besides being convinced that the balance of power was in danger, he was also disturbed over the plight of the Protestants in various parts of the empire and in Poland. Townshend, who knew how greatly the plight of the persecuted Protestants grieved the Prussian monarch, did not fail to play on his fears regarding the future of Protestantism. Furthermore, if the reports of the English representative at Berlin can be credited, Frederick William was also much alarmed because he believed that secret articles directed against the liberties of the empire had been drawn up and signed by Charles VI and Philip V.

These factors helped to banish for the time being Frederick William's scruples against entering into an alliance pointedly directed against Austria, and hence the tripartite treaty was signed at Hanover in October, 1725.[11] Its most important article was the second, in which the three powers reciprocally guaranteed all possessions "both inside and outside of Europe" held by each of the allies at the time the treaty was signed; also all "rights, immunities, and privileges, particularly those relating to trade which the said allies respectively enjoy or ought to enjoy." The two articles especially pleasing to Frederick William were those

[11] Text in Loewe, *Preussens Staatsverträge aus der Regierungszeit König Friedrich Wilhelms I*, pp. 285–294.

guaranteeing to the states of Germany the privileges and liberties accorded them in the treaty of Westphalia and to the Polish Protestants the liberties granted them in the treaty of Oliva. In case of war Great Britain and France were each to furnish twelve thousand troops, while Prussia was to furnish five thousand. But "in case of need the said allies shall assist the injured party with all their forces." Finally, the fourth article forbade any party to enter into "any treaty, alliance, or engagement whatsoever which may in any manner whatever be contrary to the interests of each other." They were "even faithfully to communicate to each other any proposal that may be made to them and not to take, upon what may be proposed, any resolution otherwise than in concert together and after a joint examination of what may conduce to their common interests."

Lord Townshend would hardly have induced Frederick William to join the alliance had he not been ready to renew the promise that England would support Prussia's claims to the duchies of Jülich and Berg and to assure the Prussian king that France would also support them. Accordingly, as a special concession to Frederick William, a secret article was added in which both Great Britain and France promised to prevent the sequestration of the disputed duchies on the death of Charles Philip of Neuburg and to endeavor to persuade the interested parties to submit their claims to arbitration before a neutral tribunal. Regarding this question Townshend wrote to Walpole:

You may well imagine that the secret article concerning the succession of Juliers (Jülich) and Berg was the chief bait that drew the king of Prussia into this alliance. You will therefore dispose the court of France not to make any objections to the said article; which is in effect no more than a confirmation of the 14th article of the treaty by which the Elector Palatine himself holds these duchys, and, to which, in truth, the king of Prussia has a right to demand our guaranty.[12]

Despite this guarantee Frederick William's adherence to the anti-Austrian party was brief. Hardly had he signed the treaty of Hanover when he began to repent the haste with which he had acted. His loyalty to the empire and the emperor came to the fore again, causing him to wonder whether his association with the enemies of the empire was not a form of treason to Germany and whether an attack on the empire might not result in the destruction of the rights of the German princes. More than this, he began to wonder whether the French and the British were not using him simply to further their own ends; in his words, "as a catspaw to pull the chestnuts out of the fire." [13] He began to fear that he might have to fight for objects in which he had no interest. Above all, he realized that if war broke out he would have to bear the brunt of it, for his territories were exposed to invasion by the Austrian armies, while England was protected by the sea and France by the line of forts Vauban had built. Nor was he alone in his doubts; some of his ministers also believed that the move had not been a judicious one. Particularly frank in his disapproval of it was Ilgen, the minister of foreign affairs, who had been opposed to the alliance from the start. Ilgen told his master that since it was extremely doubtful that France and England could defend him against any attack by the Austrian armies the risks exceeded any possible advantage Prussia might derive from the anti-Austrian alliance.

Thus the Prussian monarch was ready for the persuasive influence of Count Seckendorf, whom the imperial court

[12] Cited in Chance, *The Alliance of Hanover*, p. 64.
[13] Förster, *Urkundenbuch*, II, 64.

sent to Berlin for the express purpose of detaching Frederick William from the anti-Austrian league and of binding him to the house of Habsburg. The emperor was most anxious at the time to gain the support of Prussia for the Pragmatic Sanction. He believed that the recognition of this decree by one of the most powerful princes of the empire should induce the other princes to give it their support. Before Frederick William had signed the treaty with Great Britain and France the court of Vienna knew what was transpiring at Hanover. The emperor, as soon as he received the information, commissioned Seckendorf to go to Hanover for the purpose of finding out, if possible, what the conditions of the alliance were. Seckendorf went at once on the pretext of trying to obtain the post of Master-General of Imperial Ordnance, and he soon managed to ferret out the contents of the treaty. Despite the secrecy which was supposed to cover the agreement regarding the Jülich-Berg question, Seckendorf was able to report to Prince Eugene on the eleventh of October, the day before the final signature of the treaty: "I can report this much, that I have been assured one of the most important secret articles is a guarantee of Jülich and Berg to the king of Prussia." [14] Thereupon the emperor ordered Seckendorf to Berlin "to work on the king and to induce him to entertain better thoughts, which of course must be done in a natural and unaffected way." [15]

Seckendorf was not a stranger to the Prussian king. The two had met as far back as 1709, and a warm friendship had grown up between them. During the subsequent period they had corresponded occasionally, and at intervals Seckendorf had come to Berlin, usually with a secret commission on be-

[14] Förster, *Urkundenbuch*, II, 51.
[15] Full instructions to Seckendorf in Förster, *Urkundenbuch*, II, 101–113.

half of the imperial court. Now, in 1726, he settled permanently in Berlin, and soon afterward he became the imperial ambassador to the Prussian court. No person was probably better fitted for the task of bringing Frederick William back into the Austrian fold. Of pleasing appearance, Seckendorf also possessed considerable shrewdness and tact, cultivated during long years of diplomatic service. What was even more important, he thoroughly understood the whims and peculiarities of the Prussian monarch and knew how to cater to them. In consequence he enjoyed the full confidence and the marked favor of Frederick William. How well he knew the king can be seen in the letters he wrote to Prince Eugene from Berlin. In one, for example, he stated: "In Berlin the principal point is, to know the humor of the king and, as his temper is very quick, to avoid meeting its first outburst. This being over, he is accessible to any reasonable representations." [16] Besides having a thorough knowledge of the Prussian ruler, Seckendorf was intimately acquainted with the conditions at the Prussian court and also with most persons attached to it. This enabled him to keep informed of all court happenings.

Seckendorf's principal assistant was General von Grumbkow who was at the same time the most intimate of Frederick William's advisors and in some respects the ablest man at the Prussian court. To him the Prussian monarch confided most of his plans and projects, carefully pondering whatever advice this minister gave him. Grumbkow was, in fact, almost the only man whose objections the king would tolerate. He was a man of affable manners, with a personality that could adapt itself to all occasions, whether joyful or serious. However, this pleasant exterior served as a mask to cover a heart that was perfidious and a conscience wholly devoid of

[16] *Ibid.*, p. 10.

scruple. Wilhelmina, the eldest daughter of Frederick William, had considerable justification for describing his character as "a tissue of vices." Grumbkow had sold himself to the Austrian court in 1724 for an annual stipend of a thousand ducats and thereafter had systematically revealed to Seckendorf all the information he could gather from the king and about him.[17] The letters of Grumbkow show that nothing was so secret or so confidential that he did not betray it to the Austrian envoy.

With the help of Grumbkow the adroit Seckendorf soon succeeded in getting Frederick William to renew his old alliance with the emperor. An important inducement to the Prussian militarist was the permission to levy recruits in the Austrian dominions; but the principal bait was the promise to support Prussia's claim to at least a part of the disputed territory of Jülich and Berg. At first Frederick William had demanded both duchies; however, Seckendorf, at the behest of the emperor, had induced him to modify his demands. After signifying his willingness to accept a compromise which would give Jülich to the house of Sulzbach, while Prussia was to receive Berg and the seigniory of Ravenstein, the Prussian ruler refused to retreat any farther. To Seckendorf, who sought to exclude the question from the treaty entirely, he firmly stated that this was the *conditio sine qua non* of any treaty of alliance. Though the emperor was loath to make any promises regarding Jülich and Berg, he finally yielded. In the treaty signed at Wusterhausen [18] in October, 1726, Frederick William not only guaranteed the Pragmatic Sanction but also agreed to abandon the alliance with Great Britain and France and to support the emperor if he should be

[17] *Ibid.*, III, 325.
[18] Text in Loewe, *Preussens Staatsverträge aus der Regierungszeit König Friedrich Wilhelms I*, pp. 311–322.

attacked in Germany. In return the emperor made certain vague promises to support the compromise according to which Jülich should be inherited by the Sulzbachs, Berg and Ravenstein by Prussia. Furthermore, the emperor promised to obtain the consent of the Elector Palatine to this agreement within six months; if he did not, the whole treaty was to be considered null and void. Thus within a year after concluding the alliance with Great Britain and France, Frederick William had not only abandoned it but even aligned himself definitely with the opposition. And this despite the stipulations which prohibited him from concluding any other treaty or entering into any other alliance or engagement without the consent of the others.

Having won Frederick William to the side of Austria, Seckendorf had to exercise his ingenuity to keep him there. He knew how unstable the king's temperament was and feared that someone might reveal to him how empty the Austrian promises were. Hence he tried to be near Frederick William as much as possible. Whether the Prussian monarch was on the parade ground, at dinner, on a hunting trip, or in his Tobacco Parliament, Seckendorf was usually beside him. "One must be in the company of the king," he wrote to Prince Eugene, "from ten in the morning until eleven or twelve at night if one does not want to miss an opportunity to make the proper insinuations." [19] But Frederick William's daily routine was so strenuous that Seckendorf could not endure the pace. After some months he was compelled to take a vacation because, as he wrote to Prince Eugene, "it is hardly possible to endure perpetually the fatigues of attendance upon this lord." [20] When he was absent from the Prussian court, Seckendorf indulged Frederick William's tastes by sending him Italian truffles, Dresden fieldfares, and tall

[19] Förster, *Urkundenbuch*, II, 75.   [20] *Ibid.*, p. 200.

grenadiers. To keep himself minutely informed of everything that went on at the Prussian court the Austrian envoy bribed every person about the king who was willing to accept a bribe. Gundling, the "court fool," was bribed with a medallion set with diamonds, and even the Prussian envoy to London was induced to send false reports to Berlin so as to prevent a *rapprochement* with England.[21] In addition Seckendorf also bribed certain officers of the army by gifts of tall recruits. In November, 1726, for example, he begs Prince Eugene to send him thirty-two tall recruits "so that I may content those officers who have declared themselves to be my friends and whose friendship I cannot dispense with; for these people who might refuse a present of one hundred to one thousand ducats will accept several tall recruits for their companies with the greatest of pleasure, because they are unable to get them in any other way." [22] Thus in one way or another Seckendorf bribed a great number of persons, from influential favorites down to the personal valets of the king, to aid him in "keeping watch" over Frederick William.

There was need of constant vigilance on the part of Seckendorf. As the weeks passed without any report from the emperor regarding the negotiations he was supposed to be carrying on with the Elector Palatine Charles Philip, Frederick William's doubts regarding the emperor's sincerity began to assert themselves. He repeatedly told the Austrian envoy that he was ready to be a faithful ally if the emperor would only do something toward carrying out his agreement regarding the disputed duchies.

You will declare to the emperor that if he does not maintain me in the possession of Berg, [Frederick William stated] or appoint some equivalent, I do not hold myself bound by the treaty, and I will depart from it; for I do everything willingly for the

---

[21] *Ibid.*, II, 172; III, 326.   [22] *Ibid.*, II, 190.

emperor and it appears as if I shall do it all for nothing and in great uncertainty; truly, I will not do it.[23]

Seckendorf himself wrote regarding the Prussian monarch's state of mind: "This matter disturbs the king very much, and since three months have passed and nothing has been done, he is beginning to fear that nothing will come of the matter." [24] Frederick William's eagerness to get the other party to agree to a compromise was stimulated by the fact that he was not at all sure his claims even to a part of the disputed territory were just from a legal point of view. As Seckendorf put it; "Someone has convinced him that unless the house of Sulzbach cedes the territory to him he cannot be certain." [25]

The king's doubts regarding the sincerity of Austria were also being nourished from another side. No less a person than the Prussian queen herself was bitterly opposed to the Austrian alliance. Seckendorf, since he was endeavoring to frustrate her most cherished plans for the English marriage alliance, was distinctly *persona non grata* with her. He himself wrote: "My face is so odious to the queen that it is often very difficult to get her to answer my questions." [26] Sophie Dorothea had collected about her an anti-Austrian party, which included her children and several of the royal ministers, and she was ready to do almost anything to prevent a closer alliance with Austria. Seckendorf had even heard reports that the queen and her children were ready, as a last resort, to throw themselves at the feet of the king and tearfully beg him to fulfill their wishes regarding the marriage alliance with England. The queen herself missed no opportunity to counteract the influence of the Austrian party. On one occasion, for example, when the king declared to an

[23] Ranke, *Neun Bücher preussischer Geschichte*, I, 238.
[24] Förster, *Urkundenbuch*, III, 341.
[25] *Ibid.*, p. 375.　　　[26] *Ibid.*, p. 347.

assembly that he favored the cause of the emperor, she replied: "I will yet live to make you unbelievers believe and to show you that you have been deceived." [27]

Despite the opposition of the queen and her party Seckendorf's diplomacy prevailed. The treaty of Wusterhausen was never ratified, but the Austrian envoy soon opened negotiations for a new treaty. In 1726 Charles VI had guaranteed Jülich and Berg to the house of Sulzbach in return for its acceptance of the Pragmatic Sanction, promising to uphold this guarantee with all the forces at his command.[28] The international situation was such, however, that he desperately needed the support of Prussia; hence he wrote to his envoy in Berlin: "We are determined to bring the king to our side by any means whatsoever in order to secure his help and support for us and for the common fatherland in these perilous circumstances." [29] The immediate result was that Seckendorf again regaled the Prussian monarch with empty promises. His efforts were so successful that a new treaty was concluded at Berlin between Prussia and Austria in December, 1728.[30] In general this treaty was a renewal of the agreement of Wusterhausen, but the stipulations were made more definite. In the first main article the rulers guaranteed each other's possessions, the emperor pledging himself to furnish twelve thousand men and Frederick William ten thousand troops in case of war. Regarding the Jülich-Berg question the emperor promised to support the Prussian claims to Berg and Ravenstein "most vigorously" in case they were disputed. But as he had promised exactly the opposite to the

[27] Förster, *Friedrich Wilhelm I*, III, 337.

[28] The pertinent articles of the treaty are cited in Droysen, *Geschichte der preussischen Politik*, IV (Part 2), 452.

[29] Förster, *Urkundenbuch*, III, 381.

[30] Text of treaty in Loewe, *Preussens Staatsverträge aus der Regierungszeit König Friedrich Wilhelms I*, pp. 360–373.

house of Sulzbach, he added the specification "that this entire agreement, including all its points, clauses and articles, is to be kept in the strictest secrecy not only from the house of Neuburg but also from everyone else." Frederick William, for his part, guaranteed the Pragmatic Sanction and further pledged himself to give the Prussian vote in the next imperial election "to that prince of German descent whom the archduchess will marry." To make certain that his position was clear the Prussian ruler specifically stated in the margin of the treaty that if the archduchess of Austria should marry a Spaniard or a Frenchman he would not cast his vote for him.

In 1730, just when the Austrian influence was strongest at the Prussian court, the British government sent Sir Charles Hotham to Berlin to undermine it, if possible, by concluding the marriage alliance the Prussian queen so greatly desired. Frederick William was not averse to marrying his eldest daughter to the Prince of Wales, much to the amazement and consternation of the Austrian party, but he was unwilling to enter into an agreement regarding the marriage of the Prussian crown prince. Finally, after long negotiations had failed to influence the king's decision, Hotham had recourse to a bold stroke by which he hoped to destroy the Austrian influence. Having obtained possession of intercepted letters which gave incontestible proof of the unfaithfulness of Grumbkow and of Reichenbach, the Prussian envoy to London, he put them into the king's hands during one of his audiences. But Frederick William, instead of thanking Hotham for the disclosures, greatly resented what he regarded as the interference of a foreign government in his affairs. Flying into a rage, he threw the letters into the face of the British ambassador, and even made as if to kick him. Without doing so, however, he rushed from the room, slamming the

door behind him. Later the king repented his conduct and
sent the Dutch and Danish ambassadors to assure Hotham
that he had not meant to insult him. Von Borcke, a cabinet
minister, also apologized to Hotham for the irascible monarch's conduct, but the negotiations were not resumed. The
British envoy soon requested his letters of dismissal and departed for England.

The Austrian party had won again, but it was a short-
lived triumph. When the imperial court made no attempt to
translate its promises regarding the duchy of Berg into action,
Frederick William's doubts began to reassert themselves. In
1732 he still demonstrated his dogged loyalty to the emperor
by using his influence to help gain acceptance of the Pragmatic Sanction by the imperial diet over the protests of
Bavaria, Saxony, and the Palatinate. Soon after that, however, Charles VI's conduct in the controversy over the Polish
succession contributed greatly toward alienating the Prussian ruler from Austria. In 1733, upon the death of Augustus
II of Saxony, who had also been king of Poland, Stanislaus
Lesczynski [31] endeavored, with the support of his son-in-
law, Louis XV, to reclaim the Polish throne. The emperor,
on the other hand, took up the cause of Augustus III, son of
the dead king, because he had promised to recognize the
Pragmatic Sanction and also because the Habsburgs were
opposed to French interference in Poland. The Prussian
monarch thought the time had now come for him to force
the emperor's hand. As early as 1726 Seckendorf had written: "The king of Prussia, who is very restive, said to me
that when the king of Poland dies he will know if the friendship of His Imperial Majesty for him is sincere, that is, if he

[31] Stanislaus, it will be remembered, had been made king of Poland by Charles XII of Sweden, but had been driven from the
Polish throne after the defeat and death of the Swedish king.

will join him in electing another king." [32] Frederick William
was eager to prevent the election of Augustus III because he
believed the union of Saxony and Poland to be disadvanta-
geous to Prussia. A little firmness on his part, he believed,
would draw the emperor to his side. On October 30, 1733, he
wrote to Old Dessauer: "I shall put myself on a different
footing with the emperor and not show myself very meek in
order to try whether this will do better than civil and fair
words. He has need of me and dares not show it." [33] When
it appeared that war would break out between France and
the empire over the question of the Polish succession, the
Prussian monarch wrote to his representative at the diet of
Regensburg: "I will give neither men nor money; I must
know the whence and the whither." [34]

Once more Frederick William's loyalty to the emperor
caused him to weaken. When the war broke out, he discharged his treaty obligations to the empire by sending the
stipulated ten thousand men. He even went so far as to offer
thirty or forty thousand troops in return for a confirmation
of his claims to Berg and Ravenstein. But to his great surprise
the emperor declined the offer. Soon after this Seckendorf
was recalled from Berlin, and all Prussian recruiting agents
were ordered to leave the imperial states. These acts angered
Frederick William so greatly that he wrote a letter recalling
the Prussian ambassador from Vienna, but Grumbkow persuaded him not to send it. In 1735 Charles VI further alien-
ated the Prussian ruler by not inviting him to the peace negotiations between Austria and France; in fact, he did not
inform Frederick William of the contents of the treaty until
after it was signed. The latter first learned of them through

[32] Förster, *Urkundenbuch*, II, 205.
[33] *Briefe an Leopold zu Anhalt-Dessau*, p. 522.
[34] Förster, *Friedrich Wilhelm I*, II, 139–140.

the newspapers. Moreover, the emperor did not even inform him of the marriage of his daughter, Maria Theresa, to the duke of Lorraine. In short, feeling that it could dispense with Prussian aid, the Austrian court had abandoned Frederick William entirely. Now it finally became evident to the dull-witted king that Charles VI had been playing fast and loose with him; that the pledges the emperor had made were entirely worthless. The thought that he had been a victim of gross deception and that his plans for the acquisition of Berg and Ravenstein were shattered depressed him so that he became seriously ill. His only comfort was the hope that his son would one day avenge the perfidy of Austria. Pointing to the ill-used crown prince one day before a gathering at Potsdam, he exclaimed: "Here is one who will avenge me," [35] a prophecy which Frederick the Great literally and generously fulfilled.

But Frederick William still did not feel that the occasion for him to do something about his claims to Berg and Ravenstein was irrevocably gone. When his health improved somewhat, he made another attempt to strengthen them. After Austria joined Russia in the war against Turkey in 1737 he offered to lend the court of Vienna a considerable sum of money on the condition that the stipulations regarding Berg and Ravenstein which had been included in the treaty of 1728 be renewed. Even this offer was refused. Next Frederick William tried to conclude an agreement with the Elector Palatine for the cession of Berg and Ravenstein to Prussia in return for the payment of twelve hundred thousand taler to the elector himself and fifty thousand to each of his daughters. The old elector, however, was too devoutly Roman Catholic to consider the proposal. Frederick William's disillusionment became even more bitter when the emperor

[35] *Ibid.*, p. 152.

proposed to France, Great Britain, and Holland, in 1737, that provisional possession of the disputed territory be accorded to the house of Sulzbach.

Convinced that he could hope for no assistance from Austria, the Prussian king finally turned to France. Such a complete change of policy must have been abhorrent to his German patriotism, but it was his only hope for the acquisition of Berg. Cardinal Fleury, the regent of France, had no intention of yielding the duchy to Prussia. Besides being closely bound up with both Roman Catholicism and the house of Neuburg, he was also convinced that possession of territory along the Rhine by a state as powerful as Prussia would be a perpetual danger to France. On the other hand, he was eager to secure himself against the hostility of Prussia in case he should become involved in the war that was impending between Great Britain and Spain. Hence he offered Prussia a treaty, the provisions of which regarding Berg were much the same as those contained in the Austro-Prussian treaty of 1728. In other words, Fleury pledged himself to induce the Elector Palatine to accept an arrangement according to which Prussia was to get most of the duchy of Berg and the whole of the seigniory of Ravenstein. Frederick William, in return, promised to make common cause with France in European politics and to support France in case of war, the extent of the support to be decided later. The treaty was signed in April, 1739, in the most profound secrecy, because in the preceding January Fleury had concluded a secret treaty with Austria [36] which provided that upon the death of Charles Philip the house of Sulzbach was to rule Jülich and Berg for a period of two years and that no other power be allowed to take possession during this time. The deception

[36] For the broader diplomatic history of the period see Arthur M. Wilson's able study, *French Foreign Policy, 1726–1743.*

by Fleury constituted the final failure of Frederick William's foreign policy. He who had organized a large army as an instrument of power politics lacked the ability to use this instrument as a means of gaining prestige, to say nothing of territory. Excepting the Napoleonic period, the history of Prussia offers no parallel to the humiliations that Frederick William suffered at the hands of Austria and France.

The Prussian monarch did not live long enough to see the extinction of the Neuburg branch, for Charles Philip survived him by two years. When the Elector Palatine did die, Frederick the Great, having conquered Silesia, abandoned his claim to Jülich and Berg. During the ensuing period the duchies were ruled by various lines until 1815 when the Congress of Vienna awarded them to Prussia.

CHAPTER TWELVE

Frederick William Militarizes His Son

FREDERICK WILLIAM, as previously stated, lacked the gentler virtues which make for a happy domestic life; consequently tempestuous scenes were frequent in the royal household. It is true that the early years of his married life with Sophie Dorothea, whom he affectionately called Fieckchen, were comparatively calm and happy, marred by only occasional rifts. During this period he even permitted his consort a certain share in the government. When shortly after becoming king he had to absent himself in order to participate in the campaign against Charles XII, he left the following order for his ministers: "My wife is to be informed of everything, and her counsel is to be sought in all matters." [1] But as the years passed the differences in the natures and inclinations of the two became more and more apparent, giving rise to more frequent disagreements. Although the queen was in some respects a model of marital fidelity, bearing her husband no less than fourteen children,[2] she had

[1] *AB, Beh.*, II, 232.

[2] Most of the children were daughters. After the birth of the sixth daughter Frederick William, to whom a son would have been much more welcome, wrote to Leopold of Dessau: "This seems to be the age for girls. Yesterday another came into the world. I shall open a convent for which you could also furnish some nuns. One must either

little in common with her husband. Having been brought up at the splendid court of Hanover, she found the royal Prussian household with its lack of refinement little to her taste. A woman of her position, she believed, should have more of the amenities of life. Usually she would spend on her household and her children a sum greater than the king had stipulated. If she told him, he would upbraid her for her extravagance. When on one such occasion he asked her the price of eggs and she replied that she did not know, he, it is reported, said: "After I am gone you will die on the dunghill." In general she found the stern and parsimonious life Frederick William prescribed for her most galling, so much so that she wrote: "When one is contented and everything looks bright, one takes a different view of life than when one is always oppressed." [3]

In contradistinction to her husband, the queen loved culture and education. When he was absent she would often indulge her love of music and cultured society by inviting distinguished musicians or men of learning to the palace for a musical evening or for discussions on learned subjects. Furthermore she desired her children to acquire more culture than their father had and therefore encouraged them to follow forbidden pursuits. When Frederick William discovered these things he became greatly incensed. A despot by nature, he demanded as absolute obedience from his wife and his children as he did from his soldiers. Moreover, he believed that they should have no other tastes and ideas than his. If he discovered any manifestations to the contrary, he would vent his ill humor on any or all members of

---

drown them or make nuns out of them. They certainly will not all get husbands."—(*Briefe an Leopold zu Anhalt-Dessau*, p. 171.) Later when he did conclude marriages for them, he gave little consideration to their own inclinations.

[3] Förster, *Friedrich Wilhelm I*, III, 111.

the family. Consequently the home life of the royal family was clouded much of the time by quarrels and contentions; in fact, after some years of married life the king and the queen were almost always at loggerheads. To make matters worse, both had favorites who did not hesitate, if it was to their advantage, to aggravate the differences between the royal pair. The result was an atmosphere of contention, distrust, and suspicion in which the children became the shuttlecocks of the jealousies and disagreements of the parents.

The children most affected by the disharmony of the royal pair were the two eldest, Wilhelmina and Frederick. As the confidants of their mother they heard her many grievances and complaints and from them could not fail to conclude that their parents differed on almost every point. More than this, the queen gradually instilled in them a deep dissatisfaction with their mode of life by telling them that royal children should be better housed and dressed or by secretly giving them tidbits that were forbidden as luxuries by the king. Later she encouraged them, at least tacitly, if not overtly, in their opposition to the king. On occasion she even plotted with them to thwart the purposes of Frederick William. These things did not long remain secret from the king, for servants and others, eager to ingratiate themselves with him, conscientiously reported everything that was said or done in the queen's apartments. Wilhelmina herself has left in her *Memoirs* an account of the furious outbursts of the king over his discoveries. Her account must, however, be used with care, for her statements do not always rest on facts. Some of the purported incidents she relates are either grossly exaggerated or are even pure fiction. The whole account is tinged with a bitterness generated by the frustration of her hopes of being queen of England and by her disappointment in a marriage her father forced upon her. There is, nevertheless, considerable truth in her statement: "The pains of purgatory could not equal what we endured."

The member of the family who was the special target of Frederick William's resentment was the crown prince, later to be known as Frederick the Great. Before Frederick was born it was feared for a time that the male line of the Hohenzollern might end with Frederick William, for of the first three children born to him and his wife only Wilhelmina survived, the two sons having died soon after birth. These fears were aggravated by the fact that within a short period of time Louis XIV witnessed the death of his son, his nephew, his grandsons, and a great-grandson. Frederick I, who was still king at the time, wrote: "What a sad disappointment after everything had gone so well, that he must see his house die out and has no hope for heirs. I confess I would be inconsolable." [4] But the fears were dispelled by the birth of a son to Frederick William and Sophie Dorothea on the twenty-fourth of January, 1712. The father of the child was so overjoyed that he would have stifled it with caresses had not a resolute nurse snatched it from his rude embrace. As all the hopes of the house of Hohenzollern, particularly those of Frederick William, were centered in little Frederick, the father devoted himself conscientiously to the training of his son. He chose the lad's tutors with care, laid down precise rules for their guidance, and himself superintended his education. Since Frederick William always placed the interests of the State above everything else, he regarded little Frederick, above all, as the future head of the Prussian state and only secondarily as his son.

Frederick William ardently desired his heir to preserve and to carry out the work he himself had started; hence he

---

[4] *Aus dem Briefwechsel König Friedrichs I von Preussen und seiner Familie*, I, 271.

left nothing untried in order to mold him to his own ideas and sentiments, to imbue him with his own likes and dislikes, his own hopes and ambitions. In other words, he tried to make the prince royal an exact duplicate of himself. The Emperor William II wrote of his ancestor: "The king was deeply conscious of his mission, of his duty to his people and his country. He regarded it as a God-given mission for the completion of which he had to put everything at stake and to override all opposition. Hence he was animated by the single thought: 'Fritz must be just like me.' " [5] To this end the child was entrusted to the care of Madame de Rocoulle, who had also been Frederick William's governess. When he reached the age of six, two military men, General von Finkenstein and Colonel von Kalkstein, both of whom had distinguished themselves in the Prussian service, were chosen to direct his education. The actual instructor of the prince royal was Duhan de Jandun, the son of a French refugee, who by his bravery during the siege of Stralsund had first attracted the attention of the king. All three were men of considerable intellectual attainments, but of this fact Frederick William took little account. The merits for which he chose them were their achievements as soldiers, their conduct under fire. Being militarists, they would, the king hoped, make a militarist of his son.

For their guidance Frederick William furnished the preceptors with a long memorandum setting forth in elaborate detail the program of studies young Frederick was to follow.[6] In the main the plan was a revision and an adaptation of the instructions his father had prepared for his own education. As he was determined that only positive and useful knowledge was to be imparted to his son, he rigorously inter-

[5] William II, *Meine Vorfahren*, p. 82.
[6] Instructions in Cramer, *Zur Geschichte Friedrich Wilhelms I und Friedrichs II*, pp. 3–25.

dicted all studies he regarded as "useless or frivolous." Thus, for example, he forbade the study of Latin. "As for the Latin language," he wrote, "my son shall not learn it." [7] He gave no reasons for the prohibition, but to forestall any questions added: "I further desire that no one make mention of this matter to me." But the instructors were to see that his son developed "an elegant style in French as well as in German," a goal which Frederick never attained. In the sciences the instruction was to be confined to the practical, with special emphasis on arithmetic, the science of artillery, and political science. Since he regarded the knowledge of ancient history as "useless pedantry," the subject was forbidden. Careful attention, however, was to be given to the events of the century and a half preceding his time, particularly to the history of the house of Brandenburg and the houses with which it was intimately connected.

The specific object of Frederick William's plan of instruction was threefold. He desired his son to be a good Christian, a good administrator, and a good soldier. The task of making young Frederick a good Christian was entrusted to two of the court chaplains. According to the instructions they were to instill in his mind "a holy fear and veneration of God, for this is the only means of keeping the sovereign power, ex-

---

[7] *Ibid.*, pp. 13–14. Frederick later stated on various occasions that he did have a teacher who instructed him in Latin. One day, however, his father unexpectedly entered the room during the Latin lesson and asked the teacher: "What are you doing with my son?" "Your majesty, I am explaining the *auream bullam* (Golden Bull) to the prince," the teacher replied. Raising his cane the king angrily exclaimed: "I will *auream bullam* you, you scoundrel" and put an end to the Latin lessons. Later in life Frederick was fond of using Latin phrases, right or wrong, both in writing and speaking. Among his favorite expressions were: *non plus ultra* (sic!), *de gustibus non est disputandus* (sic!), *festina lente* and *dominus vobiscum*. See Catt, *Unterhaltungen mit Friedrich dem Grossen*, p. 34; Preuss, *Friedrich der Grosse*, I, 24.

empt as it is from human laws and penalties, within due bounds." Furthermore, they were to excite in him a distaste not only for Arianism, Roman Catholicism, Socinianism, and atheism, but also for the Calvinist doctrine of predestination, the principle bone of contention between the two Protestant confessions, which, as already stated, Frederick William feared would undermine the responsibility of his subjects. "You must not make him a particularist (believer in predestination)," he instructed the preceptors; "he must believe in universal salvation." He himself repeatedly admonished his son not to believe in "that damnable particularist heresy."[8] So that the heir to the Prussian throne might become a good administrator, Frederick William enjoined the preceptors "to accustom the prince to right management, economy, and modesty." He was to be taught to abhor extravagance and gambling; to be self-sacrificing for the state and the army.

Above all, the king wished to make his son a good soldier. This he indicated very definitely by choosing military men to educate the young prince. "Both governors," he wrote, "are to be particularly intent upon inculcating in my son a genuine love for the military profession and to impress upon him the conviction that nothing on earth can earn him more glory and honor than the sword and that he will be a contemptible creature if he does not love the sword and does not seek glory solely in it and through it." Already at the age of five the little prince was compelled to exchange the civilian garments of childhood for a military uniform. At the same time the king also formed a company of miniature cadets in the ranks of which the young prince was drilled, later being made the commander of the company. He was also taught

[8] See, for example, *Œuvres de Frédéric le Grand*, XXVII (Part 3), 60.

fencing and riding, and when he was nine a room in the palace was fitted up for him as an armory, with every kind of weapon in it. Meanwhile the king anxiously watched his son for some manifestation of love for military affairs. When on one occasion Frederick took delight in beating rhythmically on a little drum, the king was overjoyed, believing that he had discovered in his son the natural expression of a martial instinct, and he ordered the painter Pesne to perpetuate the scene. If we can accept Frederick's letters to his father at face value, then he was interested in military matters at this early age; but the letters were probably dictated by his governors, who knew what would most please Frederick William. Their contents must have filled his heart with joy.[9]

To prevent any influence which might thwart his educational plans, Frederick William carefully regulated every hour of the young prince's day. Thus, for example:

On Mondays he is to be called at six, when he shall rise immediately, without further sleep or even another turn in bed. Upon arising he is to kneel for a short prayer as on Sundays. This being done, he shall put on his shoes and spatterdashes as quickly as possible, and also wash his face and hands, but not with soap; then he shall put on his loose coat and have his hair combed and tied, but not powdered. While his hair is being combed and tied, he shall eat his breakfast, so that it is one task, and all this must be finished before half after six. Then Duhan and all his servants are to come in, and a long prayer is to be said, a chapter read from the Bible, and a hymn sung, as on Sundays. All this is to last until seven when the servants are to retire.

From seven to nine Duhan is to teach him history; at nine Noltenius, the chaplain, shall instruct him in Christianity until a quarter to eleven. Then the prince shall quickly wash his face with water and his hands with soap, put on fresh linen, be powdered and put on his coat. At eleven he is to go to the

---

[9] The letters are published in *Œuvres de Frédéric le Grand,* XXVII (Part 3), 3 *et sqq.*

king and remain with him until two, when he is to return immediately to his room. Duhan shall then teach him geography from two until three and while doing so explain the strength or weakness of all European states; also the size and wealth or poverty of their towns and cities. From three to four Duhan is to instruct him in moral philosophy, and from four to five write German letters with him so that he may acquire a good style. At five the prince shall wash his hands and go to the king, take a ride on horseback or divert himself in the open air— not indoors—and do what he likes so long as it is not contrary to the laws of God.

The same daily routine, with some slight variations, was prescribed for the other days. At no time were the preceptors to leave the crown prince alone; one of them was to be with him even during the night. He was on occasion permitted to have a limited number of guests, but the greatest care was taken in choosing them. No one who did not have express permission from the governors or the king was allowed to associate with young Frederick. "Have a care," Frederick William warned the preceptors, "for I make you responsible with your heads." [10]

But despite the careful planning and the strict supervision Frederick's education was taking a direction totally different from the one the king desired. The tutors, while adhering in a manner to the directions, were instilling in the mind of their pupil tastes, sentiments, inclinations, and prejudices which did not harmonize with those of the king. Frederick William himself had learned French under Madame de Rocoulle, but his studies had left in his mind a detestation, rather than a love, for French culture. However, when this same governess, who was a French refugee and could speak only French, taught his son, the result was totally different. Young Frederick not only adopted the French language as his

[10] Förster, *Friedrich Wilhelm I*, I, 357.

mother-tongue, but also developed a strong predilection for French manners, French culture, and French society. When Duhan de Jandun took over the task of educating the prince royal, he carefully nourished the love of French culture in his pupil, imbuing him completely with his own conviction of the superiority of French over German culture. German found a place in Frederick's education only as a medium of religious instruction. Because his father often required him to memorize parts of the German catechism or verses from German hymns as punishment for a misdemeanor or for lack of diligence Frederick gradually conceived a loathing for the German language. In later life his knowledge of German was so limited that he was unable to understand a scientific or philosophical treatise written in German.

Soon Frederick relished French literature to the extent that he read only French books. As he knew this to be displeasing to his father, he had to do his reading in secret. In these pursuits he was abetted by his sister Wilhelmina, who shared his tastes. Later, in recalling this period of his life, Frederick said to his reader, Henri de Catt:

Obliged to hide my books and to take steps not to be caught reading, I waited until my governor and my valet were asleep, then I stepped over my valet's bed, and gently, most gently, I went into another room, where, near the fireplace, there was a night light. Crouched over this lamp, I read *Pierre de Provence* and other books which my sister and people I could trust procured for me. This nocturnal reading lasted some time; but one night the marshal took it into his head to cough, and, not hearing my breathing, he felt my bed, and, not finding me, cried out: "My prince, my prince, where are you?" Everybody got up! I heard the noise, and ran to my bed saying that I had had a pressing need. They believed me; but I did not dare to do it again; the thing would have become dangerous.[11]

---

[11] Catt, *Unterhaltungen mit Friedrich dem Grossen*, pp. 71–72.

So as to have opportunity to indulge his penchant for reading, Frederick began with the help of Duhan the collection of a library which was secreted in a locality outside the palace. This library was gradually increased, until in 1730 it reached a total of 3,775 volumes. In 1727 Frederick with his own hand prepared a catalogue of this library which shows that it already included works of Descartes, Bayle, Locke, and Voltaire.

With such influences at work on his mind Frederick soon regarded the life into which his father was endeavoring to force him as cramping and began to neglect those things which his father thought most important. More and more everything connected with military life became boresome to him. Though he submitted to the restraints of his military duties, he no longer performed them with the zest his father demanded. Whenever he was able to elude the vigilance of the king and of his preceptors he would take off his tight-fitting military coat and dress in clothes of a French pattern. Best of all he liked the loose robes that were fashionable in France. Furthermore, he did not emulate the example of his father and keep an account of his ducats. In contrast to the saving propensities of Frederick William, young Frederick was liberal and charitable with whatever money he had; in fact, he evinced a mild penchant for elegance and magnificence. The allowance he received being too small to satisfy his tastes, he even borrowed money from Berlin merchants. Moreover, besides showing a lack of interest in the military and economic ideas of his father, the young prince was also becoming lax in his Christianity. He held but lightly, if at all, the religious sentiments which lay deep in the heart of the king. This was largely due to the fact that Duhan had filled his pupil's mind with his own skepticism. In contrast to Duhan's lively discussions the religious instructions which were to prepare Frederick for confirmation seemed to him dry and pedantic, and his confirmation in the Church, which took place in 1727, was purely an external ceremony.

The Philistine pastimes of his father, too, were little to his taste. The Tobacco Parliament, with its foul air, coarse jokes, and bourgeois company aroused in him a dislike which he expressed in no uncertain terms. He preferred to associate with men of intellectual achievements or to stay in his rooms for the purpose of reading or of playing the flute, both pastimes affording him the highest gratification. Another of his father's sports, the slaying of stags and boars in the chase, was repugnant to him. When required to go on a hunting expedition, he would often withdraw from the rest in the forest and sit down under a tree to read. In a letter to Camas, one of the many instances on which he expressed himself on the subject, he wrote: "I confess to you that I have no inclination for the hunt; this passion is entirely loathsome to me." [12]

All this was, of course, highly displeasing to Frederick William when he discovered it. Even before the little prince had grown to boyhood his father already harbored some resentment against him because he was not physically robust. The king could not bear to think, it seems, that the fruit of his loins and the heir to his throne was a weakling. He hoped, however, that time and exercise would make his son strong. Hence he compelled Frederick to accompany him on his hunting expeditions, his journeys through the provinces, and his military reviews. So strenuous was this routine that it taxed to the utmost the young prince's strength and endurance. Count Seckendorf, who feared for Frederick's health, wrote to Prince Eugene in 1725:

[12] *Œuvres de Frédéric le Grand*, XVI, 152.

The crown prince, though he is but fourteen, is obliged to accommodate himself to this way of life, and though the king loves him dearly, yet he harasses him with early rising and all the aforementioned fatigues in such a manner that, young as he is, he looks old and stiff, and walks as if he were a veteran of many campaigns. The object of the king is to induce him to prefer military science to all other knowledge, to learn frugality and self-denial, and to find pleasure only in such things as he himself cherishes. But it is evident that this way of life is contrary to the inclinations of the crown prince and that it will in time have precisely a contrary effect.[13]

On one occasion the king had a terrible scene with his son because the latter was wearing gloves at the hunt on a bitter cold day. Another time, despite the remonstrance of the equerry, he purposely chose for his son a hard-mouthed horse which, upon being frightened, became uncontrollable and threw Frederick with such force that he suffered severe injuries. Though the young crown prince had his arm in a sling and was hardly able to walk, he was ordered, the pleas of his mother notwithstanding, to appear on the parade grounds the following day.[14]

When Frederick William perceived that his son, in addition to being physically weak, did not share his own tastes and inclinations, he became increasingly hostile to him. Believing that Frederick's attitude could not end in anything honorable or good, he saw in it the apparent frustration of his fondest hopes. That the crown prince liked to affect French manners, to read French literature, and to play the flute were to the king indubitable marks of effeminacy, and he fumed at the idea of having a French fop for a successor. "Fritz is a piper and a poetaster," Frederick William exclaimed; "he cares nothing about soldiers and will ruin all

[13] Förster, *Urkundenbuch*, II, 43.
[14] See Bratuschek, *Die Erziehung Friedrichs des Grossen*, pp. 31 *et sqq.*

that I have done." [15] His resentment was greatly increased
when he discovered that the crown prince had covertly con-
tracted debts. To the penurious Frederick William this was
one of the most serious of his son's shortcomings, one which
urged on him the conviction that his son was on the verge
of moral bankruptcy. How could such an extravagant and
wasteful boy, he asked himself, really be a suitable ruler for
a poor state?

So eager was Frederick William to eradicate the "effeminate" habits that he reproached and taunted his son at every
opportunity. At the same time he tried to show him that
being economical and having a strong army were prime ne-
cessities for the ruler of Prussia. Von Suhm, the Saxon ambassador, reports that in 1724, at the baptism of one of Grumbkow's sons, the king turned to young Frederick and said:
"I should very much like to know what is going on in that
little head. I know well that he does not think as I do; that
there are people who instill contrary ideas in his mind and
cause him to find fault with everything I do. Such people are
scoundrels." After repeating the last word, he continued:

Fritz, remember what I am telling you! Always maintain a
large and good army; you can have no better friend, and without that friend you cannot stand firmly. Our neighbors wish
nothing so earnestly as our downfall. I know their intentions,
and you also will learn to know them. Believe me, and do not
think of vanities, but hold on to that which is sound. Concen-
trate your efforts on a good army and on money, for in these
two things lie the glory and security of a ruler.

While he was speaking these words the king, by way of
emphasis, gave the crown prince light taps on the cheek.
These taps became more and more emphatic until they were
veritable slaps. Finally, it is reported, the king emphasized his

[15] Cited in Preuss, *Friedrichs des Grossen Jugend und Thronbesteigung*, pp. 55–56.

advice by striking the table so hard with his fist that several porcelain plates broke.[16]

As the king's feelings toward him grew more intense, Frederick endeavored, probably upon the advice of his governors, to create a somewhat more tolerable atmosphere by writing his father a conciliatory and submissive letter. But it was all to no avail, for the king did not trust his son and therefore gave no credence to his avowals of regret and penitence. In his answer Frederick William stated his grievances in unmistakable language.

It is your stubborn and wicked head [he wrote] that does not love your father, for he who loves his father does everything the father desires whether he is present or not. For the rest you know well that I cannot bear an effeminate fellow who has no manly inclinations; who is shy, cannot ride or shoot, and is not neat in his person; who has his hair dressed like a fool and does not have it cut. For all this I have reprimanded you, but in vain. There is no improvement in anything. More than this, I cannot bear one who is conceited and overbearing, speaks only to a few people of his own choice, and is neither affable nor popular; who grimaces as if he were an idiot and obeys my will only when he is forced to do so; who does nothing from motives of love for his father, has no liking but to follow his own fancy, and is otherwise good for nothing. This is my answer.[17]

Frederick William's characteristic answer tended only to widen the existing breach. It does not seem to have occurred to him to win the love and confidence of his son through kindness. Compulsion was the only method he knew. Sooner or later, he was convinced, he would bring Frederick to his senses. He wanted nothing short of complete submission to his will. This he regarded as the first duty of children and as

---

[16] Weber, *Aus vier Jahrhunderten*, I, 104.
[17] *Œuvres de Frédéric le Grand*, XXVII (Part 3), 11.

indispensable as is military subordination in a soldier. When milder methods failed to achieve this submission, he did not hesitate to resort to severer ones. He could not forget that his mother, much as he respected her, had been too indulgent toward his own early transgressions. He himself would not be remiss in this respect, deeming it his sacred duty to extirpate the "frivolous" tendencies in his son. If he found the latter reading or playing the flute, he would throw the books into the fire or break the flute and then drive home his sharp reprimands with his cane, often with a severity that went beyond reasonable bounds. This habit of caning became so chronic that he struck his son for any reason whatever. Even the use of a three-pronged silver fork, which the crown prince had procured for himself because he disliked the two-pronged steel fork then in common use, was regarded by the king as a mark of effeminacy and an inclination toward luxury. When one day he surprised Frederick while he was eating with it, he caned him severely. Finally the king's resentment became so bitter that the crown prince could not venture into the royal presence without the certainty of blows.

All this, however, did not induce Frederick to comply with the wishes of his father even in small and unimportant matters. He continued to travel the path he had marked out for himself. To his friend Ludwig von Borcke he wrote in 1728:

The king is constantly in a bad mood; he grumbles against the whole world and is satisfied with no one, not even with himself. How then is it possible to please him. He is terribly enraged against me, and there is no possibility of a reconciliation. . . . One finally learns to become indifferent, and I am at present in spite of anything that might happen to me; I play the flute, read, and love my friends more than myself.[18]

---

[18] Cited in Muschler, *Friedrich der Grosse*, p. 44.

Soon he, in turn, found fault with everything the king did, openly loathed everything the king liked, championed the cause of those whom the king punished, and expressed contempt for those who stood in the king's favor. Gradually his situation became more and more intolerable to him, engendering in him the wish to escape from it all. Only the hope that the conclusion of a matrimonial alliance with England, according to which he was to marry the English Princess Amelia, and his sister Wilhelmina the Prince of Wales, would free him from the Draconian discipline of his father restrained him from making a desperate resolve. But in 1730 even this hope was dissipated, and he decided to seek freedom in flight—a resolve which was quickened by a caning the king administered to him before the assembled troops at Mühlberg.

A favorable opportunity for escape seemed near at hand. Frederick was about to accompany his father on a journey toward the western frontier of the kingdom. Accordingly the crown prince planned that when they reached a point near the Dutch frontier he would secretly cross into foreign territory. As companions for his flight Frederick chose two friends, Lieutenant von Keith and Lieutenant von Katte, both of whom the king had previously regarded as baneful influences in his son's life. The former had by royal order been transferred some weeks earlier from Berlin to Wesel to remove him from the vicinity of the crown prince; but Katte was stationed in Berlin and helped Frederick plan the flight. It was decided that the three were to meet at The Hague and thence proceed to England, but as Frederick and Katte were so frequently seen in confidential conversation, their intentions were suspected and the crown prince was closely watched. When the royal party reached the small village of Steinfurt on the road to Sinsheim early in August of

1730, Frederick decided that he was near enough to the border to make the escape an easy matter. Arising early on the morning of the fifth of August while the others were still asleep, he ordered one of the king's pages to procure him horses. However, before the horses arrived his valet, who had been instructed to keep strict watch over the movements of the crown prince, awoke and reported to Frederick's governor what was taking place. Von Rochow, the governor, managed to reach Frederick just before the page arrived with the horses and thus prevented him from fleeing.

When the king was informed of the attempted flight, his rage knew no bounds. Believing that a conspiracy of proportions was afoot, he ordered the crown prince arrested and confined under strong guard in the fortress of Cüstrin, in Pomerania. By special orders of the king Frederick was held in what was almost solitary confinement. Even the two officers who brought his meals were enjoined not to speak to him. "If he asks them what is happening here and there or questions them regarding the news of the world," the king wrote, "they must not answer. This is my strict order which they must obey or I will hold them responsible with their heads." [19] The only books the king permitted him to have were the Bible and a hymn book. While Frederick was being taken to Cüstrin, Keith successfully escaped to Holland and thence to England, despite the efforts of the Prussian authorities to apprehend him en route. Katte, however, whom Frederick had warned, but who had hesitated too long, was arrested in Berlin. Although a rigorous questioning of Katte failed to reveal the wider conspiracy Frederick William believed had been formed against him, the king vented his anger on those whom he regarded as accomplices

[19] Preuss, *Urkundenbuch zu der Lebensgeschichte Friedrichs des Grossen*, II, 153.

in the attempted escape of Frederick. Duhan was banished to Memel, and the princess Wilhelmina was treated more harshly than before. Everyone, in fact, who had been closely associated with the crown prince was made to feel the king's severity.

As Frederick and his confederates were officers in the army, a court martial was called to try them. Regarding the crown prince, this group of high officers decided that it did not beseem them as subjects to sit in judgment on a member of the royal family. Keith, having actually deserted, was condemned to death and hanged in effigy at Wesel, while Katte was sentenced to imprisonment for life. The latter sentence exceedingly displeased the king, who was in a vindictive mood. Though Frederick had taken all the blame on himself and Katte had not quitted his regiment, the punishment was not in accord with the king's idea of justice. He believed Katte guilty of desertion, at least in intent, and desertion he regarded as a crime which must be punished summarily to deter others. Above all, he wished to stir Frederick to the very depths of his soul in an effort to bring him to his senses. Therefore, believing the welfare of the state to be at stake, he stifled whatever feelings of clemency he may have had and imposed the death penalty on Katte.

We decree in the cause of right and justice [he wrote] that Katte, although he rightly deserves to be torn with glowing pincers and hanged for committing the crime of high treason, shall be put to death with the sword, in consideration of his family. When Katte is informed of his sentence by the court martial, he is to be told that His Majesty is very sorry, but that it is better that he should die than that justice should perish from the earth.[20]

---

[20] Preuss, *Friedrich der Grosse*, I, 43–44.

Upon being informed of this sentence, Katte wrote an imploring letter to Frederick William in the hope of softening his heart. It read in part:

My mind which was guiltless of bad intentions, my heart which was full of affection, pity, and the mere folly of youth are the things, my king, which most humbly plead for grace, mercy and compassion. . . . I have erred, O my king; I acknowledge it with a contrite heart; therefore pardon him who honestly confesses his fault, and grant to me what God has not denied to the greatest sinner.[21]

In vain did Katte's relatives, some of them with records of long service to the Prussian state, entreat Frederick William to be merciful. Even the supplications of Katte's aged grandfather, Field Marshal Wartensleben, who had served Prussia with distinction during most of his life, had no effect. The king remained obdurate. By his command Katte was to be beheaded in Cüstrin, and Frederick was to witness the execution. When the latter, who had been kept in ignorance of Katte's fate, was awakened on the appointed morning and apprised of the sentence, he wrung his hands in despair, requesting a reprieve so that he might send a messenger to the king with a renunciation of his right of succession in exchange for the life of his friend. While the crown prince was pleading with his jailors Katte and his executioners appeared in the courtyard of the prison. As Katte approached the window behind which Frederick was standing, the latter called to him in a voice stifled with emotion: "*Mon cher* Katte, I ask a thousand pardons," to which Katte replied: "My lord, there is nothing to forgive." [22] The condemned man then walked courageously to the place of execution and, kneeling

[21] Hinrichs, ed., *Der Kronprinzenprozess*, pp. 132–133.
[22] Ranke, *Sämmtliche Werke*, XXVII, 120; Koser (*Friedrich der Grosse als Kronprinz*, p. 240) gives a slightly different version.

on a heap of sand, firmly awaited the stroke of the sword. But Frederick did not see his friend's head fall, for he had fainted.

When Frederick recovered his senses he returned to the window and gazed fixedly at the body of Katte, which by royal order was not removed until two in the afternoon. During the several days that followed he suffered from recurrent fainting spells, according to the report of Chaplain Müller, who had been commissioned by the king to induce the prince to repent and submit to the will of his father. Whenever the chaplain entered the room to speak to him, Frederick was terrified, believing that he had come to prepare him for death. In his talks with Müller he professed contrition and remorse with such apparent sincerity that the king announced his pardon upon receiving the report of the chaplain. But the pardon was only conditional, and his freedom was still greatly restricted.

The whole town [the royal order stated] shall be his prison. He is not to leave it. I will give him employment from morning to night in the Chamber of War and Domains. He shall work at financial matters, receive accounts, read minutes, and make extracts. But, before all this happens, I will make him take an oath to act in all obedience, in conformity with my will, and in all things to do what is proper and fitting for a faithful servant, subject and son. But if he kicks or rears again, he shall forfeit the succession to the crown and to the electorate, and even, according to circumstances, life itself.[23]

A short time later Frederick took the required oath and started his new employment.

The execution of Katte sobered Frederick to a certain extent. As yet he had no intention of accepting the ideas of his father, but he did seem to realize that it was useless to oppose him any longer. He now began to conceal his real

[23] Hinrichs, ed., *Der Kronprinzenprozess*, p. 162.

thoughts and to feign contrite submission to his father until
he became a master in the art of simulation. Regarding all
men with suspicion, he deceived and cajoled them, but seldom unburdened himself to anyone. "His chief defect,"
Seckendorf wrote, "is dissimulation and falseness. One can
only trust him after the greatest precautions." [24] He knew
well, for example, that Grumbkow was betraying him both
to the king and to the imperial court; nevertheless, he addressed him with such titles as: *Mon très cher général et ami*
or *très cher et très généreux Cassubien.*" [25] For his new duties
Frederick manifested much outward zeal, though he was but
a common clerk required to report for work at six in the
morning. In time he worked his way through the various
branches of the administration, gaining a practical knowledge that was to prove invaluable after his accession. He
evinced an eagerness to gain a knowledge of the various activities of the government and the needs of the people, and he
did not fail to communicate to the king everything he
learned. Knowing that nothing would please Frederick William more than increased revenues, he was constantly on the
watch for new means of augmenting them. He further
sought to win the favor of his father by discussing military
affairs in his letters and by urging the king to reinstate him
in the army, avowing that he wished to serve "from love
rather than from duty." [26] Though he loathed the chase,
he described with embellishments the hunts in which he participated, even to the number of shots he fired and the animals he bagged. On a number of occasions he even sent some
of the game to the king.

Gradually some of the interests which Frederick feigned
in order to please his father became real ones. He still re-

[24] Förster, *Urkundenbuch*, III, 91.
[25] See *Œuvres de Frédéric le Grand*, XVI, 39 *et sqq.*
[26] *Ibid.*, XXVII (Part 3), 25.

mained passionately fond of music, literature, poetry, and philosophy; yet he was also beginning to see his future responsibility and to prepare himself for it. Frederick William was naturally pleased with the diligence his son manifested. Though he still continued to growl and grumble and there was still much distrust and bad feeling between him and the crown prince, he and Frederick were drawing nearer to each other. When the king visited Cüstrin in August, 1731, a personal reconciliation took place, and Frederick was given a better position in the administration and also granted greater personal freedom. Frederick William's heart even softened enough to permit his son to go to Berlin for the marriage of Wilhelmina to the prince of Bayreuth, which took place in November of that year. The serious mien and manly deportment of Frederick during his stay in Berlin made a most favorable impression on the king. So pleased was the latter that when the crown prince returned to Cüstrin after the close of the festivities he promised him a horse. Soon thereafter in a burst of generosity he wrote to his son:

I have three horses for you. . . . Keep God always before your eyes, and be obedient. Learn to manage your household and make the most of your allowance; spend nothing without first reflecting carefully whether it would not be possible to get what you want more cheaply elsewhere. Work hard so that I may entrust more and more work to you. Then with the help of God your position will improve, and I will give you a good establishment.²⁷

Frederick thanked his father profusely and asked for a copy of the military regulations. "My most gracious father," he wrote, "can show me no greater favor, for with it I can prepare myself for his service." Earlier the king had doubted the sincerity of his son's protestations and had written: "You

²⁷ *Ibid.*, pp. 50–51.

tell me that you wish to reënter the army. I do not think that your wish is heartfelt." Now, however, he appears to put more faith in the statements of the crown prince, for a few weeks later he reinstated him in the army, making him commander of a regiment stationed at Ruppin.

Frederick's submission to his father was soon to be put to a severe test. The king, after considering the question of a suitable marriage for his son, came to a decision early in 1732. At the suggestion of the Austrian party which still maintained its ascendancy over him, Frederick William decided on Elizabeth Christine of Brunswick-Bevern, a niece of the empress. Since Amelia, the English princess, was still single and the Prussian queen still had hopes of reviving the idea of the English marriage, the Austrian agents sought to hasten the marriage between Frederick and Elizabeth Christine as much as possible. Frederick, for his part, had no desire to marry. The only possible advantage he saw in matrimony was the promise of greater freedom and of a household of his own. Moreover, his father's choice of a wife was anything but pleasing to him. Already the king's description of her as "well brought-up, modest, retiring, and God-fearing" [28] filled him with aversion. Later, when he met her, he took an almost violent dislike to her. After the ceremony of betrothal (March 10, 1732) he wrote to his sister Wilhelmina: "She is neither beautiful nor ugly; nor does she lack intelligence, but she is badly brought up and without the least knowledge of the art of living. Here you have a true picture of the princess. You may judge from this, my dear sister, whether she pleases me or not." [29] Count Manteuffel, the Saxon envoy to Berlin, reported that when Frederick was told that if a man has a white liver his wife lives only a short time after

---

[28] Œuvres de Frédéric le Grand, XXVII (Part 3), 60.
[29] Ibid., XXVII (Part 1), 4.

marriage he replied: "Good, I hope my liver is white as snow, so that I may be rid of this beast whom they are forcing me to marry."[30]

Although the prospect of spending his life at the side of this woman caused him acute suffering, he knew well that if he refused to marry her the feud with his father would flare up anew. He therefore declared his unconditional submission to his father's will, but unknown to his father did all he could to frustrate the marriage plans. The many letters he wrote about his approaching marriage are an interesting commentary on the double game he played. To his father he wrote: "Let her be whatever she is, I shall at all times act in accordance with the commands of my most gracious father. With the most complete submission I await further orders from my gracious father."[31] At the same time he wrote to Grumbkow in a spirit of protest, speaking of his future wife as a "horrible creature" or satirically calling her his "Dulcinea" (Sweetie). In one letter he even mentioned suicide, though the threat does not appear to have been serious.

I have been wretched all my life [he wrote] and I believe it is my destiny to continue so. But I must be patient and take things as they come. However, come what may, I have no reason for self-reproach. I have suffered enough for a crime committed in error and I will not undertake anything that will prolong my suffering in the future. I have still some resources: a pistol can put an end to my troubles and my life. I do not think God will condemn me for that, but rather that he will have pity on me and in exchange for a life of misery will give me salvation.[32]

Another time he wrote:

[30] Weber, *Aus vier Jahrhunderten*, II, 237.
[31] *Œuvres de Frédéric le Grand*, XXVII (Part 3), 64.
[32] *Ibid.*, XVI, 43–44.

They are trying to cudgel love into me, but since I unfortunately do not have the nature of a donkey, I am very much afraid they will not succeed. Good God, I wish he [the king] would recollect that this marriage has been thrust upon me *nolens volens* at the price of my liberty. . . . Marriage makes one of age, and when I am so I will be the ruler of my own house, and my wife shall give no orders. No woman should govern anything whatever in this world. I believe that a man who allows himself to be ruled by a woman is the biggest coward in the world and unworthy to bear the noble name of man. *Vive la liberté!* . . . I love the other sex, but I love it with a love that is volatile. I want only the enjoyment of it; afterwards I despise it. Judge, then, if I am of the stuff that makes good husbands. I am enraged to become one, but I make a virtue of necessity. I shall keep my promise, I shall marry, but after the marriage ceremony: "Goodbye and good luck, Madame." [33]

But since Grumbkow was in the pay of Austria, all the protests of the crown prince were to no avail. Not even the efforts of the queen, who still clung desperately to the hope of an English marriage and regarded Elizabeth Christine "a dullard as stupid as a bundle of straw and without the least education," could change the decision of Frederick William. Realizing that he could not escape the marriage, Frederick sought desperately to postpone it as the appointed time drew near. Even this proved unavailing. On June 12, 1733, the marriage was celebrated in Brunswick with great festivities. Immediately after the ceremony Frederick wrote to Wilhelmina: "My very dear sister, at this very moment the ceremony has ended. God be praised it is over." [34] After the festivities he returned to his regiment at Ruppin, while Elizabeth Christine, for lack of adequate quarters in Ruppin, remained in Berlin. During his residence at Ruppin the crown prince endeavored to ingratiate himself with his father by

[33] *Ibid.*, p. 61.   [34] *Ibid.*, XXVII (Part 1), 10.

taking at least an outward interest in military affairs. "I intend to keep on my father's right side about the army," he wrote to Grumbkow, "and I shall endeavor to convince him that I know what I am about." [35] Though there is no evidence to show that Frederick took a genuine delight in military affairs, he discharged his duties with such apparent zeal that Frederick William was highly pleased. In writing to Old Dessauer the king stated that the regiment of the crown prince was "in better order, good recruits, and everything excellent." [36] Mars, it appears, was claiming some of the interest Frederick had previously reserved for the muses. The next year the king expressed his satisfaction by publicly embracing his son during a review and by promoting him to the rank of major general.

[35] *Ibid.*, XVI, 103.
[36] *Briefe an Leopold zu Anhalt-Dessau*, p. 530.

CHAPTER THIRTEEN

A Victorious General Succeeds the
Military Organizer

B Y THE time Frederick William reached the age of forty he was a prematurely aged man. His strenuous labors and his immoderate eating, drinking, smoking, and hunting had gradually undermined the constitution which had once been so robust. Count Seckendorf had foreseen this as early as 1725, when he wrote to Prince Eugene:

According to all human reckoning the king cannot continue to live in this manner without harming his mind and his body, for he is continually on the move from morning until late in the night. At a very early hour of the day he taxes his mind with various and different matters, resolutions, and tasks and thereafter incredibly fatigues himself throughout the entire day with riding, walking, and standing; he also eats immoderately and drinks to excess, although not to the point of debauchery, and thereby excites his naturally vehement temper so much that evil consequences will result therefrom in time.[1]

These evil consequences showed themselves in the form of gout, and in 1734 symptoms of dropsy set in. His legs swelled to the size of "two butter-tubs," and for a time his

[1] Förster, *Urkundenbuch*, II, 42.

life was in danger. But he improved considerably in 1735 and lived another five years, though his health was far from good.

As the king's suffering increased, and he often suffered acutely from both the gout and the dropsy, his temper became more vehement and he grew more impatient with everyone and everything. A servant reports in 1734: "The king is upset over everything; he caned a page so vehemently that we believed he would suffer a stroke." [2] When he could no longer walk, the gouty and ill-tempered monarch rode about in his wheel chair, striking to the right and to the left with his crutches if something displeased him. But his temper became almost unendurable when he was confined to his room. In 1740 Guy Dickens, the English ambassador, wrote: "The king is indisposed and keeps to his room. We are told that he is in such a horribly bad humor, that nobody can come near him without being ill used with words or blows." [3] If his commands were not obeyed with instantaneous promptness, he would fly into a furious passion and swing his bamboo upon any back or even head that was within reach. When he was bedridden and could not reach his servants with his cane, some of them would talk back to him when he berated them. This infuriated him so that he had two loaded pistols put beside his bed as a means of enforcing prompt obedience. The servants, however, straightway fled and refused to reënter the room until he had the pistols removed. A short time before his death he became so enraged at Dr. Eller, his physician, that he boxed his ears. Leaving the sick room at once, Eller refused to return when he was summoned, whereupon the king, infuriated by the refusal, vented his rage on his valets by condemning one to

[2] Förster, *Friedrich Wilhelm I*, II, 143.
[3] Raumer, *Beiträge zur neueren Geschichte*, II, 1.

serve as a private in the army and ordering the second to be punished with two hundred blows. The valets were saved only through the intercession of the queen, who chided her husband, telling him that if he did not curb his evil temper "everyone would forsake him and he would be left to die in his own filth or he would be put in chains like a madman." [4]

During such times of pain and ill-temper all Frederick William's suspicions and jealousies were aroused to the highest pitch, and all the old bitterness toward his son would reassert itself. He would demand of the crown prince that he pledge himself on oath to make no changes in the army or the government after his death, to choose his officials only from a list he himself would draw up, and to administer the finances in the most economical way. When Frederick refused to subscribe to such conditions, the king threatened to disinherit him. The fact that his son sought by various acts of charity to make himself popular with the people also infuriated Frederick William. When the king, for example, heard that the crown prince had given money to a woman whose pension he himself had revoked, he said, according to Manteuffel's report: "I am not at all sorry that I am going to die, for the man who fears death is a cur; but what I really regret is, that I shall have such a monster as my son to succeed me." [5] Another thing that irritated him was the increasing respect that was paid to the crown prince as it became apparent that he himself would not live much longer. Any display of more than ordinary civility toward the heir to the throne would evoke immediate denunciations from the king. Feeling somewhat better one day during his last illness, the king invited his generals to assemble in his apartment for a Tobacco Parliament. He was in a gay mood at having his

[4] Weber, *Aus vier Jahrhunderten*, I, 159 et sqq.   [5] *Ibid.*

cronies about him again, when suddenly the crown prince entered the room and all but the king rose to their feet, a formality which was contrary to the established rules of the Tobacco Parliament. At once Frederick William turned white with rage and shouted to his generals: "You may adore the rising sun, but I still live and will show you who is the master." Then he broke up the meeting by ordering the generals to leave the palace.[6]

In his better moods, however, Frederick William frequently expressed his satisfaction with his son, confident that Frederick would complete the structure for which he himself had laid the foundation. Rothe, the secretary of the Saxon legation in Berlin, wrote in a letter to Count von Brühl in 1739: "When last week His Majesty was seated at the dinner table with his family and other members of the royal household, he turned to the crown prince and said to him: 'Fritz, I love you with all my heart! For the first time I have really learned to know you; there is a Frederick William in you. Fritz, all is forgiven and forgotten; you are my dear son.'" [7] Pöllnitz, in a letter to Frederick, states that the king said on another occasion: "I am satisfied with him, for he has promised to keep the army and has assured me that he will abide by his promise. I know he loves the soldiers; he has sense and everything will go well." [8] One day Frederick William even spoke of intellectual occupations as something laudable. This made Frederick so happy that he wrote to his friend Camas:

I have found a remarkable change in the humor of the king. He has been extremely gracious, affable, and just. He has even

---

[6] Koser, *Friedrich der Grosse als Kronprinz*, p. 214.

[7] Weber, *Aus vier Jahrhunderten*, II, 211.

[8] Koser, "Aus den letzten Tagen König Friedrich Wilhelms I," in *Hohenzollern-Jahrbuch*, VIII (1904), 24.

spoken of the sciences as if they were something praiseworthy. I am most happy over what I have seen and heard. All this gives me an internal satisfaction. The feelings of filial affection are redoubled in me when I perceive such rational and such true sentiments in the author of my being.[9]

During the early months of 1740 Frederick William's illness took a turn for the worse. Having spent the winter in Berlin, the dying king decided to go to Potsdam at the approach of warmer weather in the spring. According to contemporary newspaper reports he said as he was being lifted into his carriage: "Farewell Berlin, I am going to Potsdam to die." At Potsdam the sight of his giant grenadiers acted upon him like a tonic, and for a time his health improved, giving him new hope. Some days after his arrival he wrote to Leopold of Dessau: "I am not yet on a horse, and so long as I am not there can be no question of real improvement. When I am again able to ride I shall no longer have doubts as to my recovery." [10] Soon, however, his condition became worse again, and the crown prince (who had spent most of the winter near his father, but had returned to Rheinsberg toward spring) was summoned to Potsdam. The day on which Frederick arrived at Potsdam saw the king so much improved that the latter had himself taken into the palace gardens to witness the laying of the cornerstone for a house that was being built for the royal smith. There Frederick found him on his arrival. As soon as he saw his son, Frederick William extended his arms toward him, and the crown prince threw himself into them and wept. For a time neither spoke, but finally the king broke the silence, telling his son that he was overjoyed to see him again and that he had always loved him even though he had been severe with him at times. Then

[9] *Œuvres de Frédéric le Grand*, XVI, 172–173.
[10] *Briefe an Leopold zu Anhalt-Dessau*, p. 712.

the king requested to be taken to his apartments and asked Frederick to accompany him.

That day and also on the succeeding days the king and the crown prince conversed privately in the royal apartments. The former, realizing that he had not long to live, desired to give the prince as much information as possible about the various domestic and foreign concerns of the government. Frederick himself wrote to Voltaire some time later:

On Friday afternoon (May 27) I arrived at Potsdam, where I found the king in such a bad state that it was evident he could not live long. He showed me great kindness and spoke to me for more than an hour on the internal and external affairs of the country with good sense and good judgment. On Saturday, Sunday, and Monday he continued these conversations, entirely resigned to his fate and bearing his excruciating suffering with the greatest fortitude.[11]

It was after one of these conversations that the king turned to the officers and officials who were being admitted to his presence and said: "Has God not been good to me in giving me so brave and worthy a son?" At these words the crown prince kissed his father's hand, while tears fell upon it. This so moved the king that he threw his arms about his son and exclaimed: "Oh God, I die content, since I have so worthy a son and successor." [12]

Having instructed his son, Frederick William faced his last hour with calm resignation. During his serious illness of 1734 he had written to Leopold of Dessau: "God may do whatever he wills. I am ready to quit the world. One ship sails faster, another slower, but both finally reach the same harbor. It is necessary to go. I am entirely content and resigned." [13] This same resignation characterized his last hours.

[11] Œuvres de Frédéric le Grand, XXII, 13.
[12] Droysen, Geschichte der preussischen Politik, IV (Part 3), 408.
[13] Briefe an Leopold zu Anhalt-Dessau, p. 536.

He had no fear of death, for he was firmly convinced that his standing with God was excellent. Upon receiving from Count Zinzendorf, the bishop of Herrenhut, a letter which admonished him to repent of his sins and to prepare for death Frederick William wrote: "Thank you for the good advice. I am convinced that I stand well with God and my Savior, to whom I commend myself and my temporal and eternal welfare in the firm belief that He will receive me by His grace." [14] He could, in fact, even joke about his death. When his condition became worse, the crown prince begged him to summon Dr. Friedrich Hoffmann, a renowned physician of Halle, for a consultation with Dr. Eller. To this the king replied that, like a soldier who had been condemned to death, he cared little whether Peter, Paul, or Hans was to shoot him. "Why," he continued, "should I summon the old man (Hoffmann was eighty). Is Dr. Eller not capable of dispatching me? I am sure he will succeed without any help." [15]

When the king felt the end to be near he asked that the oak coffin with copper handles which had been made at his request be brought into the room. "This is the bed in which I hope to rest," he said and then began to dictate the instructions for his funeral. His penchant for detail showed itself even in death as can be seen from the following:

1. As soon as I am dead, my body is to be washed, dressed in a clean shirt, and placed upon a wooden table; then I am to be shaved and made generally neat. That finished, I am to be covered with a sheet and permitted to remain that way from two to four hours.

2. In the presence of Lieutenant-General von Bodenbruck, Colonel von Derschau, Major von Bredow, Captains von Prinzen and von Haacke, and Lieutenant von Winterfeld, as well

---

[14] Krebs, *August Hermann Francke*, p. 50.
[15] Webër, *Aus vier Jahrhunderten*, I, 144.

as all the physicians who are here and also the surgeons of my regiment and my servants, all of whom must be present, my body is to be opened and carefully examined in order to ascertain the real cause of my death and the internal condition of my body. But I forbid most emphatically, under punishment of death, that any organ be taken out; only the water and the phlegm, insofar as that is possible, is to be removed; then my body is to be washed, dressed in the best uniform I possess, and put in the coffin, which is not to be draped. This done, the lid of the coffin is to be fastened with screws and left that way throughout the night.

In the same detail he continued to dictate page after page of instructions, specifying how his body was to be transported to the garrison church, how the horses that were to draw the caisson were to be placed, who was to carry the coffin, who was to be in the funeral procession, what the various people were to wear, what hymns were to be sung at the funeral service, and how the salvos were to be fired.[16] He concluded the instructions with the specific command that there must be no ceremonies whatsoever except those he had prescribed. Previously, with his characteristic thrift, he had set aside a sum of money for his funeral. "So that all superfluous expenditures may be avoided," he wrote, "we set aside the sum of twenty thousand taler, which is not to be exceeded. We shall be satisfied to have the funeral conducted with still less expense if that is possible."

Since everything was ready, he could now die. Seeing that those who were gathered about him were much affected by his approaching death, he tried to console them by saying: "It is the lot of man, a debt we must all pay to nature." During his last hours he frequently lapsed into a coma and upon

[16] Full text of the instructions in Cramer, *Zur Geschichte Friedrich Wilhelms I und Friedrichs II*, pp. 167–183; also in Förster, *Friedrich·Wilhelm I*, I, 409–412.

regaining consciousness repeatedly asked his physician to feel his pulse and tell him how long he would still live. Once he asked for a mirror to see if he was taking on the appearance of a corpse. When finally Dr. Eller in answer to his persistent questions told him that the end was near, the king said: "Thank God, it will soon be over." [17]

On the afternoon of May 31 death finally ended Frederick William's sufferings. Frederick, who was at the deathbed, was greatly moved by the calmness and the courage with which his father faced the inevitable. On the same day he wrote to his wife: "It pleased God to summon the king at half after three this afternoon. He thought of you. His death has drawn from all of us real tears of compassion. You would never believe with what firmness he died." [18] The next day he wrote to Wilhelmina: "The good God summoned our father yesterday at three. He died with an angelic firmness and without suffering much." [19] To his friend Voltaire, he wrote: "My fate is now changed; I have witnessed the last moments of a king—his agony, his death. Truly, before acceding to the throne I didn't need this lesson to inspire me with disgust for the vanity of human greatness." [20] Several weeks later he sent Voltaire a more detailed account of his father's death:

On Monday, appearing very calm and very resigned, and bearing his suffering with much firmness, he surrendered the government into my hands. On Tuesday morning he tenderly took leave of my brothers and me, we who attended him in his last hours. In his anguish he showed the stoicism of a Cato. He died with the curiosity of a scientist eager to see what was taking place within him at the very moment of his death and with

[17] See Droysen, *Geschichte der preussischen Politik*, IV (Part 3), 408 *et sqq.*; Koser, *Friedrich der Grosse als Kronprinz*, pp. 214 *et sqq.*
[18] *Œuvres de Frédéric le Grand*, XXVI, 14.
[19] *Ibid.*, XVIII (Part 1), 92.   [20] *Ibid.*, XXII, 3.

the heroism of a great man, leaving to us sincere regrets over his loss and in his courageous death an example for his family.[21]

The salvos of the giant grenadiers over the grave of the dead king announced the beginning of a new era. The king who had created the Prussian army was dead, and one who was to use that army was now king. Frederick's writings and his association with men of learning had gained for him the reputation of being a philosopher and a *littérateur*. So far as his contemporaries could see he was totally unmilitary. Seckendorf, for example, had written to Prince Eugene regarding Frederick: "He told me that he is a poet and can write a hundred lines in two hours. He could also be a musician, a philosopher, a physicist, or a mechanician. What he never will be is a general or a warrior." [22] Upon hearing of the death of Frederick William, the former crown prince's friends began to flock to Berlin, hoping to live on the royal bounty while they were enjoying the arts. The Prussian people as a whole believed that the new ruler would end the sway of Potsdam militarism and devote his reign to the cultivation of the arts. This, in fact, was the sentiment of Europe generally. Two months after Frederick's accession *The Gentleman's Magazine* of London published the following statement:

The present king of Prussia's accession to the throne hath given his subjects such an happy prospect of a mild, gracious and glorious reign; for he hath not only made the usual solemn declaration that their interests and happiness shall be inseparable from his own, but if any competition should happen to arise between them the good of his people should have the preference.[23]

---

[21] *Ibid.*, p. 12.
[22] Förster, *Urkundenbuch*, III, 75.
[23] X (1740), 347.

But Frederick was to disappoint the hopes of those who looked to him for a reign of peace. No sooner was he seated on the throne than he began to stoke the fires of war. Among the first measures of his reign were some which strengthened the army his father had left him. He dismissed the regiment of giants, added more than ten thousand troops to his forces, and increased his stock of war munitions. When Guy Dickens, the English ambassador, saw that the new Prussian ruler was strengthening an army which already was considered the best in Europe, he wrote: "We wish that this young prince's great reading, and in particular Rollin's *Ancient History*, which is his favorite study, may not have filled his head with notions of imitating a Cyrus or an Alexander." [24]

The English ambassador's surmises were not very wrong. Frederick may not have entertained ideas of imitating Cyrus or Alexander, but he did have ambitions of launching an aggressive expansionist policy. He would round out the territories under his rule and guarantee Prussia a position of respect in Europe. To the literary friends who hopefully gathered about him he said: "Those pastimes are ended." His plan was, on the approaching death of the Emperor Charles VI, to profit by the insecure position of Austria and to take possession of the province of Silesia, to which the Hohenzollern had at various times laid claim. For many years Charles VI, having no son, had striven to insure the succession of his daughter Maria Theresa to the hereditary domains of the Habsburgs. The Pragmatic Sanction which guaranteed Maria Theresa's succession to the Habsburg territories had been signed by all the states of Europe, except Bavaria. Few of the signatories, however, intended to keep their pledge. Frederick, who foresaw this, decided he would strike immediately after the emperor's death.

[24] Raumer, *Beiträge zur neueren Geschichte*, II, 74.

The new Prussian monarch did not have to wait long for this event. Charles VI died only five months after Frederick became king. What Frederick had in mind can be seen from his correspondence. Upon hearing the news of the emperor's death he wrote to his friend Algarotti: "Everything has been foreseen, everything is ready. It remains only to put into execution the plans which I have long had in mind." [25] In a letter to his friend Jordan he said: "Behold me now at a most critical but desirable juncture, one which may lay the foundation of my renown." [26] At the same time he wrote to his minister, Von Podewils: "I am ready with my troops and everything. If I do not avail myself of them, I hold in my hands a good which I do not know how to use; but if I profit by it, my skill will be praised." [27] So that Voltaire might not think that the attack on Silesia had been planned a long time in advance Frederick wrote to him: "This death upsets all my peaceful ideas." Then he went on to hint darkly of coming events. "I believe," he continued, "that in the month of June there will probably be more talk of gunpowder, soldiers, and trenches than of actresses, ballets, and the theater. The moment for a change of the entire political system is at hand." [28]

Though Frederick confided his plan for invading Silesia only to a few intimate friends, indications of what he intended to do were gradually seen by others. The English ambassador, upon realizing clearly what Frederick's intentions were, wrote to his government:

Nobody here, great or small, dares make any representation to this young prince against the measures he is pursuing, though they are all sensible of the confusion which must follow. A

---

[25] Œuvres de Frédéric le Grand, XVII, 79.
[26] Ibid., XVII, 79.
[27] Politische Correspondenz Friedrichs des Grossen, I, 84.
[28] Œuvres de Frédéric le Grand, XXII, 55.

prince who has the least regard for honor, truth, and justice could not play the role he is choosing. It is plain his only purpose is to deceive us, and to conceal for a while his ambitious designs.[29]

Others denounced the proposed invasion in even stronger language. When Frederick was told of these denunciations, he wrote to Jordan: "Let the ignorant and envious babble; they shall never form the compass by which I shall steer. My object is glory; of this I am more enamored than ever."[30] About the same time he wrote to Voltaire: "I would willingly resign my occupations to another were it not for the phantom of glory that visits me so frequently. The desire for glory is indeed a great folly, one of which man cannot easily rid himself, once he is possessed by it."[31]

On December 16 Frederick marched across the border into Silesia. "I have crossed the Rubicon," he wrote to Podewils, "with waving banners and beating drums. Everything is going according to our wishes."[32] Since Maria Theresa was unprepared for the invasion, Frederick's progress was rapid; in fact, many places surrendered without resistance. The first important engagement between the Austrian and the Prussian armies did not take place until April 10, 1741. In this battle at Mollwitz, Frederick himself made a poor start as a general. Beholding war in all its fearful reality for the first time, he became panic stricken in the general confusion, wheeled his horse, and did not stop riding until he had put many miles between himself and the battle lines. But the army which Frederick William had trained stood its first real test. Under the able leadership of Marshall Schwerin it won a victory over the Austrian forces. The king's flight gave his

[29] Raumer, *Beiträge zur neueren Geschichte*, II, 76.
[30] *Œuvres de Frédéric le Grand*, XVII, 83–84.
[31] *Ibid.*, XXII, 65.
[32] *Politische Correspondenz Friedrichs des Grossen*, I, 147.

friend Jordan, whom he had twitted for his opposition to war, an opportunity to revenge himself. Jordan wrote a poem which reads in part:

> First battle-fields, my prince, are like first gallantries,
> Skill cannot be acquired except by slow degrees;
> But you did very well; you trotted round about,
> Some fourteen miles they say, you heard the fighters shout;
> Firstly you sought to learn the art of riding,
> Next to learn conquest, last to take a hiding!
> Yet during that same ride and other daring hits,
> You won, all unawares, the victory of Mollwitz.[33]

In the end everything turned out well for Frederick. He did not again lose his self-command in the midst of battle. The Prussian advance was so rapid that within a short time most of Silesia was in Frederick's hands. Having taken the Habsburg province, he had to fight two wars to hold it. The general European war, commonly called the War of the Austrian Succession, which resulted from Frederick's invasion continued until 1748. During the course of the war Frederick wrote to his friend Jordan: "We have undergone fatigues from bad roads and worse weather. But what are fatigues, cares, and danger compared to glory. It is so mad a passion that I cannot conceive how it happens that it does not turn every man's brain." [34] When peace was finally concluded at Aix-la-Chapelle, Prussia was permitted to retain Silesia. However, the treaty proved to be only a truce. Maria Theresa, far from reconciled to the loss of her province, immediately began to conclude alliances in preparation for another war. This war, known as the Seven Years' War (1756–1763), strained the financial resources and the man power of Prussia to the utmost before Frederick finally emerged from it the victor.

[33] Cited in Eulenberg, *The Hohenzollern*, p. 154.
[34] *Œuvres de Frédéric le Grand*, XVII, 287.

In both wars the son whom Frederick William had feared would be little more than an unpractical *littérateur* acquitted himself as a soldier in a manner that would have delighted his father's heart. Frederick himself said, as reported by Henri de Catt: "My father wanted me to become a soldier, but he never suspected that one day I should be in this respect what I am. How astonished he would be if he saw me here at Schmirsitz amidst an army that is worth more than a little and a cavalry of which he would not have the least idea; he would not even believe his eyes." [35] How eager Frederick was to live up to the standard his father had set is shown by the dream he related to Henri de Catt. Frederick dreamed that he was at Charlottenburg and there met his father and Old Dessauer. "Have I conducted myself well?" he asked his father. "Very well" was Frederick William's reply. "That pleases me greatly," Frederick said; "your approbation means more to me than the approval of the whole universe." [36]

[35] Catt, *Unterhaltungen mit Friedrich dem Grossen*, p. 72.
[36] *Ibid.*, p. 427.

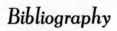

Bibliography

Bibliography

SOURCE MATERIALS

Acta Borussica, Die Behördenorganisation und die allgemeine Staatsverwaltung, ed. by G. Schmoller, W. Stolze, and O. Hintze. Vols. I–V. Berlin, 1894–1910. In the footnote references Acta Borussica is abbreviated as AB.

Die Handels, Zoll, und Akzisepolitik, ed. by H. Rachel. 3 vols. Berlin, 1911–1928.

Die Wollindustrie in Preussen unter Friedrich Wilhelm I, ed. by C. Hinrichs. Berlin, 1933.

Das preussische Münzwesen im 18. Jahrhundert, ed. by F. Freiherr von Schrötter. 4 vols. Berlin, 1904–1911.

Die preussische Seidenindustrie im 18. Jahrhundert, ed. by O. Hintze. 3 vols. Berlin, 1892.

Altmann, Wilhelm, Ausgewählte Urkunden zur brandenburgisch-preussischen Verfassungs- und Verwaltungsgeschichte. Vol. I. Berlin, 1897.

Bielfeld, Jacob F., Letters of Baron Bielfeld. 4 vols. London, 1768–1770.

Bismarck, Otto von, Die gesammelten Werke. Vol. X, 2d ed. Berlin, 1928.

Catt, Henri de, Unterhaltungen mit Friedrich dem Grossen, ed. by R. Koser. Berlin, 1894. "Publicationen aus den preussischen Staatsarchiven," Vol. XXII.

Codex diplomaticus brandenburgensis: Sammlung der Urkunden, Chroniken und sonstigen Quellenschriften für die Geschichte der Mark Brandenburg, ed. by A. F. Riedel. 41 vols. in 40. Berlin, 1737–1751.

Corpus constitutionum marchicarum, edited by C. O. Mylius. 6 vols. Berlin, 1737. A collection of many of the edicts issued by the Prussian rulers from 1640 to 1737.

Corpus constitutionum marchicarum continuatio, ed. by C. O. Mylius. 4 vols. Berlin, 1751. A collection of many of the edicts issued between 1737 and 1750.

Cramer, Friedrich, Zur Geschichte Friedrich Wilhelms I und Friedrichs II. 3d ed. Berlin, 1835. Contains the instructions for the education of Frederick the Great and for the funeral of Frederick William I.

Erman, J. P., ed., Mémoires pour servir à l'histoire de Sophie Charlotte. Berlin, 1801.

Fassmann, David, Leben und Thaten Friedrich Wilhelms I. Hamburg, 1735. A biography of Frederick William by a member of his Tobacco Parliament.

Feuquières, Antoine de, Geheime und sonderbare Kriegsnachrichten. Leipzig, 1738.

Förster, Friedrich, ed., Urkundenbuch zur Lebensgeschichte Friedrich Wilhelms I. 3 vols. Potsdam, 1835.

Frederick I, Aus dem Priefwechsel König Friedrichs I mit seiner Familie, edited by Ernst Berner. Berlin, 1901.

Frederick the Great, Friedrichs des Grossen Briefe an seinen Vater, geschrieben in den Jahren 1732 bis 1739. Berlin, 1838.

—— Œuvres de Frédéric le Grand, ed. by J. D. E. Preuss. 31 vols. in 30. Berlin, 1846–1857.

—— Politische Correspondenz Friedrichs des Grossen. Vols. I–II. Berlin, 1879.

Frederick William I, Briefe Friedrich Wilhelms I an Leopold zu Anhalt-Dessau, ed. by O. Krauske. Berlin, 1905.

—— Briefe König Friedrich Wilhelms an Hermann Reinhold Pauli, ed. by F. Frensdorff. Göttingen, 1894.

—— Correspondance inédite de Stanislas Lesczczynski avec les rois de Prusse Frédéric Guillaume Ier et Frédéric II, 1736–1766, ed. by Pierre Boyé. Paris, 1906.

—— Erlasse und Briefe des Königs Friedrich Wilhelm I von Preussen, ed. by W. M. Pantenius. Leipzig, 1913.

—— In tormentis pinxit: Briefe und Bilder des Soldatenkönigs, ed. by J. Klepper. Stuttgart, 1938.

Friedländer, Ernst, Berliner geschriebene Zeitungen aus den Jahren 1713 bis 1717 und 1735. Berlin, 1902.

Gansauge, H. von, Das brandenburgisch-preussische Kriegswesen um die Jahre 1440, 1640, 1740. Berlin, 1839. With an appendix of documents.

Hinrichs, C., ed., Der Kronprinzenprozess; Friedrich und Katte. Hamburg, 1936.

Krauske, O., ed., "Die Briefe des Kronprinzen Friedrich von Preussen an den Fürsten Leopold und an die Prinzen von Anhalt-Dessau," *Forschungen zur brandenburgischen und preussischen Geschichte*, VII (1894), 49–69.

—— "Geschriebene Zeitungen aus dem Jahr 1713," in Schriften des Vereins für die Geschichte Berlins, XXX (1896), 97–129.

Küntzel, G., and M. Hass, eds.; Die politischen Testamente der Hohenzollern. Berlin, 1911.

Lehmann, Max, Preussen und die katholische Kirche seit 1640. Vol. I. Leipzig, 1878. With documents.

Loewe, V., ed., Preussens Staatsverträge aus der Regierungszeit König Friedrich Wilhelms I. Leipzig, 1913.

Meyer, Moritz, Die Handwerkerpolitik König Friedrich Wilhelms I. Minden, 1888. "Geschichte der preussischen Handwerkerpolitik," II. With a collection of guild documents.

Morgenstern, S. J., Ueber Friedrich Wilhelm I. Berlin, 1793. A biography of Frederick William by a member of his Tobacco Parliament.

Oncken, W., "Sir Charles Hotham und Friedrich Wilhelm I im Jahre 1730: Urkundliche Aufschlüsse aus den Archiven zu London und Wien," *Forschungen zur brandenburgischen und preussischen Geschichte*, VII (1894), 377–407.

Pöllnitz, Karl Ludwig von, Mémoires. 4 vols. Londres, 1739–1740.

Preuss, J. D. E., Urkundenbuch zu der Lebensgeschichte Friedrichs des Grossen. 5 vols. Berlin, 1832–1834.

Raumer, Friedrich von, Beiträge zur neueren Geschichte aus dem Britischen Museum. 5 vols. Leipzig, 1836–1839.

Stadelmann, R., Friedrich Wilhelm I in seiner Tätigkeit für die Landescultur Preussens. Leipzig, 1878. With an appendix of documents.

Thiebault, Dieudonné, Souvenirs de vingt ans de séjour à Berlin. Paris, 1891.

Thomasius, Christian, Nachahmung der Franzosen. Stuttgart, 1894. "Deutsche Literaturdenkmale," No. 51.

Toland, John, An Account of the Courts of Prussia and Hanover. London, 1705.

Urkunden und Aktenstücke zur Geschichte des Kurfürsten Friedrich Wilhelm von Brandenburg. 23 vols. Berlin, 1864–1930.

Waddington, A., ed., Recueil des instructions données aux ambassadeurs et ministres de France depuis les traités de Westphalie jusqu'à la révolution française. Vol. XVI. Paris, 1901.

Walpole, Sir Robert, Memoirs of the Life and Administration of Sir Robert Walpole, ed. by W. Coxe. 3 vols. London, 1798.

Wilhelmina, Memoirs of Frederica Sophia Wilhelmina, Princess Royal of Prussia, Margravine of Baireuth, ed. by W. D. Howells. 2 vols. Boston, 1877.

William II, German Emperor, Die Reden Kaiser Wilhelms II, ed. by J. Penzler. 3 vols. Leipzig, 1897–1907.

Wolff, R., ed. Vom Berliner Hofe zur Zeit Friedrich Wilhelms I: Berichte des braunschweiger Gesandten in Berlin, 1728–1733. Berlin, 1914.

SECONDARY WORKS

Arneth, Alfred, Prinz Eugen von Savoyen. 3 vols. Wien, 1858.

Atkinson, C. T., A History of Germany, 1715–1815. London, 1908.

Ausländer, Fritz, Friedrich Wilhelms I Verhältnis zu Oesterreich, vornehmlich im Jahre 1732. Königsberg, 1908.

Baczko, L., Geschichte Preussens. 6 vols. Königsberg, 1792–1800.

Balk, Norman, Die Friedrich-Wilhelms-Universität. Berlin, 1926.

Beheim-Schwarzbach, Max, Friedrich Wilhelms I Colonisations-Werk in Litauen, vornehmlich die Salzburger Colonie. Königsberg, 1879.

—— Hohenzollernsche Colonisation. Leipzig, 1874.

Beneckendorf, K. F., Karakterzüge aus dem Leben König Friedrich Wilhelms I. 9 vols. Berlin, 1787–1789.

Berner, Ernst, "Die auswärtige Politik des Kurfürsten Friedrich III von Brandenburg, König Friedrich I," in Hohenzollern-Jahrbuch, IV (1900), 60–109.
—— Geschichte des preussischen Staates. 2d ed. Bonn, 1896.
Berney, Arnold, Friedrich der Grosse: Entwicklungsgeschichte eines Staatsmannes. Tübingen, 1934.
Biedermann, Karl, Deutschland im achtzehnten Jahrhundert. 2 vols. in 4. Leipzig, 1854–1880.
Borkowski, H., "Erzieher und Erziehung König Friedrich Wilhelms I," in Hohenzollern-Jahrbuch, VII (1904), 92–142.
—— "Die Königin Sophie Charlotte als Mutter und Erzieherin," in Hohenzollern-Jahrbuch, VII (1903), 223–232.
Bornhak, Conrad, Geschichte der preussischen Universitätsverwaltung bis 1810. Berlin, 1900.
Bratuschek, A., Die Erziehung Friedrichs des Grossen. Berlin, 1885.
Braubach, Max, "Der Aufstieg Brandenburg-Preussens 1640 bis 1815," in Geschichte der führenden Völker, XV, 165–367. Freiburg, 1933.
Brode, Reinhold, Friedrich der Grosse und der Konflikt mit seinem Vater. Leipzig, 1904.
Bülow, B. von, Imperial Germany. New York, 1914.
Büngel, W., "Friedrich Wilhelm I, Meister der Verwaltung," Reich und Länder, XI (1937), 253–261.
Chance, James F., The Alliance of Hanover. London, 1923.
—— George I and the Northern War. London, 1909.
—— "The Northern Pacification of 1719–1720," English Historical Review, XXII (1907), 478–507, 694–725; XXIII (1908), 35–64.
—— "The Treaty of Charlottenburg," English Historical Review, XXVII (1912), 52–77.
—— "The Treaty of Hanover," English Historical Review, XXIX (1914), 657–688.
Collenberg, Rüdt von, "Friedrich Wilhelm I zum 250 Geburtstage," Militärwissenschaftliche Rundschau, III (1938), 575–585.
Cotton, R. H. A., "English Captives in Potsdam in the Eighteenth Century," National Review, LXX (1918), 486–494.

Courbière, l'Homme de, Geschichte der brandenburgisch-preussischen Heeresverfassung. Berlin, 1852.

Crousatz, A. von, Die Organisation des brandenburgischen und preussischen Heeres. Berlin, 1873.

Dorn, Walter L., "The Prussian Bureaucracy in the Eighteenth Century, " *Political Science Quarterly*, XLVI (1931), 403–423; XLVII (1932), 75–94, 259–273.

Droysen, Hans, "Friedrich Wilhelm I, Friedrich der Grosse und der Philosoph Christian Wolff," *Forschungen zur brandenburgischen und preussischen Geschichte*, XXIII (1910), 1–34.

Droysen, J. G., Geschichte der preussischen Politik. Vol. IV. Leipzig, 1869.

Du Moulin-Eckart, Richard, Geschichte der deutschen Universitäten. Stuttgart, 1929.

Eulenberg, H., Die Hohenzollern. Berlin, 1928.

Fester, Richard, Friedrich Wilhelm I, Friedrich der Grosse und die Anfänge der deutschen Staatsgesinnung. Köln, 1938.

Fix, W., Die Territorialgeschichte des preussischen Staates. 2d ed. Berlin, 1869.

Förster, F., Friedrich Wilhelm I, König von Preussen. 2 vols. Potsdam, 1834.

Ford, Guy S., "Boyen's Military Law," *American Historical Review*, XX (1914–1915), 528–538.

Freytag, Gustav, Politische Aufsätze. 2 vols. Berlin, 1901.

Haake, Paul, "Besuch des preussischen Soldatenkönigs in Dresden, 1728," *Forschungen zur brandenburgischen und preussischen Geschichte*, N.F., XLVII (1935), 358–377.

—— "La Société des antisobres," *Neues Archiv für sächsische Geschichte und Altertumskunde*, XXI (1900), 241–254.

Hälschner, Hugo, Das preussische Strafrecht. Bonn, 1855.

Harnack, A., Geschichte der königlich-preussischen Akademie der Wissenschaften zu Berlin. Vol. I. Berlin, 1901.

Heppe, H., Geschichte des preussischen Volksschulwesens. 3 vols. Gotha, 1858–1860.

Heyck, Hans, Friedrich Wilhelm I, Amtmann und Diener Gottes auf Erden. Berlin, 1936.

Hinrichs, Carl, "Das Ahnenerbe Friedrich Wilhelms I," *For-*

schungen zur brandenburgischen und preussischen Geschichte, L (1938), 104–121.

—— "Bildungsreise des jungen Friedrich Wilhelms I in die Niederlande und die preussischen Absichten auf die Statthalterschaft im Jahre 1700," *Forschungen zur brandenburgischen und preussischen Geschichte*, XLIX (1937), 39–56.

—— "Friedrich Wilhelm I, König von Preussen," in Die Welt als Geschichte, IV (1938), 1–34.

Hintze, Otto, Die Hohenzollern und ihr Werk. 9th ed. Berlin, 1916.

—— "Die Hohenzollern und der Adel," *Historische Zeitschrift*, CXII (1914), 494–524.

—— "Preussens Entwicklung zum Rechtsstaat," *Forschungen zur brandenburgischen und preussischen Geschichte*, XXXII (1920), 385–451.

Hoese, Alexander, and H. Eichert, Die Salzburger. Gumbinnen, 1932.

Holtze, Friedrich, "Chronistische Aufzeichnungen eines Berliners," in Schriften des Vereins für die Geschichte Berlins, Vol. XXXVI (1899).

—— Geschichte der Mark Brandenburg. Tübingen, 1912.

—— Geschichte der Stadt Berlin. Tübingen, 1906.

—— Das juristische Berlin beim Tode des ersten Königs. Berlin, 1895.

—— Strafrechtspflege unter König Friedrich Wilhelm I. Berlin, 1894. "Beiträge zur brandenburgisch-preussischen Rechtsgeschichte," Vol. III.

Hoven, Jupp, Der preussische Offizier des 18. Jahrhunderts. Zeulenroda, 1936.

Hubrich, Eduard, "Zur Entstehung der preussischen Staatseinheit," *Forschungen zur brandenburgischen und preussischen Geschichte*, XX (1907), 43–123.

Hummrich, Hermann, Beiträge zur Sprache König Friedrich Wilhelms I von Preussen. Greifswald, 1910.

Hutchinson, J. R., The Romance of a Regiment. London, 1898.

Isaacsohn, Siegfried, Geschichte des preussischen Beamtenthums von Anfang des 15. Jahrhunderts bis auf die Gegenwart. 3 vols. Berlin, 1874–1884.

Jaehns, Max, Geschichte der Kriegswissenschaften vornehmlich in Deutschland. Vol. II. Munich, 1890.

Jany, Curt, Geschichte der königlichen preussischen Armee bis zum Jahre 1807. Vol. I. Berlin, 1928.

—— "Die Kantonverfassung Friedrich Wilhelms I," *Forschungen zur brandenburgischen und preussischen Geschichte,* XXXVIII (1925), 225–272.

Keil, A., "Das Volksschulwesen im Königreich Preussen und Herzogtum Litauen unter Friedrich Wilhelm I," *Altpreussische Monatsschrift,* XXIII (1886), 93–137, 185–244.

Kessel, E., "Friedrich Wilhelm I," in Schöpfer und Gestalter der Wehrkraft, ed. by Cochenhausen, Berlin, 1935, pp. 37–55.

Koser, Reinhold, "Die Abschaffung der Tortur durch Friedrich den Grossen," *Forschungen zur brandenburgischen und preussischen Geschichte,* VI (1893), 575–581.

—— "Aus den letzten Tagen König Friedrich Wilhelms I," in Hohenzollern-Jahrbuch, VIII (1904), 23–32.

—— Friedrich der Grosse als Kronprinz. Stuttgart, 1886.

—— "Die Gründung des Auswärtigen Amtes durch König Friedrich Wilhelm I im Jahre 1728," *Forschungen zur brandenburgischen und preussischen Geschichte,* II (1889), 161–197.

Kramer, G., Neue Beiträge zur Geschichte August Hermann Franckes. Halle, 1875.

Krauske, O., "Friedrich Wilhelm und Leopold von Anhalt-Dessau," *Historische Zeitschrift,* LXXV (1895), 19–37.

—— "Fürst Leopold von Anhalt-Dessau," in Hohenzollern-Jahrbuch, II (1898), 57–78.

—— "Vom Hofe Friedrich Wilhelms I," in Hohenzollern-Jahrbuch, V (1901), 173–210.

—— "Das Königtum Friedrich Wilhelms I," *Altpreussische Forschungen,* I (1924), 70–77.

—— "Der Regierungsantritt Friedrich Wilhelms I," in Hohenzollern-Jahrbuch, I (1897), 71–86.

Krebs, Albert, August Hermann Francke und Friedrich Wilhelm I. Langensalza, 1925.

Lavisse, Ernest, Etudes sur l'histoire de Prusse. 4th ed. Paris, 1896.

—— La Jeunesse du Grand Frédéric. Paris, 1891.

—— "Une Journée de Frédéric-Guillaume, le roi sergent," *Lettres et les arts*, IV (Part 2, 1889), 241–252.

Lehmann, E., "Beitrag zur Geschichte des preussischen Heeres während der Regierung Friedrich Wilhelms I," in Jahrbücher für die deutsche Armee und Marine, CXV (1900), 46–59.

Lehmann, Max, "Aus der Geschichte der preussischen Volksschule," *Preussische Jahrbücher*, CXL (1910), 209–231.

—— Historische Aufsätze und Reden. Leipzig, 1911.

—— "Der Ursprung des preussischen Kabinets," *Historische Zeitschrift*, LXIII (1889), 266–271.

—— "Werbung, Wehrpflicht und Beurlaubung unter Friedrich Wilhelm I," *Historische Zeitschrift*, LXVII (1891), 254–289.

Leineweber, Richard, Salomon Jakob Morgenstern, ein Biograph Friedrich Wilhelms I. Leipzig, 1899.

Linnebach, Karl, König Friedrich Wilhelm I und Fürst Leopold zu Anhalt-Dessau. Leipzig, 1907.

Lodge, Sir Richard, Great Britain and Prussia in the Eighteenth Century. Oxford, 1923.

Loewe, V., "Zur Gründungsgeschichte des Generaldirektoriums," *Forschungen zur brandenburgischen und preussischen Geschichte*, XIII (1900), 242–246.

Lotz, Albert, Geschichte des deutschen Beamtentums. Berlin, 1909.

Lukinich, E., "Preussische Werbungen in Ungarn, 1722–1740," in *Ungarische Jahrbücher*, VI (1926), 20–38.

Malinowsky, L. von, and R. Bonin, Geschichte der brandenburgisch-preussischen Artillerie. 2 vols. Berlin, 1840–1842.

Michael, Wolfgang, Das Original der Pragmatischen Sanktion Karls VI. Berlin, 1929.

Miosge, August, Soldatenkönig Friedrich Wilhelm I. Langensalza, 1935.

Moeller van den Bruck, A., Der preussische Stil. 2d ed. München, 1922.

Muschler, Reinhold, Friedrich der Grosse: eine Entwicklungsgeschichte des Menschen. Leipzig, 1925.

Naudé, W., "Die merkantilistische Wirtschaftspolitik Friedrich Wilhelms I und der Küstriner Kammerdirektor Hille," *Historische Zeitschrift*, XC (1903), 1–55.

Naudé, W., "Zur Geschichte des preussischen Subalterntums," *Forschungen zur brandenburgischen und preussischen Geschichte*, XVIII (1905), 355–386.

Nordmann, R., *Friedrich Wilhelm I und die Organisation der preussischen Armee.* Leipzig, 1907.

Ogilvie, Vivian, "Education under Hitler," in "Friends of Europe" Publications, No. XVII (1934), 1–13.

Oppeln-Bronikowski, F. von, *Der Baumeister des preussischen Staates, Friedrich Wilhelm I.* Jena, 1934.

Osten-Sacken, O. von, *Preussens Heer von seinen Anfängen bis zur Gegenwart.* Vol. I. Berlin, 1910.

Pierson, John, *König Friedrich Wilhelm I von Preussen in den Denkwürdigkeiten der Markgräfin Wilhelmine von Baireuth.* Halle, 1890.

Preuss, J. D. E., *Friedrich der Grosse.* 5 vols. Berlin, 1832–1834.

—— *Friedrich des Grossen Jugend und Thronbesteigung.* Berlin, 1840.

Priebatsch, F., "Die Judenpolitik des fürstlichen Absolutismus im 17. und 18. Jahrhundert," in *Forschungen und Versuche zur Geschichte des Mittelalters und der Neuzeit: Festschrift Dietrich Schäfer.* Jena, 1915, pp. 564–651.

Rachel, Hugo, *Das Berliner Wirtschaftsleben im Zeitalter des Frühkapitalismus.* Berlin, 1931.

—— "Die Juden im Berliner Wirtschaftsleben," *Zeitschrift für die Geschichte der Juden in Deutschland*, II (1930), 175–196.

—— "Der Merkantilismus in Brandenburg-Preussen," *Forschungen zur brandenburgischen und preussischen Geschichte*, XL (1927), 221–266.

Rachel, Hugo, and Paul Wallich, *Berliner Grosskaufleute und Kapitalisten.* Vol. II. Berlin, 1938.

Ranke, Leopold von, *Genesis des preussischen Staates.* Leipzig, 1874. "Sämmtliche Werke," Vols. XXV–XXVI.

—— *Neun Bücher preussischer Geschichte.* Vol. I. Berlin, 1848.

Raumer, F. von, "Das königlich-preussische General-Ober-Finanz, Kriegs und Domänen Direktorium," *Historisches Taschenbuch*, VII (1836), 399–427.

Rehtmeyer, V., *Das politische Testament Friedrich Wilhelms I* von Preussen vom Jahre 1722 im Verhältnis zu den Erfahrungen seiner auswärtigen Politik von 1713–1722. Greifswald, 1909.

Reicke, Erich, Die Schulreorganisation Friedrich Wilhelms I in den samländischen Hauptämtern Fischhausen und Schaaken. Königsberg, 1910.

Riedel, A. F., Der brandenburgisch-preussische Staatshaushalt. Berlin, 1866.

Rödenbeck, Karl, Beiträge zur Bereicherung und Erläuterung der Lebensbeschreibungen Friedrich Wilhelms I und Friedrichs des Grossen. Berlin, 1836.

Roehder, Wolfgang, Das Staatserziehungswerk Friedrich Wilhelms I von Preussen. Altenburg, 1937.

Roscher, Wilhelm, Geschichte der National-Oekonomik in Deutschland. 2d ed. München, 1924.

Schaefer, W., "Die Politik Friedrich Wilhelms I," *Deutsches Volkstum*, XVIII (1936), 721–727.

Schmid, Karl, Geschichte der Erziehung. 5 vols. in 8. Stuttgart, 1884–1901.

Schmidt, P. von, Der Werdegang des preussischen Heeres. Berlin, 1903.

Schmoller, G., "Die Epochen der preussischen Finanzpolitik," in *Jahrbuch für Gesetzgebung, Verwaltung und Volkswirtschaft*, I (1877), 33–114.

—— "Historische Betrachtungen über Staatenbildung und Finanzentwicklung," in *Jahrbuch für Gesetzgebung, Verwaltung und Volkswirtschaft*, XXXIII (1909), 1–64.

—— "Der preussische Beamtenstand unter Friedrich Wilhelm I," *Preussische Jahrbücher*, XXVI (1870), 148–172, 252–270, 538–555.

—— "Die preussische Kolonisation des 17. und 18. Jahrhunderts," Schriften des Vereins für Sozialpolitik, XXXII (1886), 1–43.

—— "Eine Schilderung Berlins aus dem Jahre 1723," *Forschungen zur brandenburgischen und preussischen Geschichte*, IV (1891), 213–216.

—— Umrisse und Untersuchungen zur Verfassungs-, Verwaltungs-, und Wirtschaftsgeschichte des preussischen Staates im 17. und 18. Jahrhundert. Leipzig, 1898.

Schmoller, G., "Die Verwaltung Ostpreussens unter Friedrich Wilhelm I," *Historische Zeitschrift*, XXX (1871), 40–71.

Schultz, W. von, Die preussischen Werbungen unter Friedrich Wilhelm I und Friedrich dem Grossen. Schwerin, 1887.

Schultz, Walter, Die ersten Lebensbeschreibungen Friedrich Wilhelms I. Danzig, 1909.

Selle, Götz von, "Zur Kritik Friedrich Wilhelms I," *Forschungen zur brandenburgischen und preussischen Geschichte*, XXXVIII (1925), 56–76.

Skalweit, August, Die ostpreussische Domänenverwaltung unter Friedrich Wilhelm I und das Etablissement Litauens. Leipzig, 1906. "Staats und Sozialwissenschaftliche Forschungen," Vol. XXV (Part 3).

Sommerfeld, W. von, "Die philosophische Entwicklung des Kronprinzen Friedrich," *Forschungen zur brandenburgischen und preussischen Geschichte*, XXXI (1918), 69–84.

Spengler, Oswald, Preussentum und Sozialismus. München, 1920.

"Statistische Nachrichten über die Armee Friedrich Wilhelms I," *Militär-Wochenblatt*, LXXVI (1891), 1031–1036.

Stern-Täubler, Selma, "Die geistigen Strömungen des 18. Jahrhunderts und das Judenproblem," *Zeitschrift für die Geschichte der Juden in Deutschland*, VII (1937), 71–76.

—— "Die Juden in der Handelspolitik Friedrich Wilhelms I von Preussen," *Zeitschrift für die Geschichte der Juden in Deutschland*, V (1935), 207–215.

—— Der preussische Staat und die Juden. Berlin, 1925.

—— "Probleme der Emanzipation und der Assimilation," *Der Morgen*, VII (1932), 423–439.

Stölzel, Adolf, Brandenburg-Preussens Rechtsverwaltung und Rechtsverfassung. 2 vols. Berlin, 1888.

—— Fünfzehn Vorträge aus der brandenburgischen Rechts- und Staatsgeschichte. Berlin, 1889.

Stolze, Wilhelm, "Friedrich Wilhelm I und die Volksschule," *Historische Zeitschrift*, CVII (1911), 81–92.

—— "Die Testamente Friedrich Wilhelms I," *Forschungen zur*

brandenburgischen und preussischen Geschichte, XVII (1904), 221–234.

Stresemann, G., Gustav Stresemann: His Diaries, Letters, and Papers; edited and translated by Eric Sutton. 3 vols. London, 1935–1940.

Toeppen, M., "Die Einrichtung der Elementarschulen im Ortelsburger Hauptamte unter der Regierung Friedrich Wilhelms I," *Altpreussische Monatsschrift,* III (1866), 302–311.

Torinus, Heinz, Die Entstehung des preussischen Beamtentums unter Friedrich Wilhelm I. Würzburg, 1935.

Treitschke, Heinrich von, Die Politik. 2 vols. Leipzig, 1897–1898.

Tümpel, Ludwig, Die Entstehung des brandenburgisch-preussischen Einheitsstaates im Zeitalter des Absolutismus. Breslau, 1915.

Tuttle, H., History of Prussia to the Accession of Frederick the Great. Vol. I. New York, 1884.

Varnhagen von Ense, K. L., Biographische Denkmale. Vol. II. Berlin, 1825.

Vollmer, Ferdinand, Friedrich Wilhelm I und die Volksschule. Göttingen, 1904.

Volz, G. B., "Die Krisis in der Jugend Friedrichs des Grossen," *Historische Zeitschrift,* CXVIII (1917), 377–417.

——— "Der Kronprinzenprozess von 1730," *Forschungen zur brandenburgischen und preussischen Geschichte,* L (1937), 1–32.

——— "Die Politik Friedrichs des Grossen vor und nach seiner Thronbesteigung," *Historische Zeitschrift,* CLI (1935), 486–527.

Waddington, A., "Frédéric Guillaume Ier," *Séances et travaux de l'Académie des Sciences Morales et Politiques,* N.S., LXXIX (1919), 472–489.

Weber, Karl von, Aus vier Jahrhunderten. N.F., Vols. I–II. Leipzig, 1861.

Weber-Krohse, O., "Friedrich Wilhelm I," *Nationalsozialistische Monatshefte,* V (1934), 646–665, 758–774.

——— "Nationalwirtschaft Friedrich Wilhelms I, der Sozialist auf dem Königsthron," *Odal,* III (1935), 506–522.

William II, Meine Vorfahren. Berlin, 1929.

Wilson, Arthur M., French Foreign Policy during the Administration of Fleury, 1726–1743. Cambridge, Mass., 1936.

Winterfeld, F. A. von, "Christian Wolff in seinem Verhältnis zu Friedrich Wilhelm I und Friedrich dem Grossen," *Nord und Süd*, LXIV (1893), 224–236.

Winters, F., "Friedrich Wilhelm I als Begründer des deutschen Beamtentums," in Beamten-Jahrbuch, XXI (1934), 410–417.

Index

Index

ised to Prussia by Charles VI,
201; emperor promised to support Prussian claims, 205; king's
offer of troops in return for confirmation of claims, 208; effort of
Frederick William to conclude
agreement with Elector Palatine,
209; emperor's proposal that territory be accepted to house of
Sulzbach, 210; Fleury's pledge to
Prussia, 210
Raw materials, only, to be imported,
162
Recruiting, forcible, 72 ff.; outside
Prussian territories, 74, 78; of
young giants, 85 ff.
Recruiting fund, officials induced
to contribute to, 110; applicants
for councillorship in *Kammergericht* paid large sums to, 125;
wealthy could atone for crime by
donation to, 138
Recruiting officers, terror of countryside, 72; excesses perpetuated
by, 88 ff.; ordered to leave Austria, 208
Reformed and Lutheran churches,
efforts to bring about union of,
149
Reich, the achievement of power
and military valor, 5
Reichenbach, proof of unfaithfulness of, 206
Reichshofrat, decisions of, invariably against Prussia, 192
Reichspatent, decisive change in,
170; proclaimed in Austria and
Prussia, 171
Religion, central factor in elementary education, 146
Rents, increasing revenues from,
60, 182
Revenue, zealous management of,
60; collection and production of,
105; king's object to increase,
163; source of, 182
Rochow, von, 229
Rocoulle, Madame de, governess to
crown prince, 216
Roermonde, bishop of, 151
Roloff, Pastor, 27

Roman Catholicism, Frederick William's lack of sympathy for, 151;
championed by emperor, 192
Roman Catholic league, Frederick
William feared formation of a
new, 192
Roman Catholics, zeal in hunting
down witches, 139; reformers ad-
vocate compulsory education,
143; freedom of conscience
granted to, 151; given permission
to worship publicly in Berlin and
other places, 151-152; many in the
army, 152; priests appointed to
minister to, 152
Rothe, quoted, 94, 99, 242
Royal Academy of Arts, founded,
15
Royal Drill Sergeant, atmosphere
created by, not conducive to advancement of higher learning, 147
Royal family, home life, 214
Royal seal, Jews fined for disap-
pearance of, 155
Rügen, occupied by Prussians, 189
Runck, Castellan, 138
Running the gauntlet, 69
Russia, army, 63; sent contingents
of tall men to Prussia, 87
Russian Company of Berlin, 178

Salaries, of court officials reduced,
55; of army officers reduced, 59;
difficult for officials to subsist on,
119; paid promptly, 120; of
judges, 125
Salewsky, Georg, tortured and
beaten, 73
Salvation, universal, 218
Salzburg, burning of witches, 140;
Protestant colonists from, 184
Salzburgers, promised churches and
schools if they would come to
East Prussia, 145
Saxons, laid siege to Stralsund, 189
Saxony, Prussian agents had list of
every tall man, 88; recruiting officer arrested in, 92; importation
of grain from, prohibited, 182
Schlubhut, von, flayed and hanged,
118